# FULL METAL JACKIE

## CERTIFIED

### THE 50 MOST INFLUENTIAL
HEAVY METAL SONGS OF THE '80s
AND THE TRUE STORIES BEHIND THEIR LYRICS

WRITTEN BY JACKIE KAJZER AND ROGER LOTRING • PHOTOS BY MARK WEISS
FOREWORD WRITTEN BY DAVE MUSTAINE

# COURSE TECHNOLOGY
## CENGAGE Learning™

**Full Metal Jackie Certified:
The 50 Most Influential Heavy Metal
Songs of the '80s and the True Stories
Behind Their Lyrics**

**Jackie Kajzer and Roger Lotring**

**Publisher and General Manager,
Course Technology PTR:**
Stacy L. Hiquet

**Associate Director of Marketing:**
Sarah Panella

**Manager of Editorial Services:**
Heather Talbot

**Marketing Manager:**
Mark Hughes

**Acquisitions Editor:**
Orren Merton

**Project Editor/Copy Editor:**
Cathleen D. Small

**Series Developer:**
Jason Miletsky

**Interior Layout:**
Shawn Morningstar

**Cover Designer:**
Jason Miletsky

**Cover Layout:**
Luke Fletcher

**Indexer:**
Kelly Talbot

**Proofreader:**
Kim V. Benbow

Printed in the United States of America
1 2 3 4 5 6 7 11 10 09

For product information and technology assistance,
contact us at

**Cengage Learning Customer and Sales Support,
1-800-354-9706**

For permission to use material from this text or
product, submit all requests online at
**cengage.com/permissions**

Further permissions questions can be emailed to
**permissionrequest@cengage.com**

All images © Mark Weiss unless otherwise noted. Image
retouching courtesy of Andrea Atis and Christopher Ivey.

Library of Congress Control Number: 2009933313
ISBN-13: 978-1-4354-5441-5
ISBN-10: 1-4354-5441-3

**Course Technology, a part of Cengage Learning**
20 Channel Center Street
Boston, MA 02210
USA

Cengage Learning is a leading provider of customized
learning solutions with office locations around the globe,
including Singapore, the United Kingdom, Australia,
Mexico, Brazil, and Japan. Locate your local office at:
**international.cengage.com/region**

Cengage Learning products are represented in Canada by
Nelson Education, Ltd.

For your lifelong learning solutions, visit **courseptr.com**
Visit our corporate website at **cengage.com**

Full Metal Jackie dedicates this book to Mom and Dad
*for supporting every ridiculous move I have ever made*

and to Jen
*for taking me to my first metal show.*


Roger Lotring dedicates this book to Cindy, Hazel, and Herman
*for their love, support, and belief.*

# FOREWORD

January 1, 1980. The start of the decade known affectionately as the '80s. Who would have known that this relatively short time span of 3,653 days would result in the creation of some of the most influential heavy metal bands on Earth—otherwise known as the Four Horsemen—and the imminent destruction of anything and everything that stood in our paths?

There was also the second wave of American heavy metal, regardless of what it was called—speed metal, thrash metal, etc.—and there was one last thing: the common thread that the music had to be aggressive, and the lyrics could not be stupid, or else!

Or else what? Or else you were a poseur! L.A. wasn't the only city trying to be metal. The Bay Area, the East Coast, Seattle, Texas, and Florida all got into the fray, too. Everyone was scrambling to produce the next stable, the next round of the new Four Horsemen.

Of course, there were the bands that were our friends. And bands that were our friends' friends. But that only meant you were several guys who jammed together, and the first believable wank was getting a record contract—"*Dude!* We just got signed!"—which is the first big lie if you got past this stage and you could get up on stage and get some able-bodied people to stand still long enough to listen. And if they actually *stayed* and *kept* listening, then you, my friend, had just earned your very own brand-new soapbox. "Step right up, sonny, and tell the world what you think. Just make sure you don't end up like Prince in *Purple Rain*." (Remember that one scene where the club owner says, "and the only one who understands your music is yourself!")

The hardest part was, if you were friends with a band and the songs sucked, especially in the lyric department. I mean, is there that much difference between 'White Metal' and 'Black Metal' lyrics? Really? I mean, come on, really?

And what happens if you are smarter than the stereotype that Brendan Fraser so aptly played in *Airheads*? But, then again, that was also the same character in *Encino Man*, *George of the Jungle*, and . . . oh, well he seems to be stuck in that role. But I digress. This is about the book you hold in your hands.

I should say that people who write books are either right on the money, somewhere in the middle, or full of shit. I know Full Metal Jackie, and we are talking about one of the smartest gals in the heavy metal radio business. A great talent, and I believe she got down what I am trying to say. Jackie aims to champion so many of these sad, affected, disenfranchised youth and their songs; songs with masterfully penned lyrics, yet until you hear them, and the fact that they exist without anyone knowing about them, is just like the sound of a tree falling in the forest.

Yet, there is something inebriating, almost orgasmic about heavy metal lyrics; granted there are the interlopers who do not belong amongst our ilk, and gratefully our genre has a way of extricating the rotten teeth from the gnashing jaws of the truth; this savage truth, that we live to sing about.

So, we hold our heads up and state to the best of our ability, ruthless in its brutality, yet as soothing as that first drink to a wino, or like the first shot of heroin to a junkie, the moment the neurotransmitter fires and the pleasure center says, "I like this!" Yep. I like heavy metal lyrics! I think you do too, or maybe you're just really brave. You know what they say: "The higher the octane, the more thrilling the ride!" Either way, read on, and don't operate any heavy machinery while reading this book! You don't want to end up like Gary Busey!

Dave Mustaine
August 2009

# ACKNOWLEDGMENTS

**FULL METAL JACKIE THANKS:** Jason for being my best friend always, Bill for bringing the woot, Roger Lotring (we did it!), Dave Mustaine for writing the awesome foreword and being a good friend, my friends at 10th Street who make it fun (even on days when it's not), Jack Ponti for saying it like it is and having my back, Five Finger Death Punch, Michael Steele, Lenny Bloch, Mike Sauter, Eric Cole and Concrete, Adan, Bob Divney, Danno, Adam, Phil and Tina Davis, KNAC.com, WSOU, Birch Hill and the many years of great shows, Indie 103.1, Miles Hlivko, Frank Webb, "Neander" Paul Marshall, Buck, Scott Less, Kayvon, and Ross Ford. To all the Full Metal Jackie listeners and supporters for the last few years, thank you! And thanks to everyone who has been a part of this that I didn't get a chance to list here. Nobody is forgotten!

**ROGER THANKS:** Mom, Dad, and Cindy, Edward Nowakowski, Jackie Kajzer, Blackie Lawless, Chip Ruggieri, Paul Gargano, Kevin Coughlin, Greig O'Brien, Valerie Potter, Chris Ingham, Phil Freeman, Katherine Santiago, Dana Smart, Michael Jenkins, Jon Vandergrift, Jason Hobart, *Prime Choice* readers and staff, *Metal Edge* readers, Alexandra Siskopoulis, David Collier, Dana Smart, George Greider, Amy Lotring Shaw for *Queen II*, 91.7 WHUS, Caffeine Bomb listeners, everyone who has read and supported my writing, and El Bombo and the Luscious Lush for all my truly horrible onstage moments that have been so much fun—now play "Breakin' Down," damn it!

**THE AUTHORS THANK:** Orren, Stacy, Cathleen, Shawn, and all the other Cengage people who made this book possible, Mark Weiss for the great photographs, Jayne Andrews, Jim Silvia, Rob Halford, Chip Ruggieri and Chipster Entertainment, Ronnie James Dio, Jason Elzy, Brian Johnson, Lemmy Kilmister, Janie Hoffman and All Things Possible, Sheryl Buckridge, Dee Snider, Frankie Banali, Doug Pinnick, Dave Brenner and Earsplit PR, Udo Dirkschneider, Louiche Mayorga, King Diamond, Mark Phillips, Ivan Moody, Vania Garcia, Rich Mahan, Todd Singerman, Dan Halen, Glenn Danzig, Heather Luke, Kurt Brecht, Gary Holt, Heidi Ellen Robinson-Fitzgerald, Kerry King, Tom Araya, Jeff Albright and RockStar PR, Geoff Tate, Jen Graham, Ross Erkers, Blackie Lawless, Kristen Mulderig, Lizzy Borden, Michael Sweet, Dave Mustaine, Scott Ian, Mark Adelman, Mike Dillinger, Rachel Bolan, Dave "Snake" Sabo, Issac Thompson, Chuck Billy, Don Dokken, Lita Ford, Phil Anselmo, Jim Baltutis, Penny Palmer, Vernon Reid, John Connelly, Gary Jay, Carly Mann, Mark Phillips, Brian Simpson, Perry Farrell, Kai Hansen, Harrie Smits, Konstanze Louden, Brian Fair, Matt Heafy, Maria Ferrero and Adrenaline PR, Rikki Zazula, Jon Freeman, Bobby "Blitz" Ellsworth, Munsey Ricci, and everyone else who made this book possible.

## JACKIE KAJZER

**Jackie Kajzer** is the developer and host of the nationally syndicated metal show, *Full Metal Jackie*, and a leading voice among metal music fans everywhere. Known for her unique, customized playlists and in-depth interviews with legendary rock artists, including Ozzy, Slayer, Zakk Wylde, and many others, Jackie has been named FMQB "Metal Host of the Year" by fans for three years in a row and counting. She is a highly sought-after host for concerts and shows, including an appearance on MTV2's first annual heavy metal awards show in April 2009.

A metal fan since birth, Jackie began her career at Seton Hall University's highly acclaimed Pirate Radio (WSOU), quickly taking her talent to larger New York-Metro commercial stations WHTG and WDHA. In 2001, Jackie moved west and settled in Los Angeles, where she joined the staff of The Firm—then the music industry's premier management firm. She quickly advanced to Radio Promotions Director, establishing an in-house heavy metal radio department and working with bands such as Korn, Limp Bizkit, Linkin Park, Staind, Audioslave, Static-X, Otep, and others, as well as discovering, signing, and marketing the metal sensation, Five Finger Death Punch.

Jackie's on-air fame continued to grow in Los Angeles, first at KBZT in San Diego and later at KNAC.com, before she launched her weekly Chaos radio show—Los Angeles and Orange County's only all-metal program—from Indie 103.1 in L.A. Currently syndicated in more than 22 markets nationwide, *Full Metal Jackie* continues to be a major influence on the metal genre. For more information, visit www.fullmetaljackieradio.com.

## ROGER LOTRING

**Roger Lotring** conducted his first interview in 1990 and never looked back. That conversation with Gene Simmons in part prompted his becoming the co-publisher and editor-in-chief of *Prime Choice*, a regional hard rock newspaper based in Connecticut.

In 1999, he was approached by the Starlog Group to contribute to *The Official KISS Magazine #2* and later their in-house heavy metal periodical, *ShockWave*. Roger was a contributing writer to Metal-Is.com, a subsidiary of the Sanctuary Group. His work has also been published in international magazines, such as *Metal Hammer*, *Zero*, and *Burn*.

He was a contributor and staff writer for *Metal Edge* from 2001 to 2009, writing cover stories and features about artists such as Black Sabbath, Iron Maiden, Aerosmith, and numerous others. Roger has appeared as an interviewer on *Headbangers Ball* on MTV2, and he is the author of the liner notes to the Mötley Crüe box set, *Music To Crash Your Car To, Volume II* and *Power Ballads Gold*, both on the UMe label.

Currently, he freelances for select outlets and contributes promotional material to the syndicated *Full Metal Jackie* radio program. He also hosts *Caffeine Bomb* on 91.7 FM WHUS in Connecticut. For more information, visit www.facebook.com/roger.lotring or rogerlotring.blogspot.com.

## ABOUT THE PHOTOGRAPHER

**Mark Weiss** began his illustrious career at age 14 by trading lawn-mowing services for a Bell & Howell 35mm camera. The family bathroom became a darkroom where images of family and friends were developed.

Subject matter progressed to his brother, Jay, who was a motocross racing enthusiast, followed shortly by rock concerts. Mark was arrested for selling prints of his photographs from the previous night's show during a run of KISS dates at Madison Square Garden in 1977. The following day, he presented his portfolio to the art director at *Circus* magazine and became the staff photographer. A few years later, he would be touring with KISS, photographing them for tour books and album covers.

Since then, Mark's photography has become recognized as some of the most iconic images in the music business. His pictures have graced the covers and pages of countless magazines, and he's shot the covers of multi-platinum albums, including Twisted Sister's *Stay Hungry*, Bon Jovi's *Slippery When Wet*, and numerous others.

He continues to photograph the legends created by his images, as well as up-and-coming new bands. Mark also showcases select portraits from his extensive archives at gallery events across the country. His portfolio can be viewed at www.markweiss.com. For more information or to purchase prints, visit www.weissguygallery.com.

# TABLE OF CONTENTS

# INTRODUCTION

Listening to a metal album used to be an event. Without the digital availability of information on the Internet, hearing an album for the first time was the single source of make-believe, a direct connection to the imagination.

Fans would slit the shrink-wrap and carefully slide the vinyl LP from the cardboard cover. The paper sleeve would rest in cross-legged laps while the listener absorbed the lyrics, word for word, studying them and staring at the photographs and artwork to make the songs come alive in their mind's eye.

Our favorite bands spoke to us—and *for* us—through their music. The lyrics expressed our joy and frustration and empowered us to be strong in an intolerant culture that laughed at heavy metal to mask their fear of it. In bedroom sanctuaries those songs were conversations between trusted friends—the bands and their fans—about politics, religion, relationships, and other topics that the mainstream considered too profound for us to really understand.

Metal fans have always been on the periphery of society. We are the outcasts, the kids forbidden from the popular cliques. Our music has always provided camaraderie and a sense of community otherwise prohibited because we are different. The lyrics have always been our voice. This book is about what that voice had to say.

*Full Metal Jackie Certified: The 50 Most Influential Heavy Metal Songs of the '80s and the True Stories Behind Their Lyrics* is an artist-driven book. Over the course of five months, the lyricists of each song were interviewed and asked to remember the creative and social circumstances surrounding their songs. Some songwriters were very certain in their recollection; others were somewhat less specific in their memories. But each person had fascinating anecdotes and opinions to share.

There are similarities between creative processes that you will read about in the following pages. In all but one instance, every songwriter claimed the music was written first. Many of the people said titles and choruses were the starting point for their lyrics.

Nearly every songwriter interviewed for this book also dismissed the idea that his or her words were such an important part of the listening experience. Most suspected their own bandmates did not even know the lyrics.

We chose songs that were not always the commercial favorites. In fact, Dee Snider, although gratified that we acknowledged songs other than "We're Not Gonna Take It" and "I Wanna Rock," thought it was a mistake to stray from the obvious popular hits.

But the intention of this book is to analyze lyrics that were influential in terms of making social and personal statements that affected the heavy metal audience, rather than mainstream pop culture. Included are songs that address nuclear armament, drug addiction, religion, suicide, governmental control, and other themes. These songs are Full Metal Jackie certified as important contributions to the metal genre that continue to make a lyrical impact on successive generations of fans.

Another criterion in choosing the songs profiled in this book was continuing relevance. Some lyrics were found to be even more pertinent in the twenty-first century.

You will likely debate the level of influence exercised by some of the songs listed herein. Metal fans are devoted to scrutinizing the validity of lists. We hope you do and that you share your own choices and the reasons why you think they were influential.

These songs are listed in chronological order by U.S. album release date. The result is a timeline that becomes a subtle illustration of how the genre developed over the course of such a prolific period.

We took some liberties with the subject matter because metal *is* about freedom and making your own rules. For the purposes of this book, our decade of the '80s concludes with 1990. In select instances, musicians who were not the lyricists but were credited as songwriters were asked to discuss the creative process as they were involved. One songwriter, whose lyrics we felt were integral to the genre during this time period, declined to discuss his work, preferring to leave interpretation to the individual listener. So we chose three listeners, who happen to have become influential songwriters in their own right, to analyze the impact of his lyrics on their own careers.

Our hope is that this book will be an informative *and* entertaining look at the creative process and the significance of songs from some of the most important artists within the metal genre.

So cue up the album tracks, print out the lyrics, and listen while you read the pages that follow. You'll never hear these songs the same way again.

Jackie Kajzer and Roger Lotring
November 2009

## 1

## JUDAS PRIEST

# Breaking the Law

FROM THE ALBUM BRITISH STEEL (1980)

Great Britain was in economic disarray in 1980. The biggest steel union in the country mounted its first national strike in decades. The Conservative Party politics of recently elected Prime Minister Margaret Thatcher were widely unpopular, and the rise in unemployment seemed insurmountable to the working-class manufacturing sector that bore the brunt of the downturn.

"There was a lot of turmoil going on around that time," Rob Halford remembers. "A lot of people were very unhappy with the government that was in power. There was a lot of friction."

The frustration and overwhelming dissatisfaction of the working class made the Judas Priest singer think about the misleading optimism impressed on people from an early age. "When you're a kid, like at school, you see other people getting successful. People lead you to believe that there's a great big world out there. It's not going to fall on your plate, so to speak, but you're going to get all the things that you aim for. Of course, that's not the reality of life in general, but I think I was trying to use that as a reference point."

Halford captured the attitude of an impoverished group with lyrics that expressed their disappointment. "It pretty much makes a statement."

"For the most part, as a lyricist for Priest, I try and be straightforward and direct with what I'm trying to say—at least in my mind. You write for yourself, basically. You write what feels right, what inspires you, what excites you, and what gets your imagination flowing."

That sense of desperation readily applied to the British working class, including Halford's roots, the steel-producing town of Birmingham, where Judas Priest formed in 1969. It also resonated with the industrial communities of Middle America, where the band established an early foothold.

The song bristled with an outrage that implied turbulence. But Rob, proud to have never written lyrics that condoned or intentionally promoted violence, maintains the words were purely observational. "It's a reflection and understanding of why these things happen, what leads to that type of thing to occur. That's what 'Breaking the Law' was all about."

*K. K. Downing and Rob Halford. Their Birmingham roots gave Judas Priest the credibility to be the voice for a frustrated working class.*

A songwriter cannot be held accountable for the perceptions of another person's imagination, he says. "The thing about music, about lyrics, is that once you let them go —if it's a lyric open for a lot of other interpretations—you're not really responsible for what another person says."

That debate over the impact of songs from artists such as Ozzy Osbourne and later Marilyn Manson would ultimately snare Judas Priest. A civil action suit in 1990 would allege the existence of subliminal content in their cover of the 1969 Spooky Tooth song, "Better by You, Better than Me," blamed as the impetus for two Nevada men to attempt suicide.

"I think a lot of people have their own perceptions, which goes into the big argument with everybody that's been accused of saying you should do bad things. It's absolute rubbish. How one person might listen to a song could be completely different than how another person could listen to a song."

# FIRST WORDS

Often, Halford says, the song title is the catalyst that sparks his lyrical ideas. "That's the touchstone that gets me going, for where I want to go next." Such was the case with "Breaking the Law," he remembers. "I'm pretty certain the song title came first. That reference, he's breaking the law, she's breaking the law, it's around us all the time—you know, somebody broke the law."

If the title was the starting point for writing the lyrics, music was definitely the precursor that motivated his train of thought. "It's a nice little song. For the verses, it's big, open chords. And then you've got that tight little riff. I suppose if you stretch your mind that could sound like a police siren. I think that maybe was what I thought of at that moment."

# URGENCY AND SOCIAL UNREST

Despite the volatile economic and political backdrop of England, Halford says he did not know how people would react to the aggressive lyrics inspired by the times. "No, not at all. You have no idea. Even now, you just don't know. If you look at everything we've done in Priest, most of the lyrics don't really carry much of a social political statement." But, as it turns out, "Breaking the Law"—and most of *British Steel* —was loaded with such assertions.

*Rob Halford thinks
the title came first.
He assimilated the
concise riffing of
Glenn Tipton and
K. K. Downing (pictured)
with a police siren.*

It was natural, he says, given the state of the country. "Watching TV, reading the news-papers, I know my mind was there." Another factor was writing the songs while the album was being recorded. The continuity of the album was that most of the tracks were charged with the same urgent energy. "We were literally writing the record as we were moving along."

Also, Halford says, the punk movement was sweeping across England, another influence of social and musical unrest. "I'm really aware of the climate of the UK, and the bulk of the *British Steel* material has that kind of attitude to it."

# BREAKING THE BAND

It was difficult to gauge response because of the limited one-on-one contact with their audience. "Now you can get a reaction instantaneously," he says. "You couldn't then. You had no contact, other than maybe seeing fans at a show. They couldn't blog or text or Tweet. You had to wait for the reviews from the press."

British Steel *was written while being recorded, giving the album an edge of urgency.*

"We started getting a lot of airplay, particularly in America, with that track, along with 'Living after Midnight.'" But Rob doesn't recall any specific response to the highly charged lyrics. The appeal of the song seemed to be musical. "Everybody ran to it," he says, "because it was such a cool, compact, tight, hooky song. For a metal tune, that was kind of rare."

"It was all over in three minutes, which is pretty amazing for a metal song. Most metal songs tend to be a little bit larger and more adventurous. People just grabbed the song because it was straightforward, streamlined—getting the point across musically and message-wise."

Given the social unrest and the overall tone of the lyrics, it's surprising there was no apparent backlash against the song. None that Halford can remember. "I don't recall anything coming back to us, where we thought, 'Oh, they haven't got a clue what they're talking about; they've completely fucked it up.' The only time we had any confrontation was from the Tipper Gore administration, with the 'Eat Me Alive' track, which was also in the '80s. Everybody was on that hit list, from Prince to Sheena Easton. Everybody was being attacked."

# SIGN OF THE TIMES

"Breaking the Law" has remained a staple of the Judas Priest live set, and Rob says he still loves the track. "I think it's a very potent piece of music, as well as a strong lyrical message. It's a song that carries a message to generation after generation."

Sadly, he says, the desperate sentiment of the song is still applicable, especially within the context of the global economic upheaval of 2009. "I would have never thought the lyric would be just as relevant as it was in 1980, but there you go."

## 2

BLACK SABBATH

# Children of the Sea

FROM THE ALBUM HEAVEN AND HELL (1980)

Ozzy Osbourne was gone. But Black Sabbath already seemed out of commission before firing their front man in early 1979. Later albums *Technical Ecstasy* and *Never Say Die!* met with increasing critical and commercial indifference, and the band was admittedly upstaged throughout their tour the previous year by upstart opening act Van Halen.

The arrival of Ronnie James Dio stimulated their songwriting, rejuvenating the music and ultimately the band. *Heaven and Hell* re-launched Black Sabbath with a more sophisticated style and a new relevance.

That vitality was readily apparent with the very first song written together, "Children of the Sea."

## FIRST SONG

The first Black Sabbath track written with Dio was his first chance to musically interact with guitarist Tony Iommi. Ronnie remembers them both being appreciative of the other's ability. "We just took each other's talent and molded it into what we became, which was very different from the original Sabbath."

*They would ultimately be regarded as heavy metal pioneers, but Geezer Butler (left) and Tony Iommi were musically treading water until Ronnie James Dio joined Black Sabbath.*

Ronnie was not yet a member of the band when he started collaborating with Iommi. That first song was more an opportunity to appraise their compatibility than the official beginning of a new partnership. As a result, the lyrics were completely off the cuff, he says. "I sat in the corner and wrote some lyrics, and it just seemed to work. I had the title. I think I had the first four lines written for something else, and I applied them to that. The rest just took on a life of its own."

The song changed the dynamic of Black Sabbath, displacing the often plodding tempo and jazz-like improvisation with more of a classical style. Dio thinks it was the contrast of delicate acoustic picking and resonant vocals with the trademark heaviness, leading away from the traditional mold. "A lot of it had to do with the intro that you really didn't hear from Sabbath before."

*The comfortable ease with which Ronnie James Dio and Tony Iommi wrote songs together reinvigorated Black Sabbath, resulting in a classic metal album.*

"We started to realize that the band could put on a bit of a different-colored jacket." Black Sabbath started to incorporate more of the classical intonation of Dio's previous work with Rainbow. But that shift was not a result of the singer blatantly asserting himself. "It just happened naturally," he says.

Ronnie did have his mind set on the kinds of songs he wanted to write. The elegant musical interlude that defined "Children of the Sea" was something he had done before and wanted to do again. "If it was anything, I'd have to point to the Beatles and maybe Pink Floyd a little bit. I wanted it to be musically a bit more progressive, which it became."

The key to applying his lyrical approach to an established band was to understand its style and write within that context. "You can't suddenly make it what you are," he says. "You have to know what the band is all about. If it's Black Sabbath, you obviously are not going to write a song called 'Good Day Sunshine.' The first thing to do, for me, was to tailor myself to what the band, in my eyes, was supposed to be. I wanted it to have my stamp of lyricism on it, of course, but not for the sake of destroying the band because of my own ego. It was a matter of knowing who you're playing with, getting the best out of them, and them getting the best out of you."

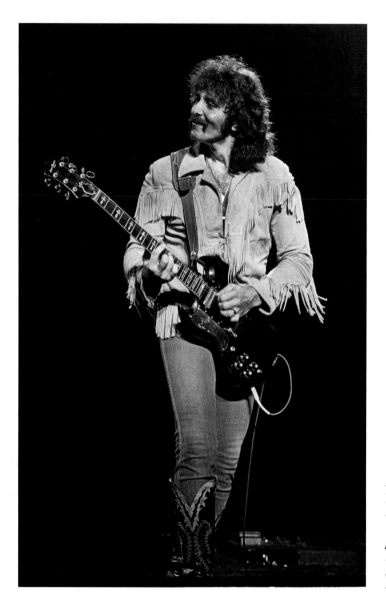

Heaven and Hell *showcased another side of guitarist Tony Iommi's playing, particularly the acoustic intro to "Children of the Sea."*

# LYRICAL BEGINNING

It was likely a matter of just a couple weeks that the ideas existed in Dio's mind before he wrote the words. After the title, the opening line definitely came first, he says.

"I had the first verse and the choruses written in about five minutes at the rehearsal, and I probably finished the rest of it that evening. It was finished the next day."

The music itself was a guide for where they wanted to navigate the song, and Ronnie offered a few instrumental suggestions from the perspective of a singer. "Everything is musical first, title after that, and then full-blown lyrics. Once the music is down, I'll know what I'm going to sing about and not necessarily have all the lyrics. Then I'll compose the melody I'm going to sing, with a few starting words."

He doesn't think the lyrics were patterned after the style of any other particular song-writer, but Dio will allow that he's always been influenced by the Beatles. "That love of what they did, so many melodic hopscotches everywhere and things that just worked so well—at some point I was probably influenced that way."

# WRITING IN METAPHORS

Ambiguity is the charm of writing in a metaphorical style, he says. "That's what I'm trying to do with a lot of the songs I write—to write in asides and a lot of similes, a lot of metaphors. It's better for the listener because they have a chance to think about it. If you just give everyone the explanation to everything and just point at it, you haven't really tickled anyone's mind at all.

"Hopefully," he says, "they do get what I'm saying. But if they don't, they've made it their own song."

Ronnie James Dio was admittedly not a conscious environmentalist in 1980. "But I was becoming concerned about what I saw, really concerned about overpopulation, which I've always felt has been the problem. Out of that feeling, being world conscious, 'Children of the Sea' came out."

But he doesn't know what moved him to tackle the subject of environmental decay. Certainly, the title illuminated the direction his lyrics would ultimately take. "I've always been a title person. Everything I'm going to write—melody or lyrics—will have a title that will eventually lead me to where I want this particular song to go."

*Dio wanted Sabbath to be more progressive, but he also understood that the character and history of the band dictated a specific musical and lyrical tone.*

# HEAVY METAL ENVIRONMENTALISM

It was not a time when people were greatly concerned with ecology, Dio recalls. But living in California, in part, made him somewhat aware of such concerns. "Say I had been living in Pittsburgh. I wouldn't have given a toss about what was going on—I wouldn't have known any different. But in California, people seem to have a lot more of a civil conscience.

"Most of my ideas come from the world around me and what society is doing—and what they aren't doing. There was probably some mention, or perhaps I read an article and thought, 'I'd like to have a go at that.'"

Although the singer previously had little environmental concern while living on the East Coast, Dio says he wasn't necessarily emotional about his statement while writing the song, either. "I was probably not so passionate about the idea as I was about writing the song that had those lyrics. When you're shaping a song, you obviously are not just doing it around your social conscience. You're doing it around how the words flow, how they work, how it works with the melody. After the song was finished, then I could become passionate about the message."

Ronnie remembers the band loving the lyrics, although, he jokes, "I don't think they had a clue what I was talking about. They probably thought I was writing one of my little fantasy pieces. They're very bright, so maybe they got it, but I told them what it was about anyway," he chuckles.

"I didn't want them to think it was about something too jolly, because I didn't mean it to be that way. I couldn't think of a darker subject than what's happening to the world, and suddenly to the children."

# INTELLECTUALISM

Ronnie says he's never been one to worry much about how people might react to his lyrics, confident that his sentiment will strike a chord with someone. But working with deliberate craftsmanship, he refuses to allow the words to be inane, either. "If you could see some of the drafts and rewrites I've done, you would be amazed." It all goes back to developing an initial idea, no matter how nonsensical, like, he says, the "ham and eggs" working lyrics that became Paul McCartney's "Yesterday."

"You need to edit, to make yourself not stupid." By the time the "Children of the Sea" lyrics were complete, "I knew it wasn't stupid at all," he says.

# EFFECTING A CHANGE

Lyrically, social awareness is what stood out most about the song. "I've not written too many of those," he says. "I've written a couple of Dio songs that were about child abuse and things like that that really bothered me."

Dio might have hoped the lyrics would become a call to ecological awareness. "I thought, 'This album is going to be so good, and this is such a great song, it's probably going to open the eyes of a lot of people.'" If he once thought it would effect social change, Ronnie now responds with discouraged sarcasm: "Wow, the world is really changed since I wrote that song, isn't it?"

"I found out you're not going to change the world by writing a song. Luckily, Bob Dylan wrote a couple great songs in the '60s that became theme songs for social consciousness. But that just happened to be the luck of the draw, really. If he hadn't been there, it would have been another song."

The track as a whole is what Ronnie thinks made an impact. "It was the way it was presented, the way it was written: the chord changes, the intro, the arrangement. It was all about being a very well-tailored and structured song. It was just a really, really good song."

## 3

## BLACK SABBATH

# ḫeaven and ḫell

FROM THE ALBUM **HEAVEN AND HELL** (1980)

Ronnie James Dio had wanted to write a song called "Heaven and Hell" for a long time. It came specifically from wanting to make use of that title. The theology of those words, applied as a euphemism for the dichotomy between good and evil, appealed to the singer. "That's what did it. It had its evil part, and it had its heavenly part.

"I had the title for a *long*, long time." The familiar first verse sounded like a natural progression from there, he says. "The opening lyric—for some reason, that sounded like the perfect opening for that song.

"That's the only thing I ever could have thought should go there. Nothing else could have fit so well." Those lines about singers, songs, and misdeeds have become beloved vernacular for Black Sabbath and Ronnie James Dio fans. "Whenever we do the song, the audience knows that part. It's become embedded in people's heads."

The sentiment sounds like an ominous warning, and Ronnie agrees that the gloomy essence of the band was definitely a platform that led to his darker approach to lyrics. "When a band is called Black Sabbath, you're not going to be writing happy songs, that's for sure."

*Ronnie James Dio and Tony Iommi. The opening lines of "Heaven and Hell" became vernacular synonymous with their era of Black Sabbath.*

# MASTER OF REALITY

Dio's fondness for writing semi-mystical lyrics allowed listeners to imagine the fantasy of an epic fable. References to carousels and dancers, along with the wicked ambiance of the title, painted broad strokes only limited by individual interpretation. A very illusionary song, he says. "You know, little idioms here and there. It's got lyrics that I'm sure people go, 'What the *hell* is he talking about?'"

Despite their allusion, the lyrics were a cautionary message grounded in reality and Ronnie's belief that the tenet of salvation and damnation is preposterous. "The illusion you believe in life—that there's a great place to go [heaven], and hell is where all the sinners go—is a load of crap. Where we live right now, this is heaven, and this is hell. Everything being illusionary, it all leads to what I'm trying to say: what a horrible and confusing place this is."

The song is also a parable about conscience. "People out there in the world are there to *screw you to the wall*. That's why life is heaven and hell, and you have to make a choice."

Good versus evil would become a Dio trademark, and "Heaven and Hell" would be regarded by many fans as his consummate expression about the matter. Ronnie acknowledges how high the bar was raised, but the caliber of that track does not mean other songs of similar emotion deserve less merit. "It doesn't matter if you lay the same feel on them." Revisiting that ambiance can be done without being creatively overshadowed, he says, as in "Holy Diver" or previously Rainbow's "Stargazer."

# WRITING IN BEVERLY HILLS

Some of the members of Black Sabbath were living and rehearsing in a rented house in Beverly Hills. "They had converted the garage into a studio," he remembers. "It was so dark and dank, and it was horrible. So, we decided to relocate. They had quite a huge living room, and the very first day we moved into that room."

During the formative days of their creative partnership, Ronnie explained his concept to Tony Iommi, describing the musical feel. "I told Tony that I had an idea for a song called 'Heaven and Hell.' Geezer [Butler] was gone, and I was playing bass at that point. We kind of put that feel down, and it went from there.

"Of course, the riff that Tony came up with, over the idea of the rhythm of the song, was absolutely stunning. Another one of those songs that just worked because we know how to write well together."

# HEART OF THE MESSAGE

The first verse came together quickly, Dio remembers. He had the title and the opening line and started from there. "The second verse wasn't too difficult. I think the third verse took me three or four days, just to tailor it the way I wanted it to be. There are bits at the end, really the crux of the song."

Those lyrics about kings and queens waiting to mislead people and take advantage of their goals and ambitions are the most important part, he says. "That's really what the song is all about, those lines. Everybody is just getting screwed out there. Everybody is going to lie to you just to get what they want for themselves. They're around the corner waiting for you."

*The mystical quality of Dio's lyrics painted the fantasy of an epic fable. But the meaning of the song was firmly rooted in reality.*

# SABBATH IN MIAMI

The line qualified by Dio as the heart of the song was written in Miami. Black Sabbath had started tracking songs at Record Plant Studios in Los Angeles before relocating to Florida. "We recorded a couple songs, then moved to Miami to finish the album."

The aggressive, up-tempo latter part of the track, including the key lyric, was developed at Criteria Studios. "We started putting the song down, and when the song was finished, we did a faster portion at the end. I had to write another part for that, so I actually wrote that in the studio in Miami."

Other than that addition, there were hardly any lyrical revisions during the rehearsal and recording process that Ronnie can remember. "There was a word or two done in ad lib, perhaps, that might have been changed. I was given free rein to do what I wanted, and I guess it worked. Everyone seemed to like what it was."

# MORALIST BACKLASH

Dio thought people would respond to the lyrics, but the album as a whole was what he expected would make the greater impact. "The quality of the songs was so good that even if there was an occasional bad lyric, it would have been overshadowed by good music." But the singer had little assumption about how people would interpret the words. "I thought they would be understood and liked by the people who followed what I had written before."

*(Left to right) Ronnie James Dio, Tony Iommi, Vinny Appice, and Geezer Butler. Black Sabbath was often perceived to represent the darker side of spirituality. The result was burnt albums, banned concerts, and a segment of the audience that startled the band.*

*Heaven and Hell* was released at the beginning of a decade during which conservatives would escalate their targeting of hard rock and heavy metal bands. Moralist groups taking aim at Black Sabbath was no surprise, given their dubious reputation throughout the 1970s. Dio, who admittedly hoped the song would instigate more controversial thought than it did, wishes he could have done more to provoke naysayers.

But the seemingly diabolical tone of the title track and its lyrics must have prompted some indignation, he says. "I guess maybe they did. Sometimes when we would play shows, they would burn our albums out in the front.

"We were scheduled to play in Phoenix, Arizona, on Easter Sunday, and they made us cancel the show. We had to shift the show to the Monday. They wouldn't allow Black Sabbath to play on Easter Sunday."

Some people did take the unearthly connotation of tracks such as "Heaven and Hell" to heart. "The name Black Sabbath has always conjured up such dark images, so there's always going to be some strange people, and there have been at the shows. People have come up on stage, dressed in robes, and kneeled down or handed us *The Book of the Dead* and scared the daylights out of us. How they got there, I'll never know. And you're thinking, 'Where's security all this time?'"

Luckily, Ronnie says, the Dio lineup of Black Sabbath has not had any such incidents since reforming as Heaven & Hell in 2006. The namesake track remains their signature song and arguably their most recognized lyrics, given the response captured by the 2007 live release, *Live from Radio City Music Hall*.

## 4

# AC/DC
# Hells Bells

FROM THE ALBUM **BACK IN BLACK** (1980)

AC/DC was recording at Compass Point Studios on the island of New Providence, 10 miles west of Nassau. Bon Scott had passed away two months earlier, and they assuaged their grief by working. Brian Johnson, their new singer, was miles from home, literally and figuratively.

"Here I was, this kid from Newcastle, and I was in the Bahamas. I had only been there about four days, and they said, 'Could you write some lyrics?'"

Not only was he attempting to follow in the cunning lyrical footsteps of his predecessor, he was essentially writing lyrics in earnest for the first time in his life. Johnson's prior experience was limited to a pair of songs with his previous band, Geordie.

The pace of the sessions was exhausting. "I was writing during the day, basically, then singing the things at night." He wrote two or three songs, but Brian was drained.

He was running out of ideas by the time brothers Malcolm and Angus Young gave him the title of the next song. "Hells Bells" was a colloquialism Brian knew from Newcastle. "If you stubbed your toe, you'd go, 'Oh, hells bells and a bucket of shit!' Some people just shortened it to hells bells.

"So, I was familiar with it, but I couldn't really think of anything to say with it." He struggled with the song in his room—his little cell, he says. "Believe me, when I say a cell, I'm not using the term loosely."

Resources were limited, so the band lodged at a cottage off the studio that consisted of four breeze-block rooms that resembled prison cells. "There was nothing but one chair, a little table—what I wrote on—a bed and a toilet. That was our living accommodations."

A storm was developing while Johnson wrestled with the blank page, and producer Robert John "Mutt" Lange stepped in to check on the Englishman who had never experienced a tropical storm. "The sky was black as fuck," he recalls. "And thunder, just the loudest I've ever heard."

*Rolling* thunder, Lange corrected. Stuck for a direction for the latest song, Brian started there. "And then this huge lightning flash cracked like I've never seen before. I went, 'Fuck, look at that lightning!'"

Torrential rain was driven by wind gusts. "I went, 'Hang on'—and basically, that's how the song was written," he laughs, "with me getting excited, waiting for new shit to happen."

"Hells Bells" was basically Brian Johnson delivering a weather report. "Sandstorm from the beach didn't fit," he jokes.

# MOTHER NATURE

Brian worked quickly and didn't slow down to think about what he was writing. "No, I didn't." He literally watched his hand scribbling the words—similar to the process of writing his book almost 30 years later. "I think it's a bodily thing—just get it down real fast before I forget, because I've got a dreadful memory.

"There wasn't much thinking to do. I didn't have to stop and think, 'What rhymes with that?' It just sort of came out. Nothing sensational—it just flowed, basically."

It was just a little exercise in the weather being the master, he says. "I was literally looking at the weather, saying Mother Nature is terrifying if you were out at sea. Or you get hit by an avalanche. Or if you're somewhere where there's a volcano or high winds—you're fucking dead."

# CREATIVE SPONTANEITY

The lyrics were written in half an hour, and Johnson literally took them right to the studio. "Mutt just said, 'Right, in you go, and we'll try it.'" The vocals were immediately tracked and played for the Young brothers. "I don't think there were many changes," he remembers. "I think the lyric just stood as it was."

The scratch track brought from England gave him the rhythm of the music, but familiarity with the song was limited. "That was probably the first time I heard it, and I just sang what I had on top of it, really."

"I would never say it was easy, because that's just cheating your trade. But it certainly *felt* easy at the time. I had to do it, simple as that. We had a specific amount of time to do this album there. We had to literally get it done as fast as possible."

Johnson was certainly aware the band was gambling with his inexperience. "We've got this new guy," he reasons. "We'll fly or fall according to our choice here, and he's not exactly what you'd call well known. And we're going to try to make a record?"

"That's why I love the lads. They had faith, and I won't forget that in a hurry."

# ALL HAIL SATAN

References to Satan were beginning to creep into hard rock lyrics, but Johnson was conscious to not fall into that cliché. But the title and his use of the unholy name encouraged fans and pious moralists to read more into the words and label AC/DC as devil worshipers.

"Sometimes translation is a bit of a bastard. I can't stop what people are thinking. And if they think it's that, and they think it's *good*, well, that's all right by me," he laughs.

The line about being snatched by Satan was basically a reference to Norse mythology that attributed brutal storms to Odin's anger. The popular misconception instead was that the song was an accolade to the devil. That designation would pester the band throughout the decade, including an instance when Johnson says the band arrived in one city lying on the floor of their tour bus for fear of extremists shooting at them.

*Angus Young's onstage striptease was the misdemeanor some conservatives hoped would get him arrested for the greater crime of AC/DC being perceived as devil worshipers.*

The Parents Music Resource Center put the band in the sights of conservative coalitions hell-bent on saving society. "It was the stupidest thing. People must be looking back and just shuddering with embarrassment. Now, AC/DC is fine, bring the kids. It's funny— now you see kids backstage and their parents going, "'Hells Bells" is his favorite song, isn't it? Go on; show them what you can do!' They do the bell thing, then the kid's singing it.

"All of a sudden they realize it's fun. It's not evil. And if there is any evil or mentions of devils or anything, it's all tongue and cheek. It's double entendre. You use words to have fun with explicit things, whether they be religion, sex, or whatever, and you have fun."

# NEW VOCAL RANGE

Johnson finally heard the finished album after returning to England. "I didn't get a copy of the bloody thing until a month afterwards." He was living with his mother but had to call on a friend in order to hear the album "because me mother and father had a real crap record player."

He laughs, remembering his friend's disbelief over the vocals. "Fucking hell, Jonah— fucking high, isn't it? Way too high. You shouldn't sing like that. I've never heard you sing like that."

"Neither have I," Johnson quipped.

His mate told him it would never last. "I walked out of there pretty despondent, but at the same time quite happy with what I'd heard."

Back in Black *showcased Brian Johnson singing in a much higher register than anyone expected.*

# TIMELESS CLASSIC

Brian says he never realized how much listeners were taken by the song and the foreboding lyrics. "I never really thought about it. In my little world, I was just happy." Modest, Johnson would simply laugh off the idea that the song could be so popular. "I still do," he says.

But he's admittedly proud of the lasting appeal of the song. "It's still standing. It hasn't aged, and that's the wonderful thing I think I'm more proud of. It's just as fresh as the first day you heard it."

Memories of writing the song bring satisfaction, but back then there was no time to reflect on a job well done. "I knew the next day there would be another song and a blank sheet of paper and me with a pen. That was it, really. When I look back at it now, I realize something very special came out of that room."

5

## AC/DC

# Back in Black

FROM THE ALBUM **BACK IN BLACK** (1980)

*Highway to Hell* was a significant breakthrough for AC/DC, especially in the United States, where the band charted in the *Billboard* Top 20 for the first time. Nearly six years since a New Year's Eve debut in Sydney, Australia, their momentum positioned the next album to potentially be an enormous success.

And then Bon Scott died.

Acute alcohol poisoning and death by misadventure was the determination of the coroner. Sleeping off a night of drinking in a parked car, Ronald Belford Scott, 33, succumbed to pulmonary aspiration induced by vomiting.

Brothers Malcolm and Angus Young considered disbanding AC/DC, but decided that Bon would have insisted they continue. Newcastle singer Brian Johnson was recruited, and the band relocated to the Bahamas to record the all-important next album.

"They already had in mind that it was going to be called *Back in Black*," Johnson suspects. "It was obviously something really important to them. Bon's passing *must* have had an effect on the boys. You cannot tell me it didn't. I think they had written that title especially for the fact that Bon wasn't there."

Brian, then a novice lyricist, knew the title track would be a tribute to Bon, but without being outwardly obvious. "What they basically said was, 'Jonah, this song's called 'Back in Black.' Now, we don't like to do maudlin things about Bon. But we do want to salute the fact that he was our singer, that he's passed on, and he was our friend.'"

"No words of bye-bye and stuff like that, just do what you think is right," he was advised. They also knew writing heartfelt, yet ambiguous lyrics would be a difficult undertaking. "But they're clever, the boys, because they knew I didn't know him."

Legend had Bon once seeing Brian perform years earlier with his previous band, Geordie. Scott supposedly mentioned prophetically to the brothers that Johnson was a formidable singer.

*Angus Young (pictured), and his brother, Malcolm, asked new singer Brian Johnson to eulogize his predecessor, who had passed away just a few weeks earlier.*

# COLLABORATION FROM BEYOND

Brian studied the songs Bon had written, taking into account his talent for ingenious wordplay, and also the circumstances of his death. Trying to sound reverent without being melodramatic was difficult. "It was pretty hard," he admits.

The opening line about hitting the sack, Johnson says, "basically means I'm gone. When you hit the sack, you go to sleep, which is exactly what he did in the back of a car."

Brian is not exactly sure what he was trying to convey. "I can't explain it. There's something there that was much more clever than I could ever be, and it just sort of tumbled onto the page."

*The nighttime ambiance of the area surrounding Compass Point Studios cast a spooky shadow over Brian Johnson while he wrote the lyrics to "Back in Black."*

The area surrounding Compass Point Studios was dangerous, he remembers. Each band member was provided with fishing spears and machetes for protection. Yorkshire singer Robert Palmer lived down the road, and Haitian drug dealers ensconced in the hills had already killed his dog and held his parents at gunpoint. "It was scary. They tried to break into our [rooms]. We put a chair up against the door, and I had these six-foot fishing spears," he laughs.

And nights were dark, he remembers. "I mean, pitch black. There was no light where we were." The ambiance felt unearthly. "Hairs were standing on end, and I was just writing away. It was just a strange, funny feeling."

"It's fucking spooky in that room," he later told Malcolm, and Brian wondered if some sort of metaphysical inspiration was channeled through Bon, contrary to his rational nature. "I'm *definitely* not like that. But I never made much of it because I didn't want anybody to start a big thing about it."

*Johnson says the song was a way for Angus Young (pictured) and the rest of the band to express mourning for their departed singer and celebrate his life.*

# MAKING THE GRADE

Producer Mutt Lange suggested a few changes, but lyrical revisions were minimal. "Some verses had a couple lines too many, so [he] would make us drop a couple because it just didn't fit."

Any extraneous words were likely because Brian was writing blind. Other than checking the key of the song by singing the title while previously in England, he had no other guide to the direction of the music. The recording cycle put him at work writing lyrics while the band tracked the song.

Recording at such a rushed pace was just another whirlwind facet of the new experience that added to the spontaneity of Brian's creativity. "Coming from England, all of a sudden I'm in this big, posh studio with posh producers and great musicians."

But the band approved of the lyrics that honored their departed mate, so he felt gratified. "They quite liked them, so I was very pleased that I passed muster."

# TRIBUTE TO A STRANGER

Johnson, coming into the unfamiliar situation of trying to write lyrics and working with a new band, was essentially asked to eulogize his predecessor, someone he never knew. His levelheaded nature allowed him to approach the situation simply as a task to be done. "The more you think about something, the less you get done. I just got it done. I just gritted my teeth and got on with it.

"'Back in Black' was just a lovely way of saying we're mourning, but we're living— basically, we're living, and we're celebrating this lad. We just want everybody to know that we love him, and we think of him a lot. But that's all you're getting out of these boys. You'll not squeeze one teardrop out of them."

Although the song was a tribute, Johnson also managed to immortalize Bon Scott as a presence that was larger than life.

"He deserves to be. He was a lad and a half. He was part of AC/DC; that turned the world upside down as far as rock-and-roll genre. [They] didn't fit within a genre," he laughs. "It was different. They were just *them*."

# RIGOROUS SINGING

The vocal attack of the phrasing and the phonetic flow of the words created a dynamic that exuded defiance and exhilaration.

"It's powerful, and it fits *right* into the groove of the music. What I did was try to make it sound like a guitar solo type of thing [with] the voice." That delivery was totally unplanned, he says. "I just sang it off the top of me head, and it was very high. I went, 'Holy *fuck*!' And Mutt's going, 'Yeah, it's a little high, isn't it?' High! It's in the stratosphere."

Johnson never considered the physical demands of the song beyond the studio. It wasn't until the first time he sang the song live that it became apparent what was necessary to belt it out. "It's a bugger for breathing, that one. It's a mouthful of words, and then you go straight into the chorus. And as soon as you finish the chorus, the second verse starts straight in. It really took me by storm."

# RITE OF PASSAGE

*Back in Black* became a rite of passage for successive generations discovering hard rock and heavy metal. The song itself earned the right to genuinely be considered timeless. Teenagers seeing the *Black Ice* tour in 2009 reacted with the same energetic headbanging as kids who bought the album in 1980. "It's quite strange when you see the arms go up as one—it's wonderful, in fact.

"Everybody's got their favorite songs. But every gig we [play]—every gig—when the guys start 'Back in Black,' the crowd goes fucking nuts. Now, for a mid-tempo song, that's pretty cool."

It became a sporting event anthem. Clicking through channels and hearing the song when televised games return from commercial breaks is wonderful, Johnson says, because the song has transcended the evil designation it used to sustain.

"Now, it's all right. There's nothing bad about it." The song has become even more mainstream from its use in the 2008 blockbuster, *Iron Man*, and Johnson says the filmmakers want it again for the sequel. "The producer said, '"Back in Black" and *Iron Man* are as one. You can't have one without the other,' which is a wonderful tribute."

## 6

## MOTÖRHEAD

# Ace of Spades

FROM THE ALBUM **ACE OF SPADES** (1980)

Motörhead was onstage at The Palace in Los Angeles during the 1996 Concrete Marketing Foundations Forum conference, performing for an audience consisting of numerous music industry attendees. The band was about to launch into "Ace of Spades" when Phil Campbell's guitar malfunctioned. Rather than disrupt the performance, he simply panto-mimed air guitar through the entire song while his tech scrambled to correct the problem.

"I couldn't believe it when I looked around," remembers Lemmy Kilmister. But what could have been an absurd scene from *This Is Spinal Tap* actually heightened the adventurous spirit of their signature song. The spontaneity made the exhilarating impetuousness of the lyrics resonate to a greater degree.

The words were a metaphor for the thrill of reckless living, an attitude that made heavy metal such an invigorating style of music. The sentiment of living for the moment with little concern for the future transcended the literal meaning for many listeners.

But Kilmister, who once considered publishing a book of his compiled lyrics, says it was never meant as such. References to blackjack, poker, and craps made "Ace of Spades" a glossary of gambling terms. "It's kind of hard to misinterpret those lyrics," he laughs, shrugging them off as a word exercise. "I put down every gambling cliché I could think of."

The irony was that his game of choice, slot machines, was not referenced in the lyrics. "I used to play the one-armed bandits a lot because we had them in the pubs in England."

Despite the vagabond temper of the metal and punk audiences listening to Motörhead, Lemmy never intended for the lyrics to directly represent their restlessness. "No, not at all," he laughs.

## SPONTANEITY IN THE STUDIO

*Ace of Spades* was recorded at Jackson's Studios, a small facility in the town of Rickmansworth, 30 miles northwest of London. The title of the first track was the beginning of the song, followed by the music. The lyrics were then written to basically fit the riff. "We all wrote the music together, [and] they just used to leave the lyrics to me. I always write lyrics in the studio, more or less under the knife."

*Lemmy Kilmister never intended the lyrics to "Ace of Spades" to be heard as a metaphor for living life to the fullest. To him, it was just a word exercise based on gambling clichés.*

That last-minute approach added to the spontaneity of the words. "We always work under the hammer. We're very lazy at rehearsing—we're no good at that shit. We're always lazing around in the rehearsal room and then panic in the studio. I'm always writing words just before I go in the [vocal] booth."

He guesses it probably took all of 40 minutes to write the lyrics. There were a couple of revisions, although he can't recall exactly what changed. "I'm pretty quick," he says. "(We Are) the Road Crew" from the same album took only 10 minutes and was recorded in one take."

# LYRICIST FOR HIRE

Lemmy has become recognized as an icon for his outlaw image and style of bass playing that is closer to that of a rhythm guitarist. But his talent as a lyricist has often been overlooked by fans who are unaware of his collaboration with artists such as Lita Ford and Ozzy Osbourne.

*His outlaw image concealed Lemmy's wit and talent as a lyricist.*

"Ozzy rang me up and offered an incredible [opportunity]," he says about penning lyrics for the multiplatinum *No More Tears* album. "Just lyrics—I didn't write the tunes. One guy said, "'Mama, I'm Coming Home" is really personal, Ozzy, isn't it?' And Ozzy says, 'Yeah, it is—Lemmy wrote it.'"

He also wrote the lyrics to "Can't Catch Me" on Lita's 1988 *Lita*. "I work good with women," he says. "I work good with men. Men don't have tits," he jokes, laughing. Although he got into rock and roll in order to socialize with women, Kilmister has never judged talent based on gender.

"You can't say you're a bad musician just because you've got nice tits. The women I've worked with are great musicians, or I wouldn't have bothered."

# NEVER GROW UP

Despite Lemmy saying it was not intended as such, "Ace of Spades" became a metaphorical anthem about spontaneity and the adrenaline rush of excitement. It fueled the adolescent anger and frustration of listeners hoping to defer adulthood. The spirit of the song—as well as Motörhead and Lemmy himself—has been to not surrender to the responsibility of becoming an adult.

"I fucking hate all that shit. They try to make you do what they did, all their mistakes. It makes them feel better about theirs."

Motörhead was always the soundtrack for that suspended adolescence, he laughs. "It keeps you from getting your hair cut and getting a nice steady job." And Lemmy himself has remained a constant example that people get older, but they don't have to grow up. "That's true, you don't."

# SIGNATURE SONG

Categorized as metal and punk, the fundamental basis of Motörhead has always been the early years of rock and roll and artists such as Chuck Berry and Little Richard. Many fans don't make that connection because they're too young to have readily heard that music.

*Lemmy has long been revered as an ageless icon of the spirit of rock-and-roll adolescence.*

"What people miss in Motörhead is the blues. The blues is the bend of the note. That's important because rock and roll comes from the blues. All the best rock and roll is blues-oriented—[Jimi] Hendrix, The Doors, all that stuff. The thrash metal bands missed it [in us]. They think just volume and speed will do it, and it ain't true."

*Ace of Spades* was released on Bronze Records worldwide and Mercury Records in North America. "The label that couldn't sell Chuck Berry," he scorns. "[We] didn't have a hit here with it because they didn't push it. The charts were full of shit, and you couldn't get the good bands on the radio."

The album—and especially the song—*did* gain attention in the United States through import albums and word of mouth. But "Ace of Spades" would become the single reference point most people connected with the band. Despite hundreds of tracks released on 20 studio albums over the course of a 30-plus year career, it has remained their signature song.

Although Lemmy says they would never not perform the song, for a period of several years he would claim during interviews to be weary of it. His opinion since has changed, and he's now happy to play it.

"You get tired of it for a little while, [but] I got back into it. I quite like the song. It's a good song, and it did us a lot of favors. But it's a cross to bear because people think it's the last thing we ever did."

It was just another track to him. "I never thought it was a particularly better song than all the others we were doing. It was just another Motörhead song. You can never tell which ones will catch on." Lemmy still has no idea why "Ace of Spades" affected people so much. "If I knew that, I'd have written 10 more."

## 7

## OZZY OSBOURNE

# Crazy Train

FROM THE ALBUM **BLIZZARD OF OZZ** (1981)

Black Sabbath concluded their first 10 years by firing Ozzy Osbourne. He had left once before, replaced for a four-month stretch by Savoy Brown vocalist Dave Walker. But by January 1979, he was gone for good, basically for the next 18 years.

Bob Daisley met the estranged singer at a Girl show in London. "I think it was September or October 1979," he recalls. The bassist himself had been signed to the same Jet Records label as the young band that featured future members of Def Leppard and L.A. Guns. "I thought, 'If I go to the gig, I'll know people there.' There was a chap named Arthur Sharpe, and he said, 'Do you know Ozzy? He's looking to put a band together.'"

Once introduced, Bob says Osbourne asked outright if he was interested in working together. They convened at the singer's home with his local musician friends, but Daisley was concerned that they were less than world-class players. "I had a word with Ozzy about that, and he said, 'Oh, I know a guitarist that I've already seen. His name is Randy Rhoads.'"

Jet Records flew the 22-year-old Quiet Riot guitarist to England. "The three of us began writing sessions and auditioning drummers."

# ALL ABOARD

"Randy already had the riff for 'Crazy Train,' and musically we worked on that together." The title, Daisley remembers, was inspired by an effects pedal that produced a chugging sound. "Even when he wasn't playing, you could hear that sound through the amp. I said, 'Randy, it sounds like a train.'"

They were both very interested in trains. "Randy was a collector of model trains, and so was I—I still am. Because [the pedal] sounded trippy and psychedelic, I said, 'Crazy train!' That's what got the ball rolling for the whole idea of the song."

The song referred to global tension resulting from the standoff between communism and democratic nations that had been omnipresent since the 1950s. "It was in the media about the threat of war. As a child, I remember the feeling of fear. I knew Ozzy would like that [concept] because he felt like that, too, having been through it himself. He was kind of frightened about the threat of World War III and how we, as young people, had inherited these troubles, influenced by the threat of nuclear holocaust through our lives." Despite childhoods lived through the Cold War, those lyrical ideas were not necessarily premeditated, Daisley says. They simply started to flow once the song musically started coming together. "One thing influenced another, which influenced another, which influenced another. The three of us—'Crazy Train' came to being before Lee [Kerslake] came in the band—were influencing each other directly and indirectly."

# BLIZZARD OF OZZ

The band was originally going to be billed as the Blizzard of Ozz, a name that signified a group dynamic while cleverly promoting that Ozzy was the singer. His father, Jack, actually thought of the name that Ozzy wanted to use when he first left Black Sabbath in 1977. "When we heard that name, we all said, 'Well, let's go with that.'"

It was definitely a collaborative partnership with real camaraderie, Daisley says. The unifying name was important because it represented their collective input. "It wasn't like an Ozzy Osbourne *solo* project. We were [all] writing, arranging, [and] co-producing."

Jet Records hoped to capitalize on the singer's popularity by listing his name on the album cover. "We actually agreed with them. We said, 'Look, you can utilize the name, so we don't mind if you have *featuring Ozzy Osbourne* on the cover.' But when the album was released, it had *Ozzy Osbourne* in big writing—and *Blizzard of Ozz* in smaller writing—which made it look like a solo album by Ozzy."

# BECOMING THE LYRICIST

Bob had written songs in the past, but he didn't consider himself a proper lyricist prior to forming the band with Ozzy. He contributed one full song and part of another to the first Widowmaker album and started becoming more interested in the process on their second release, *Too Late to Cry*.

"When I joined Rainbow, the songwriting situation was pretty sewn up between Ritchie Blackmore and Ronnie Dio. It wasn't until that situation with Ozzy, where I was the only real lyricist in the band, that I came to the fore."

Ozzy, Bob, and Randy were living at a residential rehearsal studio where they auditioned drummers. "I came down one morning, and [they] were sitting with a pad and pen, trying to jot down lyrics for one of the songs. They had been working on it for quite some time, and they had about four lines. I looked at them and thought, 'Oh God, these are dreadful. No, I'll tell you what, *I'll* write the lyrics.'

"Ozzy wasn't a lyricist, because Geezer Butler had written the lyrics in Black Sabbath. And Randy, as a lyricist, he was a great guitar player," Bob laughs. "I would definitely take over that role in the band straight away. I suppose it was meant to be, and that's what happened. I wore the lyricist hat ever after that."

Writing lyrics diametrically different from Black Sabbath was never purposely done, he chuckles. "I knew which band Ozzy had come from, that was obvious. I thought they were a good band, but to be honest, I wasn't that familiar with them. My background always lent toward the heavier stuff, so I didn't want to write anything airy fairy or pop-y. But there was no real comparison to Sabbath on my part. I just wrote according to our music and how I felt and what I thought would suit us."

# COLLABORATION MADE INSPIRATION

Although Bob says he almost singularly handled the task of writing the lyrics, the characteristics of Ozzy's voice greatly shaped which words were written. "Ozzy's vocal melodies were always strong and very important. Quite often when we were rehearsing and writing, I would tape the initial sessions. He would just be singing anything that came to his head, just nonsensical noises. But I got an idea of where the melody was going and how he would sing, [and] I wrote lyrics to fit his phrasing and melodies."

In that sense, Ozzy greatly affected the songs. "His input was very important. Not so much the content of the lyrics, but people influence things just by being there. There was definitely a chemistry with that band, those four people. Everybody brought out the best in everyone else. The whole, as the saying goes, was much greater than just the sum of the parts."

*Ozzy Osbourne and Randy Rhoads. Bassist Bob Daisley says the* Blizzard of Ozz *songs were very much a product of the camaraderie between the band members.*

"Ozzy had a couple of lines on it on the demo," Bob recalls. "But I changed them when we came to record the song for real at Ridge Farm Studios." One of his expressions did fit the context of the song, though. "He had a saying that he used to say to people: 'Oh, you're off the rails'—or 'That's off the rails'—meaning it's a bit off the wall. I thought, 'His saying will fit with my idea of a crazy train going off the rails.'"

# FISH, CHIPS, AND LYRICS

"It's funny—the last verse, I wrote that outside of a chip shop," he laughs. Recording in Surrey, he and drummer Kerslake had driven to nearby Horsham in West Sussex, "and he ran in to get something to eat. I had some paper, and I jotted down that last verse."

"Crazy Train" was one of the first four songs Bob, Ozzy, and Randy wrote together, along with "I Don't Know," "Goodbye to Romance," and "You Looking at Me Looking at You," which became the non-album B-side track on the "Crazy Train" single.

He estimates that the basis of the lyrics was probably written fairly quickly. But it took awhile to realize that "Crazy Train" and the other songs were distinctive. "I think once we started recording, we were starting to get an idea that we were onto something special. It was gelling so well. We would listen back to different takes and think, 'This is actually sounding pretty good.'"

Daisley thinks part of the success of the album and song was because they weren't contrived. "We didn't go into the studio thinking, 'How can we make money or get airplay?' or 'How can we have a hit single?' The musical environment in those days was leaning toward punk and disco. In some people's eyes, what we were doing was sort of a bit old hat. But we didn't care. We wrote and played what we loved. It was genuine, and it was from the heart, which is probably why it's held up for so long."

# GLOBAL STANDOFF

*Blizzard of Ozz*—and especially "Crazy Train"—would go on to become iconic in the history of heavy metal. "At the time of writing then recording the song, I didn't know how many people were even going to hear [it]," Daisley laughs. "We just thought it would be nice if we sold some albums and got recognition and ended up with a good product that we were proud of. But it went a lot further than that."

People identified with the sentiment of the song, especially younger listeners living through the heightened anxiety of the showdown between the United States and the Soviet Union under the leadership of Ronald Reagan and Leonid Brezhnev. "It's not just we baby boomers who went through that. This threat of war, this fear—everybody, to some degree, felt those feelings like we did."

Comparing the Cold War to a runaway train was meant to express how the nuclear threat emotionally affected people. "It's making you crazy. It's driving you off the rails,"

*The title "Crazy Train" was inspired by the sound of Randy Rhoads' (pictured) effects pedal.*

Bob laughs. "It wasn't a nice message to get as a child growing up. I'm sure other people have felt that in other ways as well. And Ozzy's saying—you're off the rails—fitted so well. It's a reflection of those feelings."

"It's an ongoing situation. Even though it's not as such a Cold War between superpowers [anymore], there always seems to be that situation brewing. And people don't like it. Deep down inside, human beings do not like war.

"Why are they living as foes? Because they've been brainwashed and mind-controlled into it through governments wanting to control them as a whole. Wars don't just happen; they're orchestrated and made to happen. People are divided through religion and politics. They think they're fighting for their country or religion or whatever it is, and they've been manipulated. They take the bait and fall in the trap. It's so unnecessary, so unnatural, and I think people relate to that."

## 8

## OZZY OSBOURNE

# Suicide Solution

FROM THE ALBUM **BLIZZARD OF OZZ** (1981)

The popular story was that "Suicide Solution" had been written about the late Bon Scott, who asphyxiated following a night of drinking in London. The beloved AC/DC singer's death was officially ruled the result of acute alcohol poisoning and death by misadventure. But Bob Daisley says his lyrics actually referred to someone else.

"Bon Scott was a friend of mine. I would be the first person to say yes, it was written about [him], but it wasn't. It was written about Ozzy."

Ozzy Osbourne spent a decade fronting Black Sabbath, the band that would become regarded as *the* pioneers of heavy metal. The singer was dismissed from the group in 1979, and Daisley remembers it had a devastating effect on him.

"[He] was very upset at being fired. It had been like a divorce for him. He was very uncertain of himself, his future, [and] his career. He was drinking heavily because of his fears."

Daisley says the singer would sometimes drink more than other times, even starting earlier during the day. Those habits became the inspiration to write a song that cautioned against coping by using alcohol. "It was an indirect message to Ozzy, but in general a warning to anybody who wants to drink their problems away."

# SUM OF ALL PARTS

Guitarist Randy Rhoads had the main riff for the song, something Bob thinks might have existed from his Quiet Riot days. "We rewrote musical parts and turned it into a new song."

All of the *Blizzard of Ozz* material was the product of close collaboration between band members. Ozzy provided the melody and vocal phrasing, which Daisley says were integral to writing the lyrics. He also remembers the singer coming up with the first line about whiskey being quicker than wine. Their ideas became a workable song while rehearsing at Easy Hire in London. "I've got a tape of that embryonic idea. It was probably [there] when Ozzy said that line. I wrote the lyrics later, once we started recording."

The word "solution" had a dual meaning within the context of the song. "Solution, as in [the] solution to a problem. And solution, as in liquid. I thought, 'That goes well with somebody drinking.'"

One line contained too many words, Bob recalls. "I had written, *don't you know what you sow can mean hell on this earth*. But it didn't sing right because there wasn't enough space for that. I'd written too many words, and he couldn't sing it. That's why *don't you know* was cut out. I've still got the bit of paper that he sang from, with that scratched out. Everything else stayed the same."

The newly formed Blizzard of Ozz band was recording at Ridge Farm Studio in Surrey, and the countryside environment of the facility likely had a positive effect on the development of the songs. It was another factor that contributed to the band camaraderie that culminated in an overall surge of creativity. "Had it been done in another studio, it may have had a different effect on us indirectly, and we might have gotten a slightly different product."

# ALCOHOLICS ANONYMOUS

Bob never knew whether Ozzy realized the lyrics had been specifically inspired by him. "I didn't say it, and I didn't make it that obvious."

"It was just a warning about drinking yourself to death for anybody, really. The liquid solution—the alcohol solution—isn't the solution to the problem. You're not going to do yourself any favors, so rethink it. That's all the message was."

*Bassist Bob Daisley wrote the lyrics to "Suicide Solution" as a warning to people drowning their problems with alcohol—specifically Ozzy (pictured), who felt uncertain about himself after being fired from Black Sabbath.*

"Suicide Solution" equated seeking solace in a bottle with slowly committing suicide. Although Ozzy's consumption was alarming, Bob says he never expected him to literally die. "I didn't really think he was going to drop dead. I've seen worse people. [He] was just the inspiration for the message."

Ozzy would famously state over the years that followed that the song was written about Bon Scott. "That would have been fresh in [his] mind because Ozzy knew Bon as well. We started that album around the 22nd of March; Bon died in February. So, with that fresh in his mind and knowing that Bon died with alcohol connections, that is probably why he connected that song to [him].

"It could be applied to the Bon Scott situation, but it was definitely not written about [him]."

# HEAVY METAL ON TRIAL

The song was alleged to have incited 19-year-old John McCollum to commit suicide in October 1984. According to court documents, McCollum—whose body was discovered wearing headphones while side four of *Speak of the Devil* still turned on his bedroom stereo—shot himself in the right temple with a .22-caliber handgun. The *Blizzard of Ozz* and *Diary of a Madman* albums were also found cued on the living room turntable.

Filed in 1986, *McCollum et. al. v. CBS, Inc., et. al.* sought to prove the song promoted desperate messages that affected distressed teenagers. The prosecution claimed it created an uncontrollable impulse and directed the young man to kill himself.

The civil suit postulated the presence of Hemi-Sync technology that could affect the subconscious and prompt an individual to enact lyrical suggestions. The plaintiffs claimed to hear the word "shoot" repeated several times as a lyrical phrase. Daisley disagrees. "If you listen closely, it's *not* the word shoot." It was actually Ozzy making a swishing sound while tracking vocals, treated with an echo and panned between the left and right channels.

He says they also connected the suicide with the phrase spoken just prior to the bridge. "The part where Ozzy says, *budge, get the flaps out*—they tried to read into those."

Budge was a Midlands colloquialism from the singer's native Birmingham that meant fuck. "And flaps," Bob laughs, "is a part of the female anatomy. End of story. There's nothing more to read into it."

But Ozzy was an easy target. "I think it was just clutching at straws or trying to get money out of somebody who was obviously having success." Daisley questions why no one ever probed the reason an intoxicated young man—who trial records indicated had emotional issues and problems with alcohol abuse—was home alone with a loaded gun and instead blamed the music.

"There was *nothing* in those lyrics to advise anybody to do anything negative. The message was, you are responsible for your life. The reaper is *you*, and the reaper is me. We all answer to the ultimate law, whether you call it God, omnipotence, the law of the universe—whatever. We all answer to that, [so] be careful what you do, that's all that meant."

Daisley says he was not indicted in the case, although his and Randy's names appeared on the appellate court documents. The 1986 case ruled the defendants could not be held liable in negligence; a 1988 appeal was likewise dismissed.

*The prosecution tried to connect an impromptu phrase spoken within the song to the suicide of John McCollum, but it was nothing more than Ozzy being cheeky with an off-color British colloquialism.*

As the principal lyricist, he reacted to the death of John McCollum with sorrow. "Very sad, very unfortunate, and such a waste of potential life. But the parents should have looked at themselves and thought, 'Well, what was wrong with our son that he should kill himself?' That's the one thing that got up my nose—they didn't look at themselves."

# BUDDHIST PHILOSOPHY

The first reaction Daisley remembers came from record company executives who visited Ridge Farm to hear playbacks of the album. He thinks it might have been representatives from CBS Records, the label that would distribute *Blizzard of Ozz* in the United States, who commented on their progress.

Still an unknown band, and Bob a relatively nascent lyricist, they had yet to hear any critical response to the songs. "They started picking out lines, and they're looking at each other going, 'Oh, this is good!' It was encouraging for me because that was some of the first reactions we got."

One line they commented on was Daisley's idea that the reaper is ourselves. "[It] means we are responsible for what we do. If you get yourself into the shit, you did it," he laughs. That line still stands out as one of his proudest favorites. "It's just an indirect way of saying we are all responsible for our own lives and our own doings. It's a message to people: Look at yourself first."

Some of the lines were simply wordplay on an old saying, he says: You made your bed, now lie in it. "Suicide Solution" contained numerous references like that to the Buddhist philosophy of cause and effect. "For every cause, there is an effect. Be careful what causes you make, because *you* get the effect. You create your own hell on this earth."

Daisley never suspected the song would become so controversial. The words were intended to convey a positive message warning against overindulgence. "It was advice *against* suicide—don't kill yourself with alcohol.

"What makes me proud is that it is a positive message for people not to drink themselves to death. Alcohol has always been around, and abuse of alcohol has always been around —been there, done that myself. Probably most people over a certain age will have, in some way or another, abused themselves with alcohol. The song won't date unless people become totally enlightened to the danger, which doesn't seem to be the case."

## 9

## Ozzy Osbourne

# You Can't Kill Rock and Roll

FROM THE ALBUM **DIARY OF A MADMAN** (1981)

Jet Records was founded by Don Arden in 1974. The independent UK label was home to Electric Light Orchestra—also managed by Arden—and later Ozzy Osbourne, whom the impresario previously represented as manager of Black Sabbath. His daughter, Sharon, estranged over her relationship with the singer, would leave his employ and take full control of her future husband's career. She would tell *The Guardian* newspaper in 2001 that her best lesson had been watching how Arden ruined his business.

Some fans speculated "You Can't Kill Rock And Roll" was an exposé about Don Arden. Bob Daisley and Lee Kerslake subsequently suing for unpaid royalties and reinstatement of performance credits lent credence to that belief. But Daisley says that's not the case. "I didn't have Don Arden in mind, or Jet Records, specifically. I would say more [about] record companies in general."

# LIFE EXPERIENCE

The title came from Ozzy, he says. It could have meant anything, but Bob wanted to make it more personal by reflecting both the disreputable aspects of the music business and his childhood rebellion sparked by the rock-and-roll lifestyle. The song was also indirectly aimed at Ozzy.

"I wrote it about being manipulated and exploited unfairly by record companies and music business management in general. I knew he had his share of that with Black Sabbath; I had my share of it, and I had seen it happen to many others."

The Australian bassist had long seen the business side of the music industry firsthand. Daisley worked his way through a series of bands in London before forming Widowmaker with former members of Hawkwind and Mott the Hoople. He then spent two years in Rainbow before meeting Ozzy in 1979.

The song applied to any musician ever cheated by the business. "We got fed so many lines—*oh, we're going to make you big stars. We're going to put you at the top.* People get sucked in by that. You concentrate on making the music, and you tend to forget about the business side of things. That's when they bend you over and stick it in—hard."

# HAIL! HAIL! ROCK 'N' ROLL

"You Can't Kill Rock And Roll" was also meant to be a bit of a nod toward Danny and the Juniors, specifically their 1958 hit, "Rock and Roll Is Here to Stay." Bob tried to echo that sentiment with his lyrics. "It was intended to be an expression of rock and roll as roots music. So much popular music tends to come from the roots of blues and rock and roll. It doesn't matter what other label you like to call it, the basis of it will always be around—it's here to stay."

Rock and roll has meant more than music for generations of fans. It has represented a lifestyle that nurtures individuality and rebelliousness against the repression of society. The song might have been written from the perspective of a musician burned by the business of the industry, but the words also heartened any disenfranchised kid ever harassed or discriminated against because of his or her belief in that culture. And that was intentional, Bob says.

*Ozzy lends Randy Rhoads a helping hand. "You Can't Kill Rock and Roll" insisted rock and roll could not be killed by conformity or authority figures. It also warned that the music industry can be an insidious business.*

"It's saying that rock and roll is a way of life. And [that] doesn't necessarily mean being a bonehead or a loudmouth yob," Daisley laughs. "I didn't go around breaking windows or stealing or getting in trouble with the law. [But] I certainly didn't like being told what to do. I did *not* like authority figures. Rock and roll, in a rebellious sense, can be a wakeup call for people against the system that manipulates and exploits them. I didn't understand it on a conscious level, but I felt it."

# BACK TO RIDGE FARM

The song really started taking shape while the band rehearsed at Rockfield Studios in Monmouth, on the Welsh border between Wales and England. "We were writing down there, and that would have been some of the earlier stuff we did for the first writing sessions for *Diary*. That was where it first came into being."

Along with the title, Bob remembers Ozzy also contributing some lyrical ideas. "And the melody is his. His melody is a very important part. When people get together and write a song, even if they write five percent of it, that five percent can be very important.

"Ozzy and I went up the pub, just for a little while, and left Randy [Rhoads] alone to work out a few chords and ideas. When we came back, he had the basis. Randy and I worked out the music for the rest of the song. Ozzy had the melody, then I wrote the lyrics to his melody. So, it was a pretty integral effort between the three of us."

*Daisley says he and Ozzy returned from the pub to find that Randy Rhoads (pictured) had worked out the basic musical structure for "You Can't Kill Rock and Roll."*

Daisley says the lyrics weren't finished until the band returned to Ridge Farm Studio, where the *Blizzard of Ozz* album had been recorded the previous year. How well the music developed was the criterion for whether Bob would ultimately write words. "It would have to musically pass the litmus test first. There were a couple of things that eventually we thought, 'No, they're not strong enough,' and we didn't use them."

The topic of the sordid side of the music business could have been on his mind for awhile, but Daisley says he probably wasn't conscious of any specific lyrical ideas prior to actually sitting down to write them. "I'd sit in my room at Ridge Farm with a tape of Ozzy's melody and write lyrics to fit it. Some of the songs I would just think to myself, 'Well, I can't do anymore today; I'll come back tomorrow.' But most of them were done in a few hours."

Bob estimates to have written about 90 percent of the lyrics for the song. "But there's a line or two, here or there, which was Ozzy's," he says, including one calling rock and roll his religion. Although Daisley says he really didn't want to reference religion, "Ozzy liked it, so I let that one go."

The line about a king being little more than a pawn was also written by Ozzy, he says. "That's just on behalf of any artist [or] musician speaking to management, record companies, people who manipulate musicians. In some ways we lose to them. A bit of a power struggle goes on, and pawn in a table sight is symbolic of [that].

"People who don't really know the art—the music, the writing—they tend to tell you what to do and how *they* want it to sound. That didn't necessarily come across in our first two records. We were given artistic control. But I had seen other examples of that with other people: *oh no, we don't like these songs. Do these, they're more commercial. Play these; they're going to get more airplay.*"

# PREMONITION

If the song bore his personal observations of the business side of rock and roll, writing the lyrics also might have been a premonition of things to come, he laughs. "Don't forget, this was only a couple weeks before [Lee] Kerslake and I got fired at the end of recording that album."

Bob claims that Ozzy and Sharon wanted to dismiss drummer Kerslake, but he wouldn't agree to the idea. "They kept asking me, and I said no. Eventually, they got rid of both of us."

*Diary of a Madman* was released in November 1981 with their songwriting credits intact. But the album cover pictured Tommy Aldridge and Rudy Sarzo, listing them as the drummer and bassist. "It took a long time for people to learn who actually played on that album. I even read a review in *Melody Maker* or *New Musical Express*—one of those papers—that said you could really hear the difference with the American rhythm section."

# ADVICE FOR THE PRACTICING MUSICIAN

Everyone in the band liked his lyrics, but Bob says the thriving creative atmosphere was not one that led to extreme reactions to the songs. "It was fairly relaxed. It was just, 'Let's see what we come up with.' It wasn't like, 'You've written a hit!' There was no whoopee, major celebration."

Asked if management or the record company took exception to his description of the often ruthless nature of the music business, Bob laughs, joking, "Yeah, they fired us.

"I don't know. I wasn't around to see. After that album was in the can, a few days later I got a call from Sharon saying you and Lee are out. So, I never even got to see what they thought of it, how they felt—any expression. Maybe that's why they fired me," he laughs.

He's not sure the extent to which the lyrics to "You Can't Kill Rock and Roll" specifically affected young musicians or outcast metalheads, either. "Over the years I've had many letters to my website saying, *oh, we loved your lyrics*, or *I grew up on your lyrics*—whatever it was. Sometimes they just generalize and say lyrics from those two albums."

Still, he knows the sentiment must have struck a chord with some people, especially those learning firsthand the pitfalls of the music business. One of his favorite lines talked about confession. "I always liked that because it just epitomized people sitting 'round a table and bullshitting you, jerking you off to all their lies and crap. It's kind of like being in a confession—we're all being honest with each other right now. Yeah, sure you are. Now can you take the knife out of my back?

*Although Bob Daisley and Lee Kerslake played on the tracks, Rudy Sarzo and Tommy Aldridge were credited on the first pressing album cover. (From left) Aldridge, Ozzy Osbourne, Randy Rhoads, and Sarzo.*

"But the line after that was a direct line to Ozzy, really. It was a way of saying, 'Look, we could be fucked here, and don't think *you're* going to get out of it just because you're Ozzy. You could be manipulated as well.' It didn't necessarily mean that it did happen; it was just a warning. The meaning—you too—is to him or to anybody who wants to listen. You *can* get screwed in this business."

## 10

JUDAS PRIEST

# The Hellion/ Electric Eye

FROM THE ALBUM SCREAMING FOR VENGEANCE (1982)

The concept of satellites tracking the activity of private citizens might have sounded like another instance of Rob Halford's affinity for science fiction. His futuristic "Metal Gods" lyrics on *British Steel* were an example of his love for that type of storytelling. But the technology described in "Electric Eye" wasn't fiction in 1982, he says. It was real.

"It was my understanding, at that time, of what was already happening, in the way that governments eavesdrop onto your private life. Musically, it's a great piece of metal, but it's a very sinister song."

Totalitarian governments watching and controlling the movement of civilians seemed to be a plot right out of George Orwell's *1984*. Popular culture was fixated with the novel and the arrival of the namesake calendar year, making "Electric Eye" particularly appealing to listeners during the proximate timeframe of 1982.

"It's interesting to think about the future. I've always been a fan of that type of futuristic, prophetic type of writing, whether it became real or not." But Halford, who had read the book, says it did not influence his lyrics.

It was the singer's awareness of technological advances, apparent through reports he saw and read in the news, which inspired the song. "They were developing these satellites that could zoom in and read the license plate of a car, and that was years ago! Now, it's unbelievable. They've got satellites that could look into the room and see two bodies in thermal imagery, sitting here talking away.

"I kind of used that as the plot," he says of the opening line about being observed from outer space. That's a great line; what does it mean? But then it leads on. It's very direct and just makes a statement."

*Rob Halford says "Electric Eye" was not prophetic. His awareness of developing technology inspired the futuristic lyrics.*

# STAR WARS

Directed-energy weapons were an early emphasis of what became the Strategic Defense Initiative. President Ronald Reagan's proposal to use land-based and orbiting systems to defend the United States against a nuclear ballistic missile attack would later be called Star Wars. Halford's perception of the information was the primary source of his lyrics.

"That was the inspiration for 'Electric Eye,' seeing what Reagan was going to do. Reagan was going to spend billions on putting up these GPS satellites, which the government eventually turned over for public use." They were originally used by the military, Halford recalls, until Korean Air Lines Flight 007 was shot down in Soviet airspace over the Sea of Japan. All passengers and crew were killed, including Congressman Lawrence McDonald. "The President said, 'Just turn this over to the public, because it's as useful in saving lives and as beneficial to the general population as it is for us in our military needs.'"

*Although the song seemed parallel to the plot of George Orwell's dystopian novel 1984, the Star Wars missile defense system was actually Halford's inspiration for the lyrics.*

Rob acknowledges the idea of a system of connected computer networks was also something that fired his imagination. "By 1990, the world was being connected globally by the Internet. But the world was already connected there on a military level. All the allies, like the UK, USA, Canada, they were already linking up."

Authoritarian surveillance was probably in the back of his mind as well. "We did that record in Miami. Some nights you would have these police helicopters flying around, and they would have these big lamps they call Midnight Sun lamps. They would just light everything up.

"I think it was a combination of that and just what was filtering around in the news that brought the idea."

# SCRUTINY VERSUS PRIVACY

"Electric Eye" is a song that is relevant within the reality of contemporary society. "Since 9/11, the world is under scrutiny, some people say for the bad," Halford says. "I personally believe that you should encourage any kind of assistance that can keep you safe. But, again, there are limits. That's why you've got civil liberty organizations. And most people in governments understand that this Big Brother thing can only go so far.

"It's a bit of a dichotomy, really, because people want their privacy. Yet they want to watch *Big Brother* on TV, or they want to see human car wrecks on *Intervention*. It's bizarre, but you can't have your cake and eat it."

# THE HELLION

"The Hellion," the 42-second instrumental that precedes "Electric Eye," is technically listed as a separate track, although their attachment makes them seem like a single song. "They are one big, long piece," Halford confirms.

Rob credits the allure of the instrumental to music theory taught to guitarist Glenn Tipton during his formative years. "He's not classically trained, but when he was at school, his mom taught him piano. He had a little bit of a lead into that world, so that's where that came from."

The title originated with Halford, who was admittedly unfamiliar with the term. "To call somebody a hellion is an American colloquialism. I either heard somebody say that, or I read it, or it was on TV or something."

Consulting *Roget's Thesaurus*, a book he still references whenever writing, the singer looked up the word. "I found it was a bit of a troublemaker, a bit of a Jack the Lad type of thing. I thought, 'God, this is so cool.' We didn't have a title for the music, and I just put that forward to the guys."

The familiarity of the sweeping instrumental evokes wild response. Halford says at the moment during the live set when the prerecorded interlude starts blaring from the speakers, the crowd goes mental. "They just go absolutely ballistic. Even though it's a little instrumental piece, everybody knows where it's going to go next. It's a very cool way to lead you into the rest of the music."

# SIGNATURE SONG

Although it was never released as a single, "Electric Eye" remains one of the more popular Judas Priest songs. Halford thinks people discovered the track because of "You've Got Another Thing Comin'." That mainstream hit drew people to *Screaming for Vengeance* and subsequently "Electric Eye," because it opened the album.

"It was a case of people finding the tune," Rob says. "It was pretty easy because it was right at the front end. It's full of melody, and it's led off by 'The Hellion,' so there it goes."

The song has become a staple of their live repertoire, but Halford says it's not unusual for an album track to grow in popularity over time. "When we released 'Painkiller,' we were convinced [that song] was going to be one of our biggest ever, but it wasn't. It took almost 10 years for that to get into the psyche of the metalheads for Priest and the metal scene in general.

"People find these songs. The fans find them in their own time, and they become more and more popular. All of that filters back to you when you're putting the set list together."

He says realizing how attuned he was in 1982 to the technological advances that would become common within the world is not overwhelming as much as fans still enjoying "Electric Eye" today. "It's the passion and fondness for a particular song that means something to you."

## 11

## QUIET RIOT

# Metal Health

FROM THE ALBUM METAL HEALTH (1983)

The initial idea for the title track of the *Metal Health* album might have subconsciously come from Randy Rhoads. The founding Quiet Riot guitarist, who left the band in 1979 to join ex–Black Sabbath singer Ozzy Osbourne's fledgling group, had returned to Los Angeles on a break.

"Kevin was asking him about road stories," says Frankie Banali. "Randy mentioned that the strangest thing he had seen were the fans in England, who would swing their heads back and forward while the band played. He said the fans called it headbanging."

Rhoads made the motion, and Frankie and Kevin burst out laughing. "That really was the catalyst for when we were first aware of the phrase and the jumping-off point for what much later became the catchphrase for the chorus."

Banali thinks the lyrics were based in part on three factors. Foremost, he says, was singer Kevin DuBrow's own frustrations that were illustrated by lyrical outbursts about being perceived as unintelligent and disruptive. "Then, there's the idea of an anthem from the fans' point of view, that teen-angst mindset. Thirdly, the necessary rhyming qualities needed for lyrical content and continuity."

Growing up, everyone has frustrations that manifest in different ways, be it relationships, school, work—or a band. "Everyone has these emotions, and with Kevin, some of that came out in his writing. Things shared by most people, to varying degrees, which made it relatable on a mass scale."

The lyrics were both a self-portrait and an observation of how metal fans were misperceived. "Kevin was both a musician as well as a fan—we all were," says Banali. "With Kevin it was more personal, because he was the main songwriter on *Metal Health*, and therefore [it was] loosely autobiographical from his perspective."

DuBrow was not one whose lyrics were shaped by paying attention to the social climate of the time. "Kevin was not a news guy—didn't read the newspaper, didn't really watch the news on TV. CNN had only been on the air since 1980, and Kevin would have none of that anyway. It was all about rock music for Kevin."

They would spend hours together, listening to music at each other's apartment or driving around in Kevin's bright yellow Opel GT while playing cassettes of The Who, Humble Pie, and Led Zeppelin. "Kevin was inspired purely by the music he loved. This was really bolstered with that new thing called MTV that appeared on our screens in 1981."

# DEVELOPING AN IDEA

"Metal Health" became a tangible idea once guitarist Carlos Cavazo joined the band. Carlos had been a member of Snow, a band that played the same circuit as Kevin, Frankie, and bassist Chuck Wright, who were together as DuBrow. Snow had had a song called "No More Booze" that served as a loose musical foundation for "Metal Health."

"The Snow song had a different direction and feel, but there was something there to build on." Frankie wanted more simplicity in the drum parts and an AC/DC feel to the tempo, without trying to replicate AC/DC.

Kevin wrote lyrics over periods of time and then bounced ideas off Frankie, who occasionally would offer simple suggestions. "I took a lot of pride in giving Kevin the vocal space that the lyrics required by playing very simple and setting the tempo of the song, to give him the optimum room for phrasing. He loved that."

*(Left to right) Rudy Sarzo, Frankie Banali, Carlos Cavazo, and Kevin DuBrow. Banali says "Metal Health" has always been the musical heart and soul of Quiet Riot.*

Banali says the song was musically a collective process. "The combination of Kevin's vocal style, Carlos's guitar style—which was different from everyone we had previously played with in DuBrow—and Chuck's wonderful abilities as a bass player made the song complete. Kevin and I always recognized that song as the real musical heart and definition of what we wanted Quiet Riot to be, but it was a work in progress over time."

Frankie thinks the first time Quiet Riot played the song from start to finish was at Uncle, a rehearsal studio in Van Nuys, California. He remembers adding it to the set and playing it live sometime in early 1982, before recording started on *Metal Health*. "We knew it was a special song—a representative song—the first time we played it from start to finish."

*Frankie Banali took great pride in his drumming allowing Kevin DuBrow the optimum vocal space to properly deliver the lyrics.*

# SIGNATURE SONG

It was Kevin's singing that stood out to the band. The rebellious lyrics were secondary to the larger-than-life character belting them out with limitless energy. Still, they appreciated the caliber of the words. "There were really clever lines that we all giggled about with enthusiasm, while raising our fists in the air like angry teamsters!"

The potential to be an anthem was not lost on the band, and Frankie says they loved playing it. "We would have played it twice in a set if we could have gotten away with it." In later years they would somewhat do that, with its familiar beginning used as an intro to whatever song opened the show. But "Metal Health" would always close the show, Frankie insists, "the position of pride and honor for us.

"We thought it was the best song on the record, certainly the most original as a complete song, and the body of the lyrics was perfect for the mood of the song."

# BECOMING AN ANTHEM

The video for "Metal Health" was the first one shot for the album, but it was largely ignored. Instead, their Slade cover became the hit single that earned Quiet Riot their initial success, in turn gaining recognition for the title track. "'Cum on Feel the Noize,' without a doubt, was the crown on the head of Quiet Riot," Banali says. "But 'Metal Health' was always, and will always be, the heart and soul of the band.

"There's nothing like the feeling we both got each time we played that song live and saw everyone with their fists raised high, slamming to the rhythm and beat, yelling out the chorus. Kevin would often turn around and look at me with that beaming, almost childlike smile of pride and yell out, 'Yeah, baby, now *that's* what I'm talking about,' and we would both crack up. I miss that now."

At the time, none of the band thought much about whether the lyrics would be fervently accepted or whether the song would continue to rouse an audience so many years later. "I think it's safe to say that the song, the music, and the lyric has become part of the fabric of the genre, as well as a pivotal point of the soundtrack of its generation."

Frankie thinks the lyrics made such an impact because they deal with angst and the fringe element that is rock society—and maybe the idea that metal fans are indeed crazy.

"Anytime a songwriter can write how they feel, it's always honest, no matter if you agree with it or not," Frankie says. They reveal in part how Kevin viewed the world and what he was about. "Defiant, defiant, defiant. The whole idea of 'You won't tell me what to do.'"

# METAL HEALTH OR
# BANG YOUR HEAD?

The title of the song has been listed various ways since the first pressing of *Metal Health*, often incorporating the "Bang Your Head" subtitle. But Banali says the correct title is simply "Metal Health." "I think because the boisterous chorus begins with 'Bang your head,' many people started referring to it as 'Bang Your Head.' At some point, I'm sure it must have been via the marketing department at CBS and Epic Records that it was decided that it would be best for print to have it listed as 'Bang Your Head.'"

*The defiant attitude and larger-than-life charisma of "Metal Health" was purely Kevin DuBrow (pictured), says Banali.*

Hearing the song now takes Frankie right back to recording it, when Kevin first laid down the vocal track. "It was the best of times—we were making a record, at long last—and the worst of times—we were all broke—and I love that memory."

For Frankie, what has always stood out has been Kevin DuBrow singing about being defiant and having the power to make a loud noise. "All of that is purely Kevin, who he was from beginning to end," Banali says about the lyrics. Frankie says he can close his eyes and imagine Kevin onstage singing the song.

Banali admits he really doesn't know why the song is still so valued today, but he speculates that maybe it just represents fun. "This style of music was fun, and the '80s were a fun decade. I think it's still relevant because a great song is a great song, for the newer fans not around for that decade, but also because, for the older fans, it takes them back to a time and place when life seemed a little more fun, a little more free—a time when you could bang your head and it meant something."

## 12

## DIO

# ⸸oly Diver

FROM THE ALBUM **HOLY DIVER** (1983)

Some listeners might have speculated that the title track on *Holy Diver* was allegorical, based on Revelations 12:9, the Biblical scripture about Satan cast to Earth and then banished to hell. "Everyone has a concept about what you've written, and that's good," says Ronnie James Dio, "because they make their own determination.

"You want to make this your song? Go right ahead," he encourages. But, the singer says, "that's not what I wrote the song about."

The Holy Diver was conceived as a messianic character. "In the way Christ was purportedly sent to Earth—in this case, we're going to call it Planet Starlet—he was sent to atone for the sins of the masses, so they won't be destroyed by God."

Dio imagined that if inhabitants of a fictional world wanted salvation, perhaps other worlds would also need deliverance—like Earth. "This messiah figure decided he was going to do the same thing for Earth. Now comes the plea from the people of Planet Starlet, saying don't go. There are bad things there. They're going to try to do horrible things to you. You'll be riding on a tiger, please don't go."

The point of the song was to illustrate the self-indulgence of humanity, assuming, Dio says, the fictitious people of Planet Starlet were human.

"It shows extreme selfishness. Stay here, then we'll be all right. Don't go away to help anyone else.

"It's the old British saying: Fuck you, Jack, I'm all right. That's what the song is about."

# GROCERY STORE TO THE SHED

"I had a house that had a tiny little room off to the side of the garage. I converted it into a little studio with nothing but a reel-to-reel recorder and things I made myself to plug in here and there."

The first song for the album that would become *Holy Diver* was written in that makeshift studio. But the idea itself came from the notion of a title Ronnie envisioned on the way back from the grocery store.

"Going from the local Ralph's in the San Fernando Valley, I came upon that title as I was driving home. It was the corner of Wilbur Avenue and Oxnard Street. That's when I thought of it, and I rushed home, whipped out to my little shed, and started putting it down."

Fragments of lyrics and phrases were in his mind for probably three weeks, he says, before coming up with the title. "I had some musical ideas for it, some chord change ideas." Once the title was established and a couple formative lines were added to reveal direction, the whole thing developed in about three weeks.

Ronnie's role in the creative process of Rainbow and Black Sabbath had primarily been composing melodies and writing lyrics, then singing them. Collaborating with guitarists Ritchie Blackmore and Tony Iommi left no need to write or play music. Prior to forming Dio, writing "Holy Diver" would be a different method. "It was the first time I consciously sat down and went, 'I think I'm going to have to write myself a blockbuster,' and attempted to do that. Not that it was a blockbuster when I finished, but I thought, 'Man, that's a great song!'"

The singer realized right away that he was writing something special. "I did, actually, yeah. I really did. I thought it was a really good piece of music."

"Holy Diver" became the cornerstone of beginning a new musical venture after leaving Black Sabbath in 1982. "It was just a song that felt good to me. I thought it was a great song to build an album around, to build a band around. After writing the second one, 'Don't Talk to Strangers,' I knew I had two complete winners, and the rest of it was easy."

*Despite the mythological fantasy that fans loved about Dio's lyrics, "Holy Diver" was actually born on the way home from the grocery store.*

# GODS AND MONSTERS

The song had nothing to do with the social culture of the time, but inspiration for the lyrics certainly came from Ronnie's early Catholic upbringing, when he would attend church school on Wednesdays. "I was told by the sisters that I should be afraid I was going to burn in hell—and it's okay to smack me with a ruler.

"That person up on that cross died for your sins—because I sinned," he remembers being told. "All the statues had no eyes, no pupils, nothing. They were just dead figures to me. I right away rebelled against that and said, 'This is bullshit.'"

A self-professed nonbeliever in any standard church regimen, he describes his background not as a lack of religiousness, but as resentment that it was subjugation.

"I thought religion, which is supposed to be such a beautiful thing, shouldn't be taught by fear. It was, to me, always taught by fear."

In addition to the self-seeking disposition of humanity, illustrated by the Holy Diver from Planet Starlet, the song was a commentary about beliefs and isms. "The inconsistency of religion, because I think it's such crap—that was the inspiration behind all that. I've used a lot of religious subjects and attitudes in the songs I've written, because it's supposed to be so good, but I find it inconsistently evil. But it's a great subject to write about!"

The album cover also reflected that conviction against religious oppression. Murray, the unearthly Dio mascot, was pictured drowning a Catholic priest. "My response was always, 'Well, how do you know it's not a priest drowning a monster?'" The increased allegations of child abuse by clergy throughout the 2000s prompted him to suggest, "I might have been right on that one."

*Denouncing the subjugation of organized religion was a theme Ronnie James Dio would regularly revisit with his lyrics, largely in defiance of his childhood indoctrination.*

# SWORDS AND RAINBOWS

The video for "Holy Diver" offered no clues to the mystery of the lyrics. The concept had nothing to do with the meaning of the song, Dio says. "It turned out to be me going through this grimy place with a sword, swinging the sword around for no reason and seeing a hawk or an owl or something."

The clip was filmed in the basement of an old, burned-out church in London. "We did that for two days, I think. We had some extra time, and someone said, 'Hey, why don't we do one for "Rainbow in the Dark"?'"

Although the premise of the video made no sense to him, Ronnie was pleased that it led to "Rainbow in the Dark" being filmed as an afterthought. "It became the most successful video we ever had, I think, aside from 'The Last in Line.'"

Positioned atop the EMI building, the additional footage was shot over the course of about five hours. "It would have been less, but it rained, then it stopped. Then it rained, and it stopped raining. Every time it rained, I got soaked, and my hair never matches in that particular video."

# LASTING APPEAL

The enigma of the title is what Ronnie suspects beckoned to fans. "No one had any clue. 'Holy Diver'? My God, what the hell is that all about? Right away, that was striking as an image—well, what's *this* going to be about? That's definitely the most important part of the song. What came after was a bonus."

"Holy Diver" would become a signature song for Dio, the band—along with "Rainbow in the Dark" and later "The Last in Line"—even though he thinks listeners might have been confused by the ambiguous symbolism of the lyrics. The attraction was simply the melody and the opening line that began with the title.

Meeting fans on tour, Ronnie says the reaction is often them bursting into song, singing the beginning of "Holy Diver." "Every place I go, everyone has to sing me the first line. It's something they remember.

"When you're lucky enough to write a few things that make a connection with a lot of people, just a small little phrase, you really lucked out with that. I'm not a poet.

*Ronnie thinks the curious title that caught people's interest was the most important part of "Holy Diver."*

Bob Dylan is a poet. I'm a singer/lyricist who does both things together. That makes my engine work."

Dio knows he's lucky that most of the songs he has written have taken on an ageless quality. But that's not entirely coincidental. "They don't point to exact episodes. If they're not written in fantasy, which should take you to a different place, then they're about reality, but in a more slanted way. And reality is always reality—nothing mind-bending in [one] generation, only that it lasts in every generation."

He thinks people will always be curious about the veiled lyrics and come to their own understanding of the meaning. The song has continually intrigued listeners since 1983, including a successful cover by Killswitch Engage in 2006. "I think it will resonate until 2083, without a doubt."

## 13

TWISTED SISTER

# You Can't Stop Rock 'n' Roll

FROM THE ALBUM YOU CAN'T STOP ROCK 'N' ROLL (1983)

The period between 1980 and 1983 was a groundswell for heavy metal. Numerous albums that would ultimately be regarded as essential classics were released, and the genre was reinforcing itself through upstart bands inspired by the momentum.

Black Sabbath, revitalized by Ronnie James Dio, released *Heaven and Hell* and *Mob Rules*. Their former frontman, Ozzy Osbourne, issued two landmark albums of his own, and Dio himself would have success with *Holy Diver*. Iron Maiden claimed dominance over the New Wave of British heavy metal, while Judas Priest hit their stride with *British Steel* and *Screaming for Vengeance*. And in Los Angeles, two kids named Lars Ulrich and James Hetfield met through an ad in *The Recycler* and formed Metallica.

Heavy metal seemed unstoppable. But Dee Snider says the title track of the second Twisted Sister album was not based on that proliferation of monumental albums and bands. "You Can't Stop Rock 'n' Roll" was actually an agenda for its survival.

The song existed prior to that pivotal three-year span, he explains. "I wrote that in the middle of the darkest times for rock and roll. It was the disco era, and it was another one of my battle cries." That song—and others with similar statements, such as "Rock And Roll Saviors"—was a staple of their club gigs in the Tri-State area of New York, Connecticut, and New Jersey.

"It was a self-fulfilling prophecy," Dee laughs. "If you yell it loud and long enough—if you write it—they will raise their fists in the air."

# DEATH BY DISCO

Disco emerged from cult status in pockets such as Philadelphia and New York City. By the latter half of the 1970s, it was the predominant genre of popular mainstream music. *Saturday Night Fever* and the accompanying soundtrack brought the dance music beat to Middle America. Studio 54 became a cultural Mecca of glittery hedonism.

The saturation of disco created a dire situation for live rock bands. "I remember the era—disco, the struggle, all those things. You couldn't find a club to play in. You couldn't work."

So, the lyrics were meant to foster determination within himself to persist. "Oh, absolutely. It was very important to remind myself and the band what the mission was and not get discouraged. You were convincing yourself that you *can't* kill rock and roll."

Recorded as an earlier demo, the song was originally planned to be the title track of their debut album. But Secret Records president Martin Hooker, who would later found the larger Music for Nations label, thought it would be a mistake.

"He said, 'Albums with rock and roll in the title are doomed to fail, so we've got to change the name of the album.' So, we changed the name to *Under the Blade* and didn't record 'You Can't Stop Rock 'n' Roll.'" By the time they released a follow-up on the Atlantic Records label, the song had already existed for nearly five years.

# SONGWRITING MACHINE

Although Dee can't recall exactly when he first had the idea, the title would have come first. "As a songwriter, I almost always start with song titles. And music *always* came before lyrics."

*The disco era proved detrimental to a working rock band in New York City. Dee Snider wrote "You Can't Stop Rock 'n' Roll" as not only an anthem for their audience, but also a rallying cry of determination for himself and the rest of the band. (From left) Mark "The Animal" Mendoza, A.J. Pero, Snider, Eddie "Fingers" Ojeda, and Jay Jay French.*

Snider would accumulate titles by jotting them down for future reference. That list and a tape recorder would be the starting point for his songwriting process. Working off the title, he would establish the beat and musical feel as a framework to influence the lyrics. "I would just start playing with song titles and create ideas," he explains. "I'll sing some sort of chordal setup, mostly nonsense lyrics, although nine times out of ten there are a handful of inspired words that wind up as a cornerstone—besides the hook—for the lyrics that build up afterwards."

Admittedly, he was finding his style as a lyricist during the late '70s, and his earliest attempts centered on overt innuendo that felt awkward to him and Twisted Sister fans. "It was like, 'Hey, there aren't any lot of girls here—who am I singing to?' The dudes in the audience weren't really into it," he laughs. "Songwriting is a craft, and I was learning and developing, but also defining myself. Songs like 'You Can't Stop Rock 'n' Roll' were hitting the mark, and I could be convincing."

# PERSONAL STATEMENT

Snider quickly became their primary songwriter, but he was unaware of what the rest of the band thought about his lyrics. Dee was very guarded about his ideas because of an early misunderstanding between himself and guitarist Jay Jay French.

The singer was a few years younger than French and other guitarist, Eddie Ojeda. And, he explains, his Long Island upbringing was comparatively innocent to their respective childhoods in Manhattan and the Bronx. "They were city kids, and I was a rube, no doubt about it. And they treated me as such."

In retrospect, he realizes their attitude was not malicious. It was a natural reaction to their obvious differences in age and background. But going forward, Dee's defensiveness would affect the creative process of the band.

"I attempted very early on to reach out to Jay Jay to write with him. He didn't realize it, but I was very nervous to bring him a song, and he inadvertently rejected me pretty hard. He sort of dismissed it, and I sort of stormed off and said, 'That's it, I'm going to fucking write by myself!' It changed a lot and created the man-on-a-mission-to-dominate-all-things-and-control-everything guy, as opposed to making a band vibe out of it."

*Lyrics such as "You Can't Stop Rock 'n' Roll" fueled Dee Snider when Twisted Sister was the antithesis of disco. During later years they helped him reconnect with the angry young man needed to sing the songs with conviction.*

Even when he demonstrated the instrumentation for a new song with rudimentary guitar playing, Snider would not reveal the lyrics. He says the band would never hear them until a complete studio demo was recorded because the vocals were tracked without them in the studio.

"To me, it was very personal. So, I wouldn't ask them what they thought. In a lot of ways it was *my* statement. If they wanted to share in the sentiment, great. If they didn't, too fucking bad."

Which is not to say he thought they would embrace every aspect of each song presented to them. But rather than alter any lyrics they disliked, Dee would simply shelve the song and move on to another one. The others were never discouraged from submitting songs, but they rarely did, he says. The disproportionate ratio of Snider's proliferative output to one or two songs from anyone else pretty much guaranteed Twisted Sister albums would be written entirely by him.

# ANGRY YOUNG MAN

Dee admittedly likes a lot of his lyrics. "Still, to this day, when I sing a lot of [them], I get real inspiration. They reconnect me to those feelings I had 30 years ago. The words were really heartfelt and passionate. They helped to fire me up every night, back in the day, and remind me what the mission was. And then, as time went by, reconnect me with the inner angry young man that needs to be present to sell these songs."

"Words are power. I do believe the pen is mightier than the sword." His use of multisyllabic words was meant to empower both himself and the audience. "Using words of intelligence is important because it makes it less easy for the mainstream to dismiss your statement. By speaking their language, so to speak, these are words they can't escape.

"If you stand there and go, 'You suck, fuck you'—which is what I'm thinking—they can just say, 'You vulgar asshole.' But when you explain your feelings with intelligence and a degree of thought, it makes it difficult for people to escape them."

"You Can't Stop Rock 'n' Roll" was supposed to be a rallying cry. But, at the same time, it was a warning for nonbelievers, he says. It was a proclamation he wanted detractors of heavy metal to understand. The care with which he crafted the words was done to guarantee the sentiment was inescapable. "By being more selective with my vocabulary, I felt like it couldn't be dismissed or written off that easily."

Snider's affinity for smart lyrics and the use of metaphor developed during his own years as a fan. He remembers consulting a dictionary to understand some of *his* favorite song-writers. *Queen II*—specifically "The Fairy Feller's Master-Stroke"—is an example of the inspiration to strive for lyrical complexity, and Dee remembers looking up every word.

"My God, it *all* made sense! It wasn't just a pile of bullshit. It was all mythology and metaphor. There was a real intelligent and thought-out statement being made. And by hearing the message, I felt empowered by saying, 'I *know* what he's saying—I know what he's *really* saying, and it's not just a bunch of catchphrases. There's a real story under this statement that Freddie Mercury is trying to make.' So, I tried to carry that forth with all my lyrics."

# METAL UPRISING

"You Can't Stop Rock 'n' Roll" struck a chord with the Tri-State audiences that were disgruntled with the profusion of disco. Twisted Sister and that song provided a rallying cry for rebellion. "Although we were unsigned, we were literally playing to a thousand to three thousand people a night, five nights a week in the Northeast. The repetitive chorus, with me throwing my fist in the air, it was simple—*Snakes on a Plane*, man. What's the movie about? It's about snakes on a plane. What's the song about? It's about you can't stop rock and roll!"

Dee tells the story of meeting a fan who saw Twisted Sister 45 times during their club days. Curious why anyone would see a band such an inordinate number of times, the answer surprised him. "In an idiot savant moment, he kind of cocked his head and goes, 'Because I believed you. You were so committed and convinced that I just had to join you.'

"The words meant something to me, and I really, truly believed it. And people were joining just because they were seeing somebody that committed and that convinced."

The song resonated with conviction and empowered listeners by reinforcing their self-worth—they were not stupid, and neither was their music. "Exactly," Dee agrees. "I never thought the audience would be lost. I always knew there was an innate intelligence, and I wasn't going to talk down to [them]. They were smart, bright young people."

Dee talks about now meeting professionals who grew up listening to Twisted Sister songs such as "You Can't Stop Rock 'n' Roll," and he laughs. "And your parents said I would fuck you up," he scoffs.

## 14

## SUICIDAL TENDENCIES

# Institutionalized

FROM THE ALBUM **SUICIDAL TENDENCIES** (1983)

Heavy metal and hardcore punk audiences converged in a flash point that was "Institutionalized." *Suicidal Tendencies* combined fundamental elements of both types of music, and fans of either genre who struggled with the confusion of adolescence could relate to that track.

Bassist Louiche Mayorga remembers Suicidal Tendencies being the center of their own scene in the Venice district of Los Angeles, despite not having a record deal. "We were different from everyone else [with] our little punk look and everything."

People would congregate around the band at the park where they hung out nearly every night. It was a society of skateboarders who attended the same punk shows and basically watched out for one another. Through that social network Louiche remembers frontman Mike Muir meeting someone with a compelling story of parental judgment.

"Mike was telling me it was one of the kids that was coming up to him, telling him what his mom was doing to him. He was like a delinquent, a juvenile on the wrong path. So, he pulled what that kid told him and wrote his own version, mixed with some of the stuff he went through with his [own] family."

# CLANDESTINE LYRICIST

Mayorga says the music was developed first. "I wrote that track on the foot of my bed with an acoustic [guitar]." He then presented it to the band where they rehearsed, near the intersection of Indiana Avenue and Lincoln Boulevard.

"Mike would never sing at practice, so we were always just doing music. We never knew what he was going to sing until we recorded. It was always a mystery."

The band practiced the song, but Louiche doesn't recall them ever playing it live prior to recording the album. And Muir would never reveal lyrics until a song was either played live for the first time or tracked in the studio. They thought the music was formidable and continued to wonder what he might sing.

It was ultimately chosen to be one of the tracks on their debut release on Frontier Records, and Mayorga says they were certainly curious to hear the words. "I remember being surprised, listening to what he was saying."

"Institutionalized" expressed the frustration of being misunderstood by parents while struggling through adolescence. Solitude and hours spent in bedrooms thinking through adolescent changes was something many kids could understand. Some parents misconstrued that seemingly antisocial behavior as a red flag signaling drug use or mental instability, in some cases even committing their children to psychiatric care as a safeguard. And teenage metalheads already viewed as problem children were even more suspect.

"If it wasn't for that kid coming up to Mike and spilling his guts, [the song] would have never been around."

# MAD REQUESTS

No one ever suspected the level to which "Institutionalized" would blow up. The band felt other songs on the album had better chances of becoming breakout tracks. "We thought other songs were going to be crazier."

Suicidal Tendencies hit the road during the week following the album release. Louiche remembers traveling in a borrowed mobile home with barely any money. But a couple weeks later they got news that the song was getting considerable attention back home.

*Mike Muir (pictured) captured the frustration of adolescence and parental misunderstanding with the lyrics to "Institutionalized."*

Rodney Bingenheimer, the influential KROQ disc jockey who championed bands such as The Ramones and The Runaways, gave the track its first airplay.

"[He] started playing it on his show, and he was getting mad requests for it. They put it on regular rotation, [and] that's when it really took off."

The lyrical story was an obvious connection for many listeners. And Mayorga likes to think he provided a springboard from which Muir could properly deliver the words. "His lyrics were definitely ear candy. But songs weren't written until the music came, so I think I have a little part of the birthing on that. I gave him a good platform to write some lyrics, just a simple little verse for him to rap over."

The bassist refers to the vocals as rap, but the delivery was more conversational than the harshly accented syllables of that style. "He ain't yelling at you like hip hop."

Louiche can be heard shouting the hook—*institution*—through the speed riffing of the chorus. "That's my little two cents," he jokes.

The lyrics became famous for Muir pleading for a Pepsi. Miscommunication stripped down to that absurdity of simply wanting a can of soda became another principal hook. But the message was serious. "A lot of people could relate to those lyrics in some sort of way." Mayorga, who left the band in 1987, says he doesn't like Muir very much now. "But I'll give it to him, he wrote some great lyrics back then."

# PUNK MEETS METAL

Louiche was a rock and roller who claims to have brought a defining element to Suicidal Tendencies. Although he simulated the writing style of Mike and Sean Dunnigan as a template for composing songs, Mayorga says his musical taste led to recruiting guitarist Grant Estes and drummer Amery Smith to replace the brothers, directly impacting the sound.

The transition was punk played by musicians who cut their teeth on bands such as Black Sabbath and Blue Öyster Cult. "Heavy metal just came natural from our neighborhood, and Mike did his thing.

"If you hear the music, there's anger to it, but there's also some classic rock tone. I mixed up these rockers with the punk rock writing and the punk rock style. Bringing in those guys, playing punk rock, we were *killing* it! When we went to record, the beauty really came out. When the record came out, jaws dropped."

Acceptance from both hardcore skateboard punks and headbanging metal fans was apparent pretty quickly. He remembers the band being booked to play the Eastern Front festival in San Francisco. That two-day event featured punk acts the first day and metal bands on the second day. "One year they had us open the punk rock [day]. The next year, after the first record came out, they wanted us to headline the heavy metal show."

# DISASSOCIATION

Many people identified with the frustration of the song. "When we were on tour, people would be like, 'Dude, the same thing happened to me.' I heard someone say, 'That came out of my diary.' People really related to those lyrics. Everyone assumed it was Mike telling his story and how it related to them."

The scenario was familiar to a lot of kids who experienced the same parental confrontation. Those emotions continued to be understood by new generations of listeners who discovered Suicidal Tendencies. Mayorga thinks the song struck a nerve because of a combination of songwriting, studio production, and lyrics that were different from typical metal lyrics. "I was just happy to lay down the music for them."

Louiche says neither he nor Muir ever thought the song would become so well-known. He actually suspects the singer tries to disassociate himself from it. "I think he's disgusted because he hasn't been able to top that. I'm not saying he hates it, but that happened to be his first one, and he hasn't been able to beat it. *I* haven't been able to beat it with my other bands."

But he doesn't regard the lyrics any differently in hindsight. "If I hear that song on the radio, I enjoy it, the whole story. It's a little book. I think it's brilliantly written. It's like, 'Damn, nobody else can touch that.' Nobody else was even coming around that style. The mold was broken after that."

## 15

## ACCEPT

# Balls to the Wall

FROM THE ALBUM **BALLS TO THE WALL** (1984)

The title track of *Balls to the Wall* was a warning that oppressed people would one day revolt against their persecutors in a violent uprising. It spoke about the determination of spirit prevailing over despotism. "Yes, that's definitely about human rights," says Udo Dirkschneider. "[It's] against slavery and all that stuff."

That sentiment was natural, given the social and political oppression observed firsthand by the German band. The fascism of Nazi dictatorship was not far removed from their post-war generation, and the subsequent allied occupation of the country resulted in a sovereign Communist state separate from the Federal Republic of Germany. "They had no human rights when East Germany had the wall around the whole country," he remembers. "So, maybe we had the feelings to write something like this."

Udo himself had family that lived in the nationalized German Democratic Republic. It was frustrating to him that Accept was not allowed to perform there. "No, never. It was not possible. We tried once, and the cultural ministry said 'No, this band cannot play here.'" The government considered their music and image too indicative of the West.

In that sense, the song could be understood as a direct reflection of their environment. But Dirkschneider thinks the band would have incorporated social themes into their songs regardless of nationality. "I think in every country there are problems, and a lot of things are not the right way. Maybe, then, you write about the country where you live."

# COLLABORATIVE SONGWRITING

"The composing situation in Accept was two parties," Udo explains. One was guitarist Wolf Hoffmann and bassist Peter Baltes. The other was the singer himself and drummer Stefan Kaufmann. "Stefan and I were always the heavy stuff," he laughs. "Peter and Wolf were more commercial. We had a crazy voice on top, and underneath we had a lot of melody and good, heavy music. The secret was to put both things together."

The track was credited to those four band members and manager Gabriele Hauke Hoffmann, née Schmidt, who used the pseudonym Deaffy. Udo says the title was her idea. "The rest, in a way, you can say was everybody—some parts from this guy, some parts from *this* guy."

So much input might seem like a perfect storm for collaborative conflict, but Udo says there was very little difficulty. Instead, the number of people heightened the level of creativity and made the process seem effortless. "Everybody had a lot of ideas, and in a way it was easy to create songs."

*The members of Accept had a firsthand view the subjugation of the Berlin Wall and the Communist state of East Germany. (From left) Peter Baltes, Wolf Hoffmann, Udo Dirkschneider, Jörg Fischer, and Stefan Kaufmann.*

Despite differing personalities and their respective musical preferences, the singer recalls no major clashes over lyrics during the five-year period between *Breaker* and *Russian Roulette*. "It was easy working. When we were doing all those albums, everything was sticking together. That was definitely the secret, that all the ideas came together in the end."

# FINDING THE MELODY

Wolf came up with the guitar riff, Udo remembers. The music was developed from that starting point, followed by attempts to assimilate a proper melody with the titular chorus, which was the most challenging aspect of writing the song.

The singer was working with Stefan in a Munich studio, improvising gibberish in search of the melody. "I was really drunk," he laughs, "and not singing but talking." That different use of his voice created the ambiance of a slow-building insurrection. The nonsense syllables led to a melody, some of the random words anchored the verses, "and we sat down and wrote the lyrics."

Once the instrumentation and melodic structure was finalized, Dirkschneider can't remember exactly how long it took to compose the lyrics. The songs were being written during the recording sessions in an incremental progression. "Sometimes you worked on a song for one or two days, then stopped [and] started working on another song—work, stop, work, stop—that was the recording process. You cannot really say it was four days or whatever, [but] I think it took not that long."

None of the band thought it would become their signature song. "When we were finished, nobody was really thinking this song would be so big. It was okay, a good song." He says "London Leatherboys" was believed to stand a better chance of being the breakout track.

# NO DRAGONS

*Balls to the Wall* was the first Accept album that really dealt with themes of human rights, explored by the title track and other songs about discrimination against homosexuals and motorcycle gangs. There were references to social concerns on previous releases, but Udo says the activism became prominent with that album. The band was becoming aware of the social consciousness of their audience, creating a greater sense of responsibility to write lyrics of merit.

*Udo Dirkschneider says his drunken attempts at finding the melody were more talking than singing and ultimately influenced the vocal delivery on the finished track.*

"A lot of people would say, 'Oh, the heavy metal fans are stupid.' They are not stupid. They are really into the lyrics. We found out we could say more. Let's write about what happens in the world, what's going on every day—political stuff, not songs about dragons," he laughs.

Accept got a favorable response to the subject matter of their songs. It was an affirmation to learn how much strength some people drew from the lyrical statements. "Especially in the Eastern countries, like the Baltic states, and especially in Russia. The Russians understood what the lyrics were all about, and they were really into this song."

## WALL TORN DOWN

"There was a big party going on when the wall came down and Germany was united again. That was a big thing. After that, the Eastern countries like Russia and the Czech Republic, Hungary, Slovakia, all opened up. We saw all these countries, how the change was going on. It's all so good now. You can play *everywhere*."

Dirkschneider left Accept in 1987 and formed U.D.O. That band has since been his priority, excluding a four-year reunion during the mid-'90s and a brief tour in 2005.

*Balls to the Wall revealed Accept really starting to address social and political themes through their lyrics. (From left) Jörg Fischer, Wolf Hoffmann, Peter Baltes, and Udo Dirkschneider.*

But classic Accept songs remain part of the U.D.O. set, and "Balls to the Wall" has always been a highlight of the show.

The singer was finally given the chance to perform in East German cities following the demise of the Berlin Wall in 1989. Fans were excited to finally hear the symbolic song played live. Hearing that anthem as free citizens was significant. "It was amazing for them, I think."

# GLOBAL INTERPRETATION

Dirkschneider thinks the song is still recognized in the United States, most recently through its inclusion in the 2008 Mickey Rourke film *The Wrestler*. But American fans were less aware of the political statement than their European counterparts. The title created a sexual connotation that actually made the song seem lascivious, especially in conjunction with the album cover artwork that resembled a sadomasochistic pose.

"We had the feeling when we came to America that people didn't get the meaning of the song. Maybe they were thinking *balls*—you know, [literally] put your balls on the wall or whatever—but they never got the real meaning for a long time. But now I think they know."

The music video did little to translate the song. The performance clip showcased the band but made no visual reference to the meaning of the lyrics. "If somebody was asking us now to do a video for 'Balls to the Wall,' I would put together a lot of things from the news, real documentary stuff. That would be right for this song."

# HUMAN RIGHTS ANTHEM

The continued relevance of the song is disheartening because it means that human rights are still being violated somewhere in the world. Dirkschneider thinks the lyrics will likely still make sense in another 20 years. "I don't think we live in a world [where] everything is okay.

"It still happens in the world. A lot of people still get treated very badly. You can see it now in Iran and Afghanistan. The females have to be clothed to [their] face. They have no rights."

Udo says the most fun part of performing the song live is hearing the empowered chanting that follows the guitar solo. "For me, it's the best part. We had some shows with Accept when the people didn't stop—10 minutes, 20 minutes, the people were still singing. That was amazing." The most recent instance was a U.D.O. Christmas show in Germany. At the end of the song, the crowd picked up the chant. "It was really amazing. We had to start the whole song again."

"Balls to the Wall" is the song singularly most identifiable with Accept and Udo Dirkschneider, but he never tires of singing it with U.D.O. He's actually prouder now than when it was written. "When you're onstage, it's amazing to see how this song still works. We cannot do a show without this song. It's not possible. I see what's going on with this song. It doesn't matter where we play, people go nuts. That means you did something. I think it's one of the greatest songs Accept ever did."

## 16

## JUDAS PRIEST
# Eat Me Alive

FROM THE ALBUM **DEFENDERS OF THE FAITH** (1984)

"It's a cartoon," Rob Halford says about the track that put Judas Priest in the crosshairs of the Parents Music Resource Center. "Eat Me Alive" ranked third on the Filthy Fifteen, a list of songs the task force considered most reprehensible to the moral fabric of American families. "That was the one that started the stink with the Tipper Gore people."

The committee, formed by then-Senator Al Gore's wife, Tipper, Susan Baker, Pam Howar, and Sally Nevius, was informally referred to as the Washington Wives. They proposed that the Recording Industry Association of America institute a rating system, similar to that of the motion picture industry. The resulting Senate hearings and Parental Advisory stickers were criticized by numerous musicians and fans as censorship.

## NIHILISTIC CARTOON

The lyrics were comparable to the absurdity of *Penthouse Forum* letters, hard for rational listeners to hear and not laugh their asses off. "That's exactly what we were doing when we were in the studio in Ibiza," says Halford, "because we were all shitfaced drunk."

Judas Priest was in Spain, recording their *Defenders of the Faith* album. Halford's recollection of the song is vague, literally a case of being drunk, and a stream-of-consciousness flow of ideas while meddling in the studio. "I don't think, in all honesty, I could sit down and write that lyric if I was sober," he admits.

He doesn't remember who came up with the riff, but they were all trying to think of lyrics to fit the song. "It was a combined effort. 'Eat me alive,' I think [producer] Tom Allom came up with that suggestion.

"It's a fuck song, basically," Halford confirms. "It's a song to get drunk and fuck to. That's it, to be perfectly honest."

The lyrics were intentionally nihilistic, like a film noir movie, Halford explains. "It's like that wonderful *Watchmen* or that thing with Mickey Rourke and Bruce Willis—a *Sin City* vibe. It was a spoof; that's basically what it was."

The line about oral sex at gunpoint could have been—and was—interpreted as a penis metaphor. Halford laughs, acknowledging differences in interpretation based on the psychology of the individual listener. "I'm sure I've read my own theory or idea into another person's lyric. It's that misconception of, *excuse me while I kiss this guy*—no, it's kiss the *sky*. That's the beauty of music, isn't it? It filters into the mainstream, and people have their own ideas."

Despite the outlandish lyrics, the vocal performance is delivered with a seriousness that understates the absurdity of the song. But Halford says that doesn't mean the band is promoting violence. The idea that the line could be literal is wrong.

"In terms of a deeper reference—what do you mean, what are you trying to say—you can't legitimately say we're condoning rape at gunpoint. That would be absolutely abhorrent." Instead, he likens the content to the make-believe of an R-rated video game.

"All of us in this band hate violence against women. Guys get fucked in prison [too], and it's terrible." But the song never defines its characters as male or female. "It's a very ambiguous song, sexually."

That ambiguity was perhaps a subconscious means of expressing his sexuality, but Rob isn't sure. "I don't know. Maybe it was; I have no idea. It's difficult to think straight when you're drunk," laughs the singer who would reveal his homosexuality to MTV 14 years later.

*"That's another perception,"*
*Halford says about people*
*assuming his stage attire*
*confirmed an S&M lifestyle.*
*"I've never been the least bit*
*interested in that."*

# WILD SONG

"Eat Me Alive" was perceived by some fans to be a sadomasochistic narrative. "It's a pretty wild song," Halford says. "I've had some people say to me, 'Is that an S&M experience?' No, not at all. But that's just their take on the lyric. There are some people that get off on that type of thing."

Neither is the song autobiographical, he says. "A lot of people thought, you know, the way Rob dresses, with the whips and chains, he's into bondage and tying people up. It's a load of bollocks. I've never been the least bit interested in that, but that's another perception."

# COMING UNDER FIRE

The band viewed "Eat Me Alive" as nothing more serious than a surreal lyrical cartoon, and they had no idea it would catch the attention of a group of political wives, much less a Congressional hearing.

"I think we were in the UK when we first heard about all this PMRC stuff," Halford recalls. "We didn't know what was going on." Once informed that one of their songs had come under fire, the band followed the proceedings as best they could. "We saw what was happening with the Senate hearings, and Dee [Snider] saying what he said, which I thought was very, very cool.

"It's sad, really, all that crap—whether it's been the horrible perception of [Marilyn] Manson and Columbine, suicide and Ozzy, Priest and all this stuff—has come from America. We really love this country, and America's been great for Priest."

*(From left) Ian Hill, Glenn Tipton, Rob Halford, K. K. Downing, and Dave Holland. Judas Priest were targets of the Parents Music Resource Center's political witch hunt. "Eat Me Alive" was ranked #3 on the Filthy Fifteen, their list of objectionable songs.*

Aside from the persecution by the PMRC and a civil suit in 1990 that alleged one of their recordings compelled two young men to attempt suicide, Halford says Judas Priest has never had any issue with their music anywhere else in the world. "It's the misperception of another person's point of view, trying to convince people that this is an evil band promoting this, that, and the other. That's absolute rubbish. Why would a band like Priest want to condone anything that would seriously damage our career?"

Speculating why the PMRC chose the farcical "Eat Me Alive" out of a catalog of nearly a hundred songs at the time, Halford laughs. "I think they were looking at lists. From what I understood, they had their committee: Who could we get? Who's on the list? We were on the list. Judas Priest sticks out as a name, and we were successful in America.

"Radio was on our side; the fans were on our side. The vast majority of America was on our side." What confused him was the campaign being mounted by Democrats. "You would expect this from the hardcore, rightwing, Christian evangelical people—the Bush end of things—but it came from there. But it didn't take two minutes to think, 'Oh, this is all politics. This is all politics, and politicians will do *anything* to advance themselves. They'll lie, they'll cheat—they'll do whatever, as we saw.'"

## Conscious People

Musically, Halford thinks it's a great song. "The energy of the riff is very intense and powerful. It's got these great big opening guitar chords, and then it just slams into the riffage. It's a great song to play live."

But Rob says he hears the lyrics differently through time and sobriety. Thinking too much about the lyrical content, he admits, makes him not want to perform the song. "It's not representative of me, of the kind of person that I am."

He likens that hesitance to artists who dislike their most revered paintings. "They think, 'Fuck, that's a pile of shit. But people love it, so I better put it on display.' That's the dilemma you're faced with. Of course, you could be downright stubborn and say, 'I'm not going to do that song again.' But we have a democracy in Priest. If the majority want to do something, then that's fine. It's within the context of a stage show, and it worked the last time we played it."

Halford won't go so far as to say he was outvoted to include the song on their 2009 album, *A Touch of Evil: Live*. "It's wrong to say outvoted. It's just a discussion that we have. We have really straightforward discussions about these kinds of things"—like, he says, conversations about naming an album *Painkiller* in the wake of the 1990 trial.

*"It's a great song to play live," says Halford. It occasionally returns to their live set and appeared on the 2009 album* A Touch of Evil: Live.

"We're very conscious people. But, at the same time, we go, 'No, this is us. This is Priest. This is what we're all about.' We're this band that wants to do these things, and we shouldn't be pushed or cajoled into doing something, just because of an opinion or reaction, because then your music isn't coming from a true source. It's being guided by somebody else, and that's not the way to be creative. You put your heart and soul into what you believe is right for you at that given moment in time as a musician."

## 17

# TWISTED SISTER
# The Price

FROM THE ALBUM **STAY HUNGRY (1984)**

Elton John producer Gus Dudgeon built his dream studio in Cookham, a village in the southeastern English county of Berkshire, but a downturn in fortune led to guitarist Jimmy Page acquiring the property. Phil Carson, then the European general manager of Atlantic Records and longtime confidant of Led Zeppelin, brokered a deal that afforded Twisted Sister the opportunity to record there.

"We couldn't have been more broke or desperate," recalls Dee Snider. "We were coming off *Under the Blade*, and we had nothing. We had just about packed it in before we got signed to Atlantic Records."

Their time in the English countryside would be his most enjoyable studio experience. "Sol Studios was in the middle of nowhere. It was a really beautiful studio—windows *in* the recording booth that looked out over a river and an open field with horses. You could be in the studio all day and look outside. You literally walked over a covered bridge to the living quarters—they called it the Wheelhouse."

Recording *You Can't Stop Rock 'n' Roll* in a world-class facility was a godsend for the struggling New York band. But the experience would be bittersweet for their singer. Dee's son, Jesse, was born in September 1982, and by the following January he was in England. "I was married. I just had my first child. At the time I couldn't afford to bring them over. We couldn't afford phone calls. Once a month, maybe, we spoke on the phone, so I would write a letter home every day."

It was Dee who answered a phone call from guitarist Jay Jay French's sister-in-law. Smalltalk led to her asking how he was holding up. "I said, 'It's going great, but it's really tough. I miss Suzette; I miss Jesse. I'm watching him grow up with pictures.' She said, 'Well, Dee, I guess that's just the price you have to pay.'

"The phrase just hit me. I handed Jay Jay the phone, grabbed my tape recorder, and went into the bathroom and wrote 'The Price.'"

# SUBJECTIVE INTERPRETATION

The literal meaning of a husband missing his wife and son was a powerful message. But making that emotional connection would be easier in hindsight, when most listeners would then have reached a more relatable time in their lives. The specific context of Dee's loneliness would be lost on teenage fans, many of whom had yet to experience dating, let alone marriage and parenthood.

But he understood that their audience could not yet relate to that specific circumstance. "My [own] bandmates couldn't understand! Back then, they had no perspective on how tough it was for me. Now that they have their own kids, they couldn't imagine doing that."

Making the situation obvious would have been detrimental to the overall impact of the lyrics. "Really, when you start to make it that personal, I think it's being a little selfish. You've got to give people room to put themselves in there. It's the larger message that's important, not the specifics of [it].

"Lyrically, I always tried to not be too specific in what I was talking about. I didn't mention being away from my son and wife in actual words. I always want people to be able to put their situation in the lyric, read their price that they're paying for *their* goal, their dream."

Ultimately, the ambiguity of the words created an open plane for subjective interpretation. In that sense the song was not relegated to loneliness and missing a family. Instead, it suggested the determination of anyone who has sacrificed to succeed at an unspecified ambition.

"I do hear from people that the song was inspirational to them and meant a lot. That was important to me, that people be able to identify with it for their own situation."

# THE PRICE OF SONGWRITING

The Twisted Sister dynamic in 1983 was very much a team function, Dee says. And living together while recording in England was socially one of their best times as a band. "It was just the band members—work in the day, watch movies together at night, joking around. We got along great. Our live performance was very physical, so we wanted to stay in shape. Jay Jay and I were jogging and working out, going to the gym together and training."

Despite the camaraderie, Dee was the odd man out when the rest of the band would go out. "I was married, a very dedicated husband. I didn't party. So, while we were recording, I would work on the next album. When we recorded *You Can't Stop Rock 'n' Roll*, I was writing the *Stay Hungry* record."

*Dee Snider's longing to be with his wife and infant son was the heart of the lyrics. But "The Price" was crafted so individual listeners could interpret their own sacrifices as the meaning of the song.*

In that sense, songwriting—or the decision not to write—was yet another price. Its payment would differ for Snider and his bandmates. "I would sit in my room and work on songs and ideas. That's one of the reasons why I never shared the writing or royalties or any of that stuff. I was committing a lot of time and effort, making a choice: My art is more important to me than having a good time. Other people, no one was stopping them from writing music. They were choosing to go out and have a good time. I sacrificed that to write with no guarantee of anything."

# THE LOST HIT

Dee believes the song should have been much bigger, definitely a hit single. But following the success of "We're Not Gonna Take It" and "I Wanna Rock," the record company appraised the album as having run its course. "The Price" was released as a single, but only as something of an afterthought. "The concept of the credibility track followed by the power ballad had not been established," he explains. "So, they did a video for it—a much lower budget video—but it was sort of like, 'Yeah, we'll put another track out, but this thing's done.'

"I'm often told [it] tested incredibly well at radio, but the record company didn't really put any promotion behind it or work the track to make it connect. [Producer] Tom Werman, to his credit, was livid because he was a big advocate of radio mixes. He really believed that a car radio or home radio required a different mix to make it pop. They didn't even mention to him that they were releasing it, and he felt the song suffered from not having that mix."

# NEW MEANING OVER TIME

Asked what his wife thought about the song inspired by their long-distance separation, Snider admittedly doesn't know. "You know, I don't know how much she pays attention," he laughs. In fact, only later in his career did Dee learn that she never really cared for his singing voice, preferring bands like Journey. "She never really said anything. But she knows that song was about the torment of the sacrifice of my chosen path."

But the meaning has changed and continues to do so for him and the band with each year. "The dream didn't exactly turn out the way we wanted it to turn out. It wasn't as we dreamed it. We achieved it, but there's a lot we sacrificed. We didn't have the ongoing career in the sense we thought we would. We didn't have the longevity we thought we would.

*Dee Snider spent his free time during the recording of* You Can't Stop Rock 'n' Roll *writing songs for the following album,* Stay Hungry. *(From left) Eddie "Fingers" Ojeda, Jay Jay French, actor Mark Metcalf, A.J. Pero, Snider and Mark "The Animal" Mendoza.*

"And then there's the era [of] the band's demise and the money drying up, and not having planned an exit strategy—not having anywhere to go career-wise. Suddenly, you're paying a price in a whole other way. You're paying the price of still being recognized, yet you're broke."

Twisted Sister released five studio albums over a six-year span during the 1980s. But the band remains categorized largely by "We're Not Gonna Take It" and "I Wanna Rock." Another price—one that dissuaded Dee Snider from writing more songs.

"I stopped writing years ago because I was getting frustrated. Once you have hit records and television and mass radio exposure, it becomes frustrating to pour your heart out and put your soul into songs, and they don't get released.

*Two hit songs singularly defined Twisted Sister to the point of overshadowing the rest of their catalog. No longer wanting to write music is one price Dee Snider paid for that success. (From left) Mark "The Animal" Mendoza, Eddie "Fingers" Ojeda, Snider, A.J. Pero and Jay Jay French.*

"I feel blessed to have had any kind of sales and reach people on a mass level like we did. But, at the same time, it's not satisfying to me to write songs to just sing them in my basement. It actually hurts. My songwriting was getting better, [but] the business wasn't going to allow me the opportunity for people to hear it, to see if they liked it. There was no way to get through that impenetrable wall of rejection. So, many years ago, I just stopped writing.

"So, every year I always say the message—the meaning in the song—mutates and changes. It's actually a bit haunting in the sense that it's almost like it's following me. There continues to be a price."

## 18

## MERCYFUL FATE

# Welcome Princes of Hell

FROM THE ALBUM **DON'T BREAK THE OATH** (1984)

King Diamond says his fascination with the occult has always been much different than the public misperception of some nefarious allegiance with Satan. He calls it a good-hearted fear. "[It] goes all the way back to my childhood in some ways, from horror movies and stuff, thinking these monsters would come out from under your bed."

But it was a supernatural occurrence that happened in his Copenhagen apartment, shortly after Mercyful Fate formed in 1981, that really kindled his interest in the subject.

The singer, his brother, and drummer Kim Ruzz were waiting for guitarist Hank Shermann to listen to the debut Mercyful Fate demo for the first time. "We were in my living room. My brother and Kim were sitting [on] a couch, and I was sitting on a chair on the opposite side of the coffee table. We had just opened the first beer and poured it in a couple of glasses."

They debated listening to the demo before Shermann arrived. "At that point, my brother's glass rose up into thin air—at least two feet—full of beer. It got so quiet, and no one said anything, until I said, 'I *know* you both saw that.' They just nodded their heads. We just stared at each other and didn't know what to say."

Their conversation resumed, but all three of them refused to discuss what they had just seen. "It was not until about a week later that we actually started talking about what happened that night. That brought the interest for me to go to the library and start reading books about the occult."

It also became the basis for "Welcome Princes of Hell," he says. "That is in the song, where I say to these princes of darkness that they are always welcome at my home."

# SATANIC PHILOSOPHY

Books about Satanism always seem to be written from a one-sided perspective, he says. "They always talk about crazy stuff, cults—things that in my mind are completely [mistaken]."

He explains that his god is not Satan. "No, I am my own god. I don't believe in any god. That never attracted me." Instead, the singer developed a belief in free will that would later be validated by Anton LaVey, author of *The Satanic Bible*. "Of course, that book isn't really a Bible. It doesn't deal with religion. Satanism—the LaVey side—is a lifestyle. It's a life philosophy. I had that philosophy before I ever read the book and could totally relate to it."

"I respect that people believe in different religions. The only problem is the lack of respect between them. Religion has so often been the root of wars and still is today. It's crazy that people have wars with each other because of different beliefs. No one has been able to stand up and prove that they believe in the only right God.

"I don't think you should think of yourself as higher than others, just because you believe in a certain god that you think is the right one. If somebody doesn't have respect for me, for the simple reason that I don't have a religion, they can go to hell themselves."

# SONGWRITING PROCESS

King says it's impossible to know exactly when the song became a conscious idea because songwriting was such a different process. Technology has since advanced to musicians using computers and software to track entire songs in full demo format without a band. Ideas used to be more rudimentary, existing as simple chords or riffs that were presented at rehearsal. "Back then we rehearsed four, five times a week.

*As an adult, King Diamond believed in the philosophy of free will, further validated by reading* The Satanic Bible. *But his interest in the occult can be traced back to watching horror movies as a child.*

I would say, 'Hey, I have this [idea].' The drummer would kick in and try to find the beat, [and] songs were built like that.

"The music was done first. Hank would write a lot of stuff. He would start playing the riffs, [and] I would get ideas, then make cassette tapes so I could listen at home and fool around with stuff. That apartment was where most of the old stuff was written—my share of it."

Despite being not very proficient at communicating in English, King Diamond says he stands by the content of his earlier songs. Some lyrics admittedly sounded disconnected, but the lack of flair caught people's attention, he reasons. "The thing about being a little clumsy, a little edgy, it made them stick out more.

"*Melissa* was a little more sophisticated, better worded sentences," he says, compared to their first four demos. "With *Don't Break the Oath*, I think it was taken even further. There are intricate, better written lyrics there."

The language barrier also made it difficult to explain his otherworldly lyrics, adding to the misunderstanding that he was professing devotion to Satan. "I was pretty good at understanding English, but when someone asked me a question, in my head I would quickly translate what they said to Danish. I would come up with a Danish answer and translate that [back] to English. So, I was a little slow in that way."

# CONTROVERSY

Considering the growing number of political and religious factions pointing fingers and denouncing heavy metal as devil music, it's surprising that King Diamond remembers very little controversy surrounding *Don't Break the Oath* in the United States.

"I don't think there was that much at all. I think Black Sabbath got 10 times more shit than we ever got," he laughs. "And we're probably 10 times worse than they are, in that direction."

Negative reaction to the album was more noticeable in Europe. Despite interviews that clarified the meaning of songs such as "Welcome Princes of Hell," one Danish priest was relentless in trying to ban Mercyful Fate, claiming their true purpose was recruiting for Satan.

"There was not that purpose," King Diamond insists. "There was a purpose with the *priest*, I can tell you, so he would be in the newspapers and on the radio. The guy had it out for us, and he just didn't get it." The band ultimately appeared on national radio to debate their adversary about the lyrical content of their songs.

He thinks the band and their lyrics were not misinterpreted, rather misunderstood because of the demonic imagery. "I can understand why people would have that first impression. They see a picture of this lunatic with makeup on. They see a horned skull on the [album cover]. But that was not for shock. These are the lyrics; we want something that illustrates some of these things."

Some of the more amusing instances of protest were Bibles hurled at the stage during some European concerts, or the occasional two or three people demonstrating outside a venue and offering to pray for the band. "I would say, 'Well, thank you very much.' That I don't believe it's going to work is another thing, but, hey, it was a nice gesture, so thanks."

# HORROR MUSIC

People responded to the songs musically, he thinks. They were the soundtrack for a rambunctious night out. He also thinks fans wanted to feel scared when they listened to Mercyful Fate, similar to the sensation of watching a horror movie. But the listeners could frighten themselves far more than anything King Diamond wrote. For that reason he was never extremely detailed with his lyrics.

"I left a lot for the listener's imagination, because [they] can scare themselves *much* better than I ever can. If I leave some open space, they can make it worse than it really is."

Music is such a subjective medium that knowing what aspect of the song made the greatest impact on the audience is impossible. "It depends on what kind of pictures I try to paint and how they get transferred to the listener. How do they absorb those pictures and what do they build on them?"

"Welcome Princes of Hell" and the whole *Don't Break the Oath* album set the bar high for Mercyful Fate and King Diamond. "A lot of fans discovered us with that album. It has that impact—*where were you when you heard it for the first time*—[and] the first impression is always the strongest. When people get used to what you're doing, some of that edge is lost. You've *got* to keep getting better all the time, because people will judge most things by [that album] and *Melissa*, too."

# STARTLING METALLICA

If King Diamond felt passionate about the lyrics to songs like "Welcome Princes of Hell," it was because they expressed a very personal side of the singer. "There is *so* much more of me in there than anyone would ever know, things I've experienced."

*King Diamond suspects the imagery of the band, rather than the lyrics, caused people to misunderstand Mercyful Fate.*

The paranormal activity that happened frequently in his apartment was also a common experience for his guests—including Lars Ulrich and James Hetfield.

Metallica used the Mercyful Fate rehearsal room during the recording of their *Ride the Lightning* and *Master of Puppets* albums at Sweet Silence Studios in Copenhagen. King Diamond recalls one night when they were at his apartment with bassist Timi Hansen and a woman visiting from Los Angeles.

"We had a little party, and we got drunk. There were *so* many bottles on the coffee table in the living room. Lars and James and I had gone into my bedroom to give Timi and that girl some free space. I had a foosball table in there, [and] we were playing. Suddenly, we heard from the living room, it sounded like Timi had fallen over the table and all the bottles had fallen over."

They opened the door to see what had happened. "I had an altar at that point, [and] everything from the altar, including the altar cloth, was spread all over the living room floor. He was just sitting with the girl on the couch, and he was white as a sheet. A little later, the girl was crying in the bathroom."

King Diamond assessed the incident as a visit from the Princes of Hell and reassured his guests: "Continue drinking, everything's fine."

*Mercyful Fate lyrics were based on specific aspects of singer King Diamond's life. But they were written with a level of ambiguity, allowing a listener's imagination to create an even scarier scenario.*

# 19

## METALLICA

# fade to Black

FROM THE ALBUM **RIDE THE LIGHTNING (1984)**

Ivan Moody remembers exactly when he became aware of Metallica. "I was in junior high school, and a friend of mine, Clayton, used to wear the back patches on jean jackets.

"He came to school one day and had this *Master of Puppets* jacket [with] a *Ride the Lightning* patch going down the sleeve. I thought it was so outrageously cool, I was like, 'You've got to turn me on to this.'"

The future Five Finger Death Punch singer had been more interested in punk, especially the Misfits. "That was the first music that really pissed off my parents. But I hadn't really dug my jaws into [metal] at that point and found my niche, so to speak."

So his friend started him with *Kill 'Em All*. "A couple days later, he bought me *Ride the Lightning* and *Master of Puppets*. I bought patches, picture discs, the singles—anything I could get my hands on that was Metallica. When *...And Justice for All* came out, I was one of those kids waiting in line for the store to open. I was *completely* drawn in."

The speed and aggression that he already liked about punk was appealing. But the intensity of the lyrics *spoke* to him. Struggling with adolescence and living in foster care, Metallica songs voiced his feelings. "It was a whole new world of release for me."

*(From left) Cliff Burton, Lars Ulrich, James Hetfield, and Kirk Hammett. Metallica voiced the inner feelings of listeners struggling with adolescence. Five Finger Death Punch singer Ivan Moody remembers the lyrics to songs like "Fade to Black" seemed like a page taken from his own reality.*

# SUICIDE NOTE

"Fade to Black" affected Ivan the first time he heard it. The despondent lyrics were relatable to the frustrations of his own life. "I was going through a lot of family issues. I didn't really have a father figure, and the lyrics of that song hit me deeply and created such an emotion in me.

"I'm not going to lie—I was suicidal a lot of the time back then, in and out of mental wards and situations like that."

The lyrics felt like someone had taken a page from *his* reality, he says. "It blew me away. It made the way I was feeling acceptable. Somebody else actually understood it. It was the first time I felt like somebody actually understood what I was going through.

"That was probably one of my first and foremost favorite songs of all time. Even the title, there's just something about it. It's really dark, but, at the same time, hopeful."

He heard it as a suicide note to the world and wondered what James Hetfield had experienced to write lyrics so close to his own despair. "I tried to think about what he was thinking, and that was part of it for me. He must have been in such a mind state, such a heart-wrenching place when he wrote that. Or else he was just so open to relating to other people's problems that he saw it that clearly."

Moody was not the only listener who recognized themselves in the lyrics. Contending with feelings of loss and despair was something relatable to many misunderstood metal fans.

*Ivan Moody was a hardcore Metallica fan. He says, "I bought patches, picture discs, the singles—anything I could get my hands on. I was* completely *drawn in." (From left) James Hetfield, Kirk Hammett, Lars Ulrich, and Cliff Burton.*

"It seemed like he was manic when he wrote it. He was going through something in his head, [and] the only way he could ever express that was to put it on paper and throw it on a piece of music."

Despite the dejected emotion, Moody heard the lyrics as an expression of hope that would be a source of strength to him. The knowledge that someone else could experience his level of despair and write a song as a means of catharsis showed him an alternative to committing suicide. He directly attributes the power of the song as a primary reason why he pursued a musical career. "Somebody [in] a situation they don't want to live through, to have a single song change your mentality and the way you look at the world around you, it made me want to do the same.

"That's why it's so touching to me, when I get kids coming up and saying, 'You changed my life; you got me through my divorce.' I had one kid tell me that his wife lost their baby, and one of our songs [made] it easier to overcome it."

## STUDENT OF METAL

Ivan was the kid who would read the lyrics printed on the album sleeve while listening to the songs. Although he had always been interested in music and even sang in the choir, Moody had yet to write lyrics or think about being in a band. "That was probably one of the breaking points when I said, 'Okay, I want to be a heavy metal singer.'"

Hetfield was admittedly a leading influence on his early attempts at writing lyrics. "Fade to Black" was a primary example that helped develop his craft. "I studied the way he sang it. I listened to the cadences and the different ways he said things and the instrumentation. Even though I'm a singer, I was into the way a guitar solo felt or how they placed a drum roll, *where* they placed it—the timing of things.

"The way he put it together, it's so genius. It's one of the first songs that showed me a good verse into an impactful chorus, into a pre-chorus, into a bridge. I can actually see the structure in it and the way it needed to be placed to be as painful as it came out."

Moody initially heard the words as a poem, and he says it took a long time to learn how to structure his own poems to fit music. "A chorus should be a few lines that are so beautiful—or so painful—you can actually repeat them and make them worthwhile the second time you hear them. The second verse doesn't have to be what the first verse was about. You can change topics and still have the chorus relate to both and connect the two."

*Moody says "Fade to Black" was a primary example that helped develop his own songwriting craft.*
*He studied everything from the cadences and vocal phrasing of James Hetfield, to guitar solos, and*
*even where Lars Ulrich (pictured) played drum rolls.*

# DYNAMIC INTENSITY

Years later, Moody would equate fans connecting Five Finger Death Punch songs to
the solace he found within Metallica songs such as "Fade to Black." "I'd be naïve not
to. To forget that you have that kind of power to change somebody's life with lyrics or
a progression of chords, I'd be an ass to overlook it.

"That's why I don't take it for granted when I shake kids' hands or sign autographs.
I know how important it was to me as a kid."

The singer says Metallica is not necessarily a sentient influence when he writes songs,
but it's definitely there. "It's embedded in you. I wouldn't say it's conscious, but when
I wrote 'The Bleeding,' I *definitely* thought of songs like 'Fade to Black' that were
powerful without having to be heavy.

"It was definitely one of those songs that made you realize this does not have to be scream-in-your-face brutal for the [metal] world to listen and take it seriously." Moody says it made him realize that intensity was about more than tempo or power. It's also about dynamics.

"'The Bleeding' could have been about anything. But the music called for something so deep and painful, it hurt me to write it. That's probably the same scenario with 'Fade to Black.' I can only imagine what was going through his soul when he wrote it."

# LIFE-CHANGING SONG

Moody admits wondering what his musical heroes might think about his own lyrics. The scenario of looking toward Stage Left and seeing someone like James Hetfield watching and listening is something he can imagine. "I want my icons and idols to be proud of what I'm doing. There may be things about it he doesn't like, but in the long run I think he would have a deep respect for what I stand for and what we do."

He regularly listens to the old Metallica albums. Age and experience now allow him to interpret them as a songwriter. "Being on the road and being a musician, I definitely hear it with a different ear. But I still have the same emotions I did when I was young. It still digs just as deep. The blade of that knife will never become dull.

"When you have something that mind-altering and soul-changing, it carries you for years and years. It still does to this day. I can turn on 'Fade to Black' when I'm in one of those down moods and still feel the same power I felt when I was that young.

"I wish I could talk to James about this, because it's a big deal. And I hope he realizes how *huge* songs like 'Fade to Black' were to the rest of the metal community."

## 20

# D.R.I.

# Shame

FROM THE ALBUM **DEALING WITH IT!** (1985)

Kurt Brecht never considered himself a social activist. "I always thought of myself as a writer first. I was just lucky enough to get a job singing my lyrics." But since they would be saying *something* by virtue of writing songs, he and guitarist Spike Cassidy thought the content should be interesting and possibly influence people.

D.R.I.—Dirty Rotten Imbeciles—formed in Houston, Texas, in 1982. The following year the fledgling band relocated to California and the punk scene of political bands like Millions of Dead Cops and The Dead Kennedys. Brecht and his band were part of an anti-establishment community making statements through its music. "We were living in our van in San Francisco. At the time I was young and idealistic, probably a little naïve," he laughs.

"Definitely, we wanted to have a message, even though the message [was] nothing positive, really."

"Shame" addressed the most prominent negative aspects of society that they encountered directly and indirectly. "Just our day-to-day existence [and] things we saw on the news and read about in the papers and magazines. You saw racism—it talks about that a little bit—border problems, with us trying to get into Canada and that sort of thing, problems moving around the country."

*D.R.I. were living in a van, and singer Kurt Brecht says he was young, idealistic, and probably a little naïve. (From left) Josh Pappe, Felix Griffin, Spike Cassidy, and Brecht.* (Photo by Naomi Peterson.)

The lyrics were a barbed commentary, and although Kurt says no one specific problem or event was the singular inspiration for the song, the reference to war was the social transgression that infuriated him the most. Selective Service required all 18-year-old males to register for military service in the event of a draft. "As a young adult, you were thinking about that a lot. We knew that we were ready to go, basically at the drop of a hat. All it would take is a phone call, and I would have to report."

Although, he retorts, "they would have had a hard time finding me, since I was living in a van."

# EFFECTING SOCIAL CHANGE

In addition to his lyrics, Brecht and D.R.I. rallied for social change through benefit concerts in support of organizations such as the anti-racism John Brown Anti-Klan Committee and the counterculture Youth International Party. "That was one of our first U.S. tours," he says of the latter, "opening up for Crucifix and a bunch of other bands. We just set up on college campuses, and nobody had to pay. They were basically forced to listen to whatever you were screaming out as they were walking by, and that was kind of fun."

Brecht—who actually lived for a time in a tree in Golden Gate Park, chronicled by his 1990 book, *Notes from the Nest*—and the band did not live a nine-to-five lifestyle. They did not want to work their life away without enjoying it. "I didn't care if I had to starve. We just didn't care because we didn't want to work, except for what we were doing in our band, so that gave me a lot of time to read and be creative."

# MACARONI AND CHEESE

The music for "Shame" came first, and Kurt remembers the tempo originally being very slow. The first draft of the lyrics professed a love for the inexpensive food that was a staple of their diet. "Back then, we were living on stuff like hot dogs and macaroni and cheese from the soup kitchen, whatever we could scavenge."

"It was just some silly kind of song," Brecht says. He later had the idea to inject more serious subject matter into the words. The slow tempo was altered to slow-to-fast, before becoming an entirely fast-paced tune. "It went through several phases. I said, 'Try playing it faster,' and it sounded better."

They were fans of California hardcore bands such as Black Flag and Fear, whose influence had an effect on "Shame" and other early D.R.I. material. "This is before we ever heard about Slayer and Exodus, Metallica—any metal bands, really. We were into very short songs that were just in your face, [without] a lot of long lead guitar parts and packed with angry words, I guess you could say."

The song was barely a minute long, but delivering the lengthy diatribe in such a short amount of time was not a challenge. "That's what we do," he laughs.

*(From left) Kurt Brecht, Spike Cassidy, Josh Pappe, and Felix Griffin. The original lyrics to "Shame" were about the soup kitchen sustenance of hot dogs and macaroni and cheese.* (Photo by Naomi Peterson.)

The exact timeframe from initial ideas to recording is hard to recall, Brecht says. But he thinks the first two lines that blasted racism and the Ku Klux Klan started the lyrical process. "I knew I had to come up with something better than hot dogs. As soon as I had the first line, I thought, 'Well, that's pretty cool.' I knew the guys would like it because that's the kind of lyrics they were wanting me to write."

But the rampant words were not written specifically to suit the musical framework. The components naturally matched. "The first line just happened to fit, luckily. Once I had that rhythm of the music down in my head, I wrote along to that [and] just continued along."

He was a prolific writer who maintained multiple journals, writing in one of several notebooks that were designated by the caliber and status of the ideas—good, not so good, and some that were suitable and yet to be used. The process of combining different words and fragments of ideas and phrases was a jigsaw puzzle, he says.

"I was constantly combining bits and pieces here and there. Sometimes I was just waiting for the right song to use [one] line. Sometimes I wrote a whole song around a good line."

# BRIDGING MUSIC SCENES

D.R.I. was one of the bands at the forefront of bridging punk and heavy metal. Brecht thinks they ultimately influenced the latter style with their instrumental speed and, to a degree, their politically charged lyrics. But fans of the two genres were yet to be confederates against the mainstream in 1985.

"Metalheads didn't get along with punks, and they were fighting and throwing bottles at each other. The skinheads hated the metalheads even more." D.R.I. were in the middle of that cultural divide, and it made little sense and discouraged his hope for social unity. "I always thought it was the most ludicrous thing. With all the other problems going on—racism and everything like that—people in the music scene couldn't even band together.

"It took a lot of people getting ostracized at shows and a lot of people getting beat up. It took several years before it homogenized into a thrash metal scene, where a skinhead could go to a Slayer show or vice versa. Metalheads with long hair could come to one of our shows without being so concerned about getting their asses kicked or having to kick somebody's ass."

# REALIZING THE EFFECT

Kurt, half-joking, says he's still ashamed to be a human being. "Yes," he laughs, "I am. I just look at it and laugh at myself. Now that I've been around the world and been alive longer, I realize some parts of that song were very idealistic. I do believe in borders now, for obvious reasons. But I still feel the same about the human condition and how messed up humans can be."

Much of his commentary continues to make sense because the global scenario remains the same, but with present-day participants. "Different war, different countries, [but] pretty much the same as it's been for a long, long time. I don't think anything is going to change anytime soon."

"Shame" was just another song to the singer. He admittedly had little thought about how it might affect anyone. "When you're writing records with 20 songs, you've got to come up with a lot of words. Our goal was to get albums out so we could go on the road. We were a touring band, and that's all we really cared about at the time, getting out there.

Dealing with It! *was the beginning of D.R.I. incorporating elements of heavy metal that ultimately made fans out of bands such as Anthrax and Slayer. (From left) Josh Pappe, Spike Cassidy, Felix Griffin, and Kurt Brecht.* (Photo by Naomi Peterson.)

"I never realized until recently how many people got through their young adulthood because of us. Something about the lyrics just kind of opened them up, especially a lot of the metalheads that were more into headbanging and death metal lyrics."

The influence of D.R.I. and other punk and hardcore bands that would affect the social consciousness of metal during the latter half of the decade surprised Brecht. "That's pretty cool. They said, 'Hey, this is pretty cool. I need to start reading up on some of this stuff and see what this guy is talking about.'

"You know how it is when you talk to somebody and they think like you do, how you make that connection? I think that's how a lot of people felt. I just didn't really hear about it until later, after the fact."

In hindsight, Kurt admits that a lot of his lyrics highlighted negative aspects of society without any suggestion for how to solve the problems. "Later, I started thinking more about that, and thinking, 'Man, I need to write some songs that actually give some sort of help.' I'm not sure I ever accomplished it, but I thought about it."

## 21

**EXODUS**

# Bonded by Blood

FROM THE ALBUM **BONDED BY BLOOD** (1985)

The members of Exodus had an affinity for the ritual of becoming blood brothers with their friends, and guitarist Gary Holt says the band had *lots* of them in the early days of the Bay Area thrash community in San Francisco.

"It was something we did at parties. You're my friend; let's be blood brothers," he says. Exodus had "a million blood brothers," the most notable being Dave Mustaine of Metallica and later Megadeth fame. Hindsight makes Gary admit that such profuse blood-letting probably wasn't the wisest practice. "Now, you think AIDS, hepatitis, all these blood-borne diseases."

That rite, plus the experience of playing at Ruthie's Inn for the first time, inspired the lyrics to the title track of their debut album, *Bonded by Blood*.

The Berkeley club was a hotspot for the growing northern California thrash scene. The first time Exodus performed there, fans of the support band left their drink glasses along the edge of the stage, Holt explains. "When we came on, all that glass got broken, and everybody was slamming their fists in it. There was all this blood all over the stage, literally—a *lot* of it."

# BLOOD MEANING

The meaning of the song was a description of Exodus gigs and also their tribal act of bonding. But "Bonded by Blood" came to signify the camaraderie of an audience that was championing a new, more aggressive style of heavy metal. Thrash was still an underground derivative of the genre, and its early devotees were even further disenfranchised than the closer to mainstream audience listening to bands such as Def Leppard and Mötley Crüe.

The song became a rallying cry for an audience of social pariahs, but the result was unintentional. There was never a conscious attempt to impart cultural relevance through the lyrics, Holt says, "just a good dose of violence, which Exodus was renowned for at the time."

The album *Bonded by Blood* was instead based on "some good teenage Satanism and some devil worship violence," Holt says facetiously, "with a touch of political commentary. Everybody had to have at least one song about nuclear war back then." Exodus was no exception, with "And Then There Were None" being an obligatory track about disarmament. "To some people it was a genuine fear, due to the Cold War and the mood at the time."

But the standout song on *Bonded by Blood* was the title track.

# WRITING THE WORDS

Gary can't pinpoint exactly when the lyrics were written, but he's sure they developed quickly. "Sometimes you go through a bunch of rough drafts, and you make some changes, but the lyrics to that [song] were written in probably two or three tries.

"We were writing about spilling blood and killing people," he laughs. "It's not like I was writing the great American novel. We weren't trying to write the next *Walden*. As long as it was metal and it was violent and made us throw up the horns, we were stoked."

Classic literature might not have been a source of inspiration, but the New Wave of British Heavy Metal was admittedly a major influence on Exodus and their songs. "We all had our personal favorites," Holt remembers. "For me, it was Venom, Mercyful Fate, and Angel Witch. Those are the three bands that shaped my whole career."

*Exodus in 1989: (From left) Rick Hunolt, Gary Holt, Steve Souza, Perry Strickland, and Rob McKillop. Holt jokes that the lyrical content of "Bonded by Blood" was far from the great American novel.*

Guitarist and the band's principal lyricist, Holt's style of songwriting has always started with a guitar riff. During the early years of the band, his creative process was to disappear into the park adjacent to his family home, smoke marijuana, then return to his bedroom to write music. "I told my mom I was going to the store. I'd go and get stoned around the corner, then come back and jam."

In spite of writing the bulk of Exodus lyrics, Gary says his primary role as a guitarist makes the lyrics secondary to him when performing the songs onstage. "It's usually the riffs that are on my mind, even if I'm singing along. Once they're recorded, lyrics are the domain of the singer."

And if the music came first, Exodus lyrics would usually then start with a title. Gary would bounce those ideas off singer Paul Baloff, but little thought was given to how an audience might react. "We never concerned ourselves with anything but our own opinions. We were just writing songs that made us happy, that in turn made our fans happy."

The band *did* assume people would react enthusiastically to the song and its lyrics, once the album was released after various delays. "We were playing the song in the Bay Area well before the album had come out. Everybody was familiar with the song, and everybody loved it."

*A Lesson in Violence* was meant to be the title of the album, until poor-quality third- and fourth-generation bootleg cassettes circulating in the network of metal tape traders prompted the differentiating *Bonded by Blood* title. "In the end, it was the best thing that could have happened," says Holt. "It was destined to be the title of the record."

But he isn't sure the extreme lyrics alone are what struck a chord with people, rather than the album as a whole. "Being one of two or three pioneering thrash albums, I think it was a *genre* thing more than a lyrical thing. I think it had more to do with giving metal the kickstart it needed."

# LOOKING BACK

Exodus and "Bonded by Blood" *did* stimulate the genre and its fans. "A lot of people have told me that that song—and that album—is what turned them on to more extreme forms of metal. I've also had people tell me our songs are disgusting and should be illegal, and I like that even more, actually!"

Fans enacting the gory lyrics by lacerating themselves and bleeding became customary during Exodus shows, continuing long after the band themselves stopped practicing the blood brother tradition. "Dude, get away from me, you're bleeding!" Holt narrates. "I don't want your blood on me. These are new white hightops; please get away."

Holt maintains that, despite the brutal overtones and drastic response, he has no regret about the lyrics for that track or the album as a whole. "There's nothing I would change. That album, as far as being one of the pioneering albums of the genre, it's perfect. We had our share of delays, so there were other albums that beat it to the release date. But I think everybody pretty much knows, if you go back to the birth of thrash metal, it boils down to two bands that were doing it first: Metallica and Exodus."

And the *Bonded by Blood* lyrics still make Gary smile. "Some of them are actually really good, as far as lyrics about violence and Satan are concerned. Some are still quite humorous and funny. Paul's lyrics to 'Piranha' will always make me smile, 'cause he lived that shit. He meant every word of it.

*Steve Souza (center) replaced original singer Paul Baloff in 1987. As time went on, Exodus also curtailed their blood brother ritual.*

"I still love playing the songs, and 'Bonded by Blood' is always part of the set—probably always will be. It's the same song it was, to me, when I was just 21 years old."

*Let There Be Blood*, a rerecorded version of *Bonded by Blood* that was released in 2008, is a statement of continued relevance to successive generations of metal fans. Holt thinks the attitude and fervor that Exodus was trying to convey with the title track still resonates today. "People still bleed at our shows, so I think they do." And bands naming themselves after the title indicates that the song continues to have weight within a contemporary metal community. "Guys tell me what an influence that album had on them, and I find it to be the ultimate compliment."

## 22

## Dio

# Rock 'n' Roll Children

FROM THE ALBUM **SACRED HEART** (1985)

Heavy metal fans have never been highly regarded by mainstream society. The social community—particularly the nonconformity of its artists and the devotion of its audience—has long been devalued and dismissed as counterculture. Successive generations of young metalheads seeking refuge in the lifestyle have felt alienated by the compliant demands of a moderate norm.

"Rock 'n' Roll Children" told the story of two teenagers exiled by the predatory cliques of high school society. Ronnie James Dio describes the girl as a metalhead and her boyfriend as a musician forced to get a job, rather than devote himself to playing guitar. "It's what they went through, how they were affected by the cheerleader faction versus the more avant-garde—the geeks, as they probably would call them."

Dio tapped into a powerful sentiment that was relatable to anyone struggling through the adolescent turmoil of finding their identity. Insecurity, multiplied by ostracizing from other teenagers that was a defense mechanism to conceal their own awkwardness, was especially hurtful for metal fans. The disapproval of parents and other adult authority figures created further isolation that increased allegiance to the music.

The heart of the song was the desperation to escape the torment of their classmates and the burden of disapproving adults. "Just a matter of wanting to run away from it all and get away from all this abuse. It was abuse—not severe child abuse—a psychological thing that goes with peer pressure."

Typical of his creative process, lyrical ideas were mostly nonexistent until Ronnie decided the subject of disenfranchised kids would make for a good song. But unlike many of his other songs, once the title was determined, writing the song became an arduous task. "The process from there to the end of the song was quite a while, actually. We recorded for quite a while."

# WORDS AND MUSIC

Ronnie would typically flesh out ideas beforehand, but "Rock 'n' Roll Children" was built over a longer period of time. The song actually developed as the studio sessions progressed. "It took us quite a while to do that song. Once you have the idea, you're okay. But I wasn't quite satisfied until pretty close to the end of the recording."

The music and lyrics were written concurrently, rather than devising words to fit an existing musical structure. That made it easier to write the lyrics, and the first line about their rainy-night decision to run away established their direction.

"The first line would certainly be the one that spurred me on to write the rest of it. It always comes with the title, with the first line. [They] take me where I'm going to go. If I don't have a great first line, there's no reason to go anywhere else."

One reason why the song took longer to evolve was perhaps the space within the instrumentation. It was one of the few instances in which the singer was afforded more time within the musical structure to tell a story with a greater number of words. "That's the difficulty in writing a song," he explains. "You only have a short period of time to write what in your mind might be an epic. That's why we do concept albums, I guess—so we can fill in the gaps."

The result was copious lyrics that were more literal than other Dio songs. Compared to his songs that relied heavily on grammatical functions such as metaphors and analogies, in turn creating a mystical ambiance, "Rock 'n' Roll Children" was fairly direct in its message. "I had a little bit more of a chance to make it go where it had to go and be a little more sensible, rather than analogous all the time."

*Dio onstage in 1986: (left to right) Craig Goldy, Ronnie James Dio, Vinny Appice, Jimmy Bain, and Claude Schnell. Ronnie identified with the lyrics and sometimes even felt choked up singing "Rock 'n' Roll Children."*

# MINI-MOVIE

The song itself spoke to a metal community painfully aware of the emotions borne of being a social pariah. But Ronnie thinks the allure of the music video probably increased the reach of the song beyond its core audience. "That really made a difference. If there had not been this blockbuster video, I think [the song] would have been not quite as popular."

Video was an important line item in the budget of promoting an album. MTV was becoming an indispensable promotional tool by 1985, and longer-established acts were starting to take their cue from up-and-coming bands by contracting big-budget clips. "A lot of money was spent on videos. And a lot of money was spent on that particular video."

*Dio played the part of the mystical owner of a curio shop in the music video, which depicted a scenario painfully close to the lives of many ostracized metal fans.*

Filming was a large-scale production that involved an elaborate treatment. The fantasy setting of the two teenagers confronted by familial and social intolerance—based on gender and their lifestyle choice—that devalued them as individuals. The clip brought the lyrics to life with a clarity that was literal to metal fans already struggling against the same pressure to conform.

"It was *so* well done, featuring three or four really good actors and actresses from the Hollywood community. It was well written [and] well performed by the two young people who did it."

# SOCIAL CONSCIENCE

Much as the video reflected a literal interpretation of the song, Dio thinks some misperception was created by the assumption that it singularly represented the lyrics. One clue to a deeper meaning might have been a line sung during the fade-out that referred to the runaways as children of the night."I was starting to get very involved with a charity called Children of the Night. It really made me so much more aware of runaways and what they go through, what they don't have when they get to the place they think is going to be heaven."

The private, nonprofit organization was established in 1979 by Dr. Lois Lee to aid children who turned to prostitution as a sole means of survival. The charity is committed to rescuing those victims and providing subsequent shelter, education, and psychological counseling. Wendy Dio, Ronnie's wife and manager, serves as chairperson of the board of directors, and the singer himself has been a longstanding proponent of their work.

# EMOTIONAL CONNECTION

Despite the age difference between them, the song validated the connection between the singer and his audience. He clearly understood the torment of feeling different. Ronnie says he really got inside the song to perform it.

"I really got inside the song, to the point that there are times when I perform [it] that there's a line toward the end that I really get choked up about. I really do."

The lyric about the rainy-night escape touched the singer. "Maybe the words aren't emotional to anyone else, but singing [them] is sometimes just as satisfying as having a lyric people might recognize or admire." Singing those lyrics is a new experience for Ronnie whenever he performs the song. The sentiment always makes a fresh impact on him. That newness is something he tries to bring to the performance of every song because the vocals are essential to the words.

"To me, it's part and parcel. I'm not a poet, I'm not a narrator—I'm a singer. The lyrics that I sing are just that; they are sung. They're not just to be left on their own."

## 23

## METALLICA

# Master of Puppets

FROM THE ALBUM MASTER OF PUPPETS (1986)

Brian Fair had already decided to be a musician before he ever heard of Metallica. He even played in a couple of grammar school bands with friends. "I wouldn't call us musicians yet, but we were a band—you know, whoever got a bass for Christmas was the bass player."

The future Shadows Fall singer was already scratching band names on textbook covers and attending arena concerts and local punk shows at a young age. "I was a little punk rock skater kid. [But] when I was 12 or 13, the name [Metallica] started floating around."

*Ride the Lightning* was the first Metallica album he heard. "That was it—instant favorite band," he laughs. "I went back, got the first record, and from then on continued to follow them.

"They combined the virtuosity of metal with the total attitude of bands like Bad Brains and Black Flag, all the stuff I had been listening to. It bridged the gap perfectly for me, between my early influences and [then] current influences."

At 12 years old, he wasn't necessarily a junior political activist, but the social awareness displayed at punk gigs made an impact on him. Information about everything from vegetarianism to communism to Hare Krishna was readily available. "That helped me get beyond the MTV example of what a band should be. Metallica solidified that, that it *could* be more.

*Lars Ulrich (pictured) hangs out with the fans. "Average guys" like Metallica made the jump from audience to the stage seem more feasible to Shadows Fall singer Brian Fair.*

"I wasn't out there starting petitions, but I wasn't into *Dungeons & Dragons* or reading fantasy novels. That didn't appeal to me as much. I was definitely more into something beyond the party or the fantasy."

The ragged denim and leather image of Metallica made Brian and other kids believe it was possible for them to write songs and form metal bands, too. "Seeing them as average guys was an inspiration, as well—wow, it *can* happen. You don't have to look like you're in Stryper," he laughs.

# OLD-SCHOOL STEALING

Fair admits he ripped off his first copy of *Master of Puppets* from Comics, Records and Fun, a now-defunct retailer in Milford, Massachusetts. "I stuck it in my pocket after school and walked out. That day, I stole [that] and my second copy of *Never Mind the Bollocks* by the Sex Pistols."

In 2000, Metallica sued Napster, the file-sharing service that enabled listeners to illegally obtain their music, and the irony is not lost on Fair. "I know, I know! And here I am ranting at kids about downloading our record and pirating it. At least I had to *physically* go get it! I couldn't just drag and drop on the computer. I had to pull some shady maneuvers, you know?"

The owner of the store eventually caught Brian stealing a copy of the Anthrax EP, *I'm the Man.*

*Master of Puppets* made an immediate impression on him. "This is now my *new* favorite record," he thought at the time. And that designation still stands. "It's not only my favorite Metallica record, but what I consider the blueprint for the perfect metal album. That's how a metal record should cover all the moods and implements, from fast and technical, to slow and heavy; to simple and sing-along, to melodic with classical overtones."

It made a permanent impact on the young musician, who listened to the album countless times. "The text [wore off] my cassette, and I had to write 'Metallica' on it with a Sharpie."

# LYRICAL REALISM

"There wasn't a lot of illusion," Brian says about James Hetfield's lyrics. The realism appealed to the beginning songwriter. "A lot of metal before that had almost a fantasy slant or the sleaze slant. Those were the two directions. What I noticed right away about Metallica lyrics was, not only were there everyday situation and problem lyrics, there were also political lyrics."

That aspect was the same thing that had attracted him to punk. "The lyrics were more than just wizards or banging chicks. They had much more of a personal connection, as opposed to just fantasy." Brian could better relate to the realism of songs about war, such as "Disposable Heroes," or the harsh reality of addiction of "Master of Puppets."

Although he could not grasp the severity of addiction at such a young age, "Master of Puppets" made an impact on him. "It definitely left a lasting impression that it could be that powerful. That was the lesson learned from those lyrics. The way he broke it down so simply—like chopping [cocaine] on a mirror—was not pulling any punches. He was letting you know *exactly* what he was talking about.

"He had such a great way with words that those [lyrics] became instantly memorable and iconic. That's a rarity in lyrics."

"It was probably my first warning about what [drugs] could do, and those lessons were definitely lasting. Honestly, as a musician on the road, you constantly see the living examples of it happen around you. Between songs like that and your own warnings, if you haven't learned the lesson, you weren't paying attention."

# DOING THE HETFIELD

More than anything, Brian thinks the complexity of "Master of Puppets" influenced his approach to song structure and fitting lyrics within a musical framework. "That had a real flow from beginning to end, through so many transitions. That's usually your biggest challenge as a metal lyricist and vocalist, trying to complement crazy, technical changes in a way that doesn't lose sight of the song, [so] it all feels cohesive from beginning to end. That's something [James] did incredibly well.

"Also, to complement the impact of such great riffs and have your voice carry just as much power, that comes from things like diction and choice of phrasing. He was a master of that at a time when some thrash metal vocals were throwaways—it was more about the intensity of [the music]. He added something *to* the songs with his lyrics and vocal patterns.

"A lot of it has become metal convention at this point. Doing the Hetfield is now the musical pantheon. It's become an inherent part of metal, something you don't even need to describe to someone. But back then it was totally new."

Admittedly, Brian was not conscious of those aspects when he first heard the song as a kid. "Oh, hell no! I was just like, 'This is fucking amazing!'" he laughs.

But those dynamics *did* affect his developing attempts at writing lyrics, although he was probably not conscious of the influence, he says. The repetitive chanting of the word "master" in the chorus taught him the importance of allowing for audience participation. "You know everyone in the arena is going to be hitting that with him. But beyond the chorus that's stuck in your head, you also need the verses to have something that sucks you in."

*James Hetfield's (pictured) lyrics, plus his diction and choice of vocal phrasing, differentiated Metallica from typical thrash metal singers. Brian Fair says using those dynamics— doing the Hetfield—has become a conventional heavy metal technique.*

# LYRICAL SALVATION

Brian remembers being able to put faces within the Massachusetts metal scene to the lyrical warning about drug addiction. "Fortunately, no one I knew very close, but it's something I've seen. [Hetfield] definitely nailed the portrait of what it means to give yourself entirely over to a substance. He created that image in such a stark and realistic way; you can definitely see all those characteristics in people going through that.

"Because of that term, *master of puppets*, I wonder how many people may have been at the depths and realized, 'I'm a slave.' I'm sure there have been people who had their path turned because of something like that. That's the power and beauty of music, that it can inspire in so many different ways, even if it's the last place you thought inspiration would come from."

The song can almost be heard as a self-fulfilling prophecy. James Hetfield warned listeners about the danger of addiction years before the 2004 documentary *Some Kind of Monster* revealed his own struggle with alcoholism.

"That's the thing about lyrics," Fair explains. "You may honestly be going through those things in your own mind, putting it all together. It may not be until years later that you realize you were warning yourself or writing about an ideal that you yourself haven't been able to live up to."

*James Hetfield (left, with Kirk Hammett) created a stark and realistic description of dependency with the lyrics to "Master of Puppets." Brian Fair says the song was his first warning about the danger of substance abuse. "He had such a great way with words that those [lyrics] became instantly memorable and iconic."*

Brian explored the subject of addiction within his own lyrics. "My Demise," the opening track on the 2009 Shadows Fall album *Retribution*, is about cycles of destructive behavior. "It's about knowing that something is spiraling out of control and ignoring it. If you do, it ultimately leads to your demise.

"It's funny, because now that I think about it, that song [also] has the acoustic break in the middle and all this stuff. Maybe it's more 'Master of Puppets' than we realized," he laughs.

# TIMELESS BLUEPRINT

Although Brian says he no longer listens to *Master of Puppets* with the same fervent regularity, the album and songs such as the title track are practically imprinted upon his DNA as a metal musician of his generation. "Albums like that and *Reign in Blood*, you may not need to spin them as much because the impact is everlasting.

"It's going to influence and set the standard for what I look for in what we do. You are always trying to reach your *Master of Puppets* as a metal band—we haven't," he laughs. "And no one ever will."

# 24

## SLAYER
# Jesus Saves

FROM THE ALBUM **REIGN IN BLOOD** (1985)

"They would have games set up in the corner, so I could occupy myself while the rest of the class caught up," Kerry King remembers. A smart kid, his tendency to ace exams led to advancement into a program for gifted elementary school students.

His intellect would come into play during summer vacation. The future Slayer guitarist was not raised in a particularly religious household, so he isn't sure why he attended—or even who suggested that he do so—summer Sunday School classes. "Six weeks into it, I just went, 'This is fucking horseshit,'" he laughs. "I told my mom I didn't want to go anymore."

No one specific aspect of the doctrinal curriculum aggravated him, other than the general sense of inaccuracy. "There are so many historical facts that it just didn't make sense. I would be very interested to find out everything that religion covered up, because they have the ability to do that."

Kerry would later be the admitted leading proponent of religious cynicism in Slayer. "As we got older, I'm the one who really took it by the horns and got on the religion bashing." The apprehension formed during summer Bible school notwithstanding, Kerry isn't sure what led to the contentious lyrics to "Jesus Saves."

"Just who we were as a band, I guess. Some things are obviously conducive to being a Slayer song, and other things are more conducive to any other band."

The growing number of evangelists crusading against heavy metal throughout the decade caused some bands to retaliate in song. But retribution didn't factor into the lyrics. Kerry was more concerned with finding a provocative title. "I did it to catch people's eye, more than anything. People looking at an album back then would go, 'I can't believe Slayer wrote a song called "Jesus Saves."'"

# JESUS ADVERTISES

The title is something King thinks he remembers seeing while driving down the street. "It could have been a church with one of those signs outside that says 'Jesus Saves.' I'm like, 'That's a great title!' That memory might be a little faded, but I really think that's how I came up with it.

"If there was [another] reason, I'd probably have a better story," he laughs.

"Jesus Saves" was a pronouncement of Kerry's childhood disbelief with the tenets of Christianity. His lyrics ridiculed the idea of a lifetime of faith without tangible evidence of salvation as irrational. It was a good idea for a song, and he knew it immediately. "I didn't waste time on something if I knew it was a bad idea. I got married to the title right away, and it was just a matter of time until I came up with how I wanted it to be."

"I knew what I had to do to make it Slayer." Kerry deliberated about the title, trying to shape it into a theme that could be conveyed in slightly less than a three-minute song. He doesn't remember how long it turned in his mind, but probably not long, he says. "We did albums more quickly back then, so I can't imagine it taking long—probably a week or less."

Part of the chorus might have come first, he says, referring to the line about seeing pearly gates. "That was pretty early. I would imagine that was probably at the beginning, then making a song make sense around it. A lot of times I'll write down phrases that start out similarly or reflect on the same kind of thing, and there will be a twist in the second one."

Despite the references, Kerry says he's never been one to source the Bible while writing about religious-based themes. "The only thing I use is a dictionary and a thesaurus, because I'm a rhymer. I'll look for similar words that mean the same thing. I can rhyme all day, but the trick is to make sense and make it to the point."

*Devotion to an intangible savior made little sense to an adolescent Kerry King. As an adult, that disbelief would be the basis for numerous Slayer songs, including "Jesus Saves."*

## MUSIC, THEN LYRICS

"That one was definitely music first," he says. "Most of our stuff is." His method has always been to restructure lyrical ideas to fit the instrumental framework of a song. Although Kerry and other guitarist Jeff Hanneman drafted lyrics to "Raining Blood" during the recording sessions, "Jesus Saves" and the other songs were already written before the band entered the studio.

Revisions during rehearsals and recording were not part of the Slayer routine. Before bringing the song to front man Tom Araya, Kerry made sure the words were singable by reviewing them in his head or recording himself singing them. "I make sure it fits before I have him waste his time learning it."

# REIGNING METAL

*Reign in Blood* would be the album that defined the band, solidifying their musical and lyrical style. "We really came into our own with what Slayer was going to sound like for the next 20 years or so," he agrees. After two albums and an EP, they had developed an identifiable archetype that was no longer affected by other songwriters.

"Sure, I looked up to people when I was a fan—I mean, I'm still a complete fan of music, mostly metal and punk—but not as an influence to writing that particular song."

The lyrics were a precursor to Kerry's developing progression as a songwriter. "I think it came out pretty cool. It was a stepping stone to more intelligent lyrics later in my career."

Hanneman, Araya, and drummer Dave Lombardo seemed to like the song, Kerry says, and it fit the vision of what Slayer was about to become. "Everybody was probably gung ho and excited about it. Historically, looking back, people always say *Reign in Blood* is the best Slayer album. That was part of it. We were getting on this locomotive, and it's just one big ride from then."

"Jesus Saves" and the other nine *Reign in Blood* tracks made an impact, both on moral propagandists and the heavy metal community. "It was a very different sound for us. It was right in your face, and it was blatant, and it was brazen. It was far more abrasive than the other records."

# PROVOCATION

Kerry remains adamant that he cared little about how anyone might rebuke the lyrics. He actually wanted to incite some sort of backlash. "I was *hoping* to provoke," he says. Ultimately, "Angel of Death," Hammeman's heinous tale of Nazi surgeon Josef Mengele, bore the brunt of controversy. But King thinks the uproar was more about their imagery as a whole, rather than one specific song.

During the latter half of the '80s, an evangelist traveled with the band for a subsequent magazine article. "The shit that would come out of that guy's mouth," Kerry laughs. "We would say, 'Okay, we'll listen.' And then we would [respond], and he's like, 'No, that's not how it is!' Well, you're not even being reasonable, dude.

*(From left) Dave Lombardo, Jeff Hanneman, Kerry King, and Tom Araya. Slayer songs that attacked the validity of religion fueled public outrage over the course of their career.*

"To write stuff that attacks religion or religious-based icons, you've got to have a pretty reasonable head on your shoulders to be able to argue with them, because they're very unreasonable, almost to a brainwashed sense."

The uproar that started with *Reign in Blood* trailed Slayer throughout their career. As late as 2006, *Christ Illusion* was banned in India when the Catholic Secular Forum issued a statement that censured the lyrics and album cover artwork.

"There are countries that still think what I have to say, and what my band has to say, is so out of control that it's going to change the way that entire nation thinks. I think that's pretty awesome, on our behalf."

# ACQUIRED SKILL

Mainstream opinion about Slayer—and Kerry King—has typically been based on songs like "Jesus Saves," he says. "Because of the way it's written, people assume I'm a Satanist, and I'm not. I'm an atheist, but atheism isn't fun to write about."

The misperception doesn't bother the pragmatic guitarist. "Not really. I know who I am. I've got to be true to myself, first and foremost, and then true to my genre, being a fan. I really don't have to think about being true to my music. We've done it so long, it just comes out that way, I think."

"Jesus Saves" was mostly intended as a trick. "When you can't see the lyrics, and you can't hear it, people think, 'Wow, they're not going to be a devil band anymore.'

"I like to play with people that way, like 'Supremist' on *Christ Illusion*. It's not about a racist. But if you call something a supremist, everybody is going to assume, 'See, I told you they were racist.' Then you get the song, and it's not what it's about."

He enjoys pushing those buttons. "People are going to jump to conclusions, and I like turning that screw. I like saying, 'See, I knew you were going to think that about me, but that ain't what it's about.' It's an acquired skill to learn how to manipulate that."

## 25

## LIZZY BORDEN

# Generation Aliens

FROM THE ALBUM MENACE TO SOCIETY (1986)

Heavy metal unsettled the complaisance of moderate America through-out the 1980s. Regarded as a corrupting style of music that led to moral decay, the Parents Music Resource Center sponsored an album-labeling system under the guise of protecting adolescent listeners. Many musicians considered the practice to be censorship. Lizzy Borden saw it as enforced conformity.

"We've got to stomp this out because these kids think on their own and think about what they want, not what someone wants from them."

The theme of *Menace to Society* was rebellion against that sort of social control. "I wanted to create something that came from my brain instead of clocking in somewhere," says the namesake singer. "They just wanted you to be a worker bee and fall in line, get a job and be happy you're there."

# LEGIONS OF OUTCASTS

Although metal was growing in popularity and attracting a larger audience, its fans were still a minority in the social hierarchy in 1986. "In junior high and high school, you're either in a clique or you're not. I was kind of on the fringe, personally," he remembers.

If Lizzy Borden and their fans were snubbed by the popular kids, the singer says the band also had little camaraderie with the rest of the outcast metal community. Simply put, they felt alienated from *everybody.*

"We weren't a thrash band, and we weren't a pop metal band. We were stuck right in the middle. I liked it fast and hard, but I liked my lyrics a certain way, and I wasn't willing to compromise. *That* led to being alienated."

The extreme image of the metal genre, and more so a band that looked like Lizzy Borden, induced trepidation from the general public. "Back then, heavy metal wasn't the norm. Even though you look at it now and go, 'Oh, everyone dressed like that,' it was few and far between.

*Heavy metal was viewed by many outsiders as a corrupting style of music that led to moral decay. Lizzy Borden explored that social fear through his lyrics and the band's image.*

"I remember playing one show in a really rich area. We could see people in their cars locking the doors, and we're thinking, 'What the hell? We're just musicians.' That made me think, 'Wow, we are really expressing ourselves in a way that is making people frightened.' That was a social behavior I had never seen before. It was interesting, and I explored it."

Lizzy Borden was not playing arenas, but they were filling smaller venues on the club circuit and building a legion of like-minded fans. "I thought of it almost as a military thing," he says. "Each stop in each different state, we had troops waiting for us. That made it into the [chorus], the legions we were putting together."

His own sense of alienation, and that of their likewise antagonized audience, sparked *Menace to Society* and acknowledged the connection between them. "I think they saw it in my lyrics and what we did onstage. That was an identifiable release they were able to grab hold of and say, 'Yeah, I believe in the same things.'"

# CUT AND PASTE

The band was on tour in the Midwest supporting *Love You to Pieces* when "Generation Aliens" was realized as an idea. They were walking across the street when it floated into his imagination. "I usually never tell my band anything about what I'm writing," he laughs. "I remember saying it out loud, going, 'I really like this title, and I want to do something with that.'

"I think I had written the melody line for that song first, and then we came up with pieces of music that would go along with that. It was lyrics and melody first, and then we finished off with the music."

Lizzy Borden albums were conceptual, rather than unrelated individual tracks. "Generation Aliens" was just one piece of a simultaneously written bigger puzzle, he says. But the lead track set the tone for the anti-indoctrination theme of the album. The self-professed film buff was influenced by totalitarian movies such as *1984* and *A Clockwork Orange*. "Big Brother and all that, taking over the way we think and taking away our individualism. That's what I rebelled against, so I think that's what poured into those lyrics.

"I'm a *massive* procrastinator," he laughs. Lizzy would labor over songs, taking his time and then putting them aside for a few days to regain perspective. "I like to step back and think about it. Some of the greatest songs were written in five minutes, but the way I work, usually I just chip away at the stone."

Many songwriters affected his compositional style, but the most important was David Bowie, he says. Bowie's use of the nonlinear cut-up technique, randomly rearranging fragments of phrases to create scrambled ideas, was fundamental to the lyrics. "You would take scissors and cut sentences in half until you had a mass of different words, then put them together completely abstract. You didn't have to make sense; it was more about the poetic flow.

"I kind of like the bridge parts, where it was basically a sarcastic way of saying, 'Tell us what to think. Tell us what to eat, tell us what to watch.'" It wasn't done consciously, but he likens those parts to Pink Floyd and the classroom indoctrination of "Another Brick in the Wall." "That's the thing that made me most proud. There were some interesting moments, [and] if we didn't move on to the next record so quickly, we might have been able to exaggerate some of that stuff."

# NO REST FOR THE WICKED

*Menace to Society* was planned to be a fast, heavy album, extreme compared to their previous album and EP. "We were in strange territory because I had never sung that fast. There were a lot of new things on that record that were different."

The singer was already writing songs for the album in his mind while they toured to support *The Murderess Metal Road Show* live album and video. "It was a little bit ahead of the game, as far as coming up with the concept. I had *some* ideas."

Lizzy Borden would record their first four albums over the course of just 14 months, so there was little time for revisions, he says. "We kind of got a template on the first record [for] how to do things. When we did *Menace*, we used that template [and] just blasted through everything.

"We rehearsed like crazy back then—six days a week, every day just blasting away. Our rehearsals were our pre-production. When we got our engineer, he sat for [just] two days [before] going, 'Okay, let's go in,' and we recorded it."

*Namesake singer Lizzy Borden thought mainstream America tried to eradicate heavy metal because it championed freewill and free thinking. "They just wanted you to be a worker bee and fall in line, get a job and be happy you're there."*

# SHAKESPEAREAN COMPLEXITY

When he's writing, Lizzy always hopes to make a connection with an audience that sees the world in a similar way. "That song is one where I thought maybe I *could* connect.

"'Generation Aliens' had that rallying cry. I knew that if people did discover it, they would identify with it. Even if they didn't understand it, they would still have some sort of reflection in there that they could grab hold of.

"We toured on the *Menace* record—we actually opened for Motörhead—and I remember some strong reactions," he laughs. "We used to open up with that song. I could see in their eyes from the stage that they were ready for this, and they were part of this. That's what I liked the most, that intensity."

He thought people would identify with the resistive sentiment, but Lizzy also wanted listeners to interpret the words in a poetic way that transcended basic metal lyrics. "I always hope people will read my lyrics and say, 'There's something interesting there. I want to dig in and see what else is there.' I also try and have two or three different meanings for everything. I like that, where you leave things open for their own interpretation.

"If you read it, you can really grasp the storyline—[but] is there a storyline? Really, with any great poetry, you either understand it or have no clue. I know people who read Shakespeare and go, 'I have no understanding of what this person is saying,' even though there are so many great meanings there. It's the same thing with lyrics. If it's so extreme, and you've gone down a road to throw out some emotion, sometimes it's hard to understand. And I love hearing the misunderstandings."

# WHOLE PACKAGE

"Kids now, they don't get to use their imagination. Back then you just had the album cover and the lyrics to hold on to. You had no choice but to read those lyrics and look at the pictures and artwork and kind of imagine what this whole thing meant. Right now, you just go to YouTube, so imagination goes out the window. Even if you do a great CD package, the lyrics are [printed] so small, you need a magnifying glass to read them. So, I don't see a lot of people doing it. But that doesn't stop me from [still] trying to write interesting lyrics."

The criteria for writing lyrics haven't changed since *Menace to Society*, he says. The words need long-term believability. Lizzy has always been conscious that he would have to sing them for the length of his career. "I didn't want to sing anything I didn't believe in, because you have to sing some of these songs hundreds of times. When you're in character on stage, and you're really belting something out, it can't be something you've outgrown. It has to be a part of your personality that you're going to throw out there year after year.

"I look back at the person who wrote that and try to remember what I was thinking," he laughs. But Lizzy says lyrically he would not change much, maybe just a line or two. "I'm proud of it. I think I nailed it, as far as the poetic aspect of it. It does have an open interpretation. But, at the same time, I am leading you down a certain way of thinking. This song, it was all about individualism.

"That song was about being a puppet to a puppet master who is thinking for you, telling you what to do, how to do it, when to do it, where to do it—not letting you think for yourself. Now, in this day and age when people are screaming socialism and everything else, it's still valid to me, what it's saying in those lyrics, probably even more so.

"There's a little bit of fear in there. You're fearing what may happen. Will it happen? Will there be a rebellion? I think there always will be a rebellion. This song kind of speaks for that."

**26**

## STRYPER

# More Than a Man

FROM THE ALBUM **TO HELL WITH THE DEVIL** (1986)

If the sex, drugs, and rock-and-roll subject matter of heavy metal lyrics was taboo to mainstream society, songs about Jesus Christ were denounced by metalheads as incongruous to headbanging. The overt Holy allegiance of Stryper was dismissed by many fans as contrary to the genre.

Michael Sweet did not attend church until the age of 12, when his family became active members of a local congregation after televangelists guided them to Christ. "I fell away at the age of 16," he remembers. During that time the singer says he lived the rock-and-roll lifestyle in Hollywood, playing clubs like Gazzari's on the Sunset Strip. He returned to the church four years later. "That's when Stryper was [born]."

Most of their lyrics between 1984 and 1988 were directly about God with little analogy or metaphor. "You knew exactly what we were talking about," he says. "We decided to take a bold stand for God with the music He gave us the ability to write. We were passionate about that, just as someone else is passionate about writing about the devil, drugs, motorcycles, or whatever it is."

But lyrics based on such an exact subject admittedly led to creative limitations that challenged Michael to avoid redundancy. "Yeah, sometimes," he says. "What started out as something we sincerely wanted to do turned into something we felt pressured to do. We were getting pressure from the Christian community, the Christian marketplace, so to speak. We felt like we *had* to say the word Jesus in every song. If the song didn't have the name in it, we would hear about it."

Ultimately, Sweet made the connection that, God being the architect of all things, he could write songs less specific to Christianity and more about the impact of the creator. Starting with *Against the Law* in 1990, his lyrics were less evangelical. "Obviously, love is the foundation. Let's write about love. Let's write about relationships. Let's write about how we struggle with pride in society.

"I branched out as a writer, and it's not just about God, Jesus, and salvation [anymore]. It's about everything God stands for, which is everything good."

# MELODY MAKES THE SONG

"More Than a Man" was an instance of Sweet wanting to write a song that was an example of unadulterated salvation. Michael says he always wanted to write a song that could be the pathway for someone to dedicate himself to Christ. "You died for me, your blood was shed for me. That's what those lyrics are, basically a prayer of salvation."

Although he can't remember the moment it became a fully conscious idea, like all his songs, the singer knows the music came first. "It started with the riff. Once I wrote the riff and arranged the song—and taught it to the guys—then the lyrics came later. That's the way it is with pretty much any song I write."

No specific word or phrase initiated the writing process, but he says it usually started with the chorus to establish a hook. "Once I write the chorus, I go back and start writing the verses. I usually do it in one shot, whether it's a one-day timeframe or starting on a specific day and writing on and off for a week or two until the song is lyrically complete."

Oddly enough, the caliber of the lyrics has never been the signal that a song is good enough to record. For Michael, it's the music. "Being a Christian band, you might think it would be the message. But first and foremost, it's really the music and the melody. Then, at that point, it comes down to powerful lyrics that work with and enforce the music and step it up a level.

"If I'm humming the melody in my head—I can't get that melody *out* of my head and have no problem remembering [it]—that's really the foundation for me. The ones that stay in my mind, I'll come back to them a month later and they're right there. There are a lot of songs where I'll be at the supermarket and come up with a melody, but I'll forget it and never remember it again. So, obviously, it wasn't that good."

# LAST-MINUTE LYRICS

The Bible has always been an obvious reference tool for writing Stryper lyrics. Sweet says he doesn't favor any particular version, although he typically sources the New King James edition. "Really, more than anything, I rely on a dictionary. That is always my go-to book. Boy, that's helped me out in a pinch a thousand times."

*Michael Sweet ultimately branched out and wrote songs that were more about the influence of God. But early Stryper lyrics, such as those in "More Than a Man," were unwavering evangelicalism. (From left) Tim Gaines, Robert Sweet, Michael Sweet, and Oz Fox.*

He thinks the lyrics to "More Than a Man" were actually written right before the vocals were recorded. "I put it off to the last minute. I did that with a number of songs. There are a few songs where I was actually writing the lyrics in the car on the way to the studio.

"You're budgeted, and each guy is allotted so much time, and there was a timeframe for me to do vocals. I was out of time, and there were certain lyrics I didn't have. But those lyrics written last minute wound up being some of the best we've ever had."

# CLASSIC METAL INFLUENCES

Lyrically, his influences were predominantly spiritual. "My only influences have been Biblical points of view—my family, my relationships, my love for others, all based back to the word in the Bible. But his musical preferences were more secular. Michael grew up listening to bands such as Iron Maiden, the Scorpions, and UFO. "You can hear it in a lot of the songs I've written over the years, the Van Halen or Judas Priest influence, *absolutely*."

Some religious traditionalists could not assimilate Christianity with the boisterous music and exorbitant image. "They saw the hair, the makeup, the spandex. That was hard for them to get cozy with."

If the fundamentalist audience failed to appreciate the presentation, metal fans in general could not equate musicianship with the evangelical message. Their assumption was that Stryper must be musically inadequate. "A lot of times, people would say, 'Give me a break, those Christian guys [are] a joke. They can't be good.' They would come see us play and basically have to eat their words. Saying this as humbly as I possibly can, we were certainly every bit as good as, if not better than, most bands from the '80s.

"I don't say that in a prideful way," he explains. "I say that in a matter-of-fact way. We worked our butts off, and I think it showed. We would spend weeks and months and years in the studio and in the garage, rehearsing guitar solos, where other bands would just kind of throw stuff out, and it would sometimes sound like that. We really worked to write melodic, sensible parts and solos and songs."

Stryper might not have been credited for being musically accomplished, but Michael claims to have no regrets about it. "The most important thing is we've encouraged people. It's more important than being revered as great musicians. We helped encourage lives; we helped change lives. That, in the end, is what I want to be remembered for, not how fast I could play or how high I could sing."

*Michael Sweet and Oz Fox. Metal fans tended to regard Stryper as musically inadequate, based on their overwhelming evangelical message, despite highly regarded influences such as the Scorpions, Judas Priest, Iron Maiden, and UFO.*

# ROCK AND A HARD PLACE

The absence of demonic references and non-orthodox imagery caused some fans to reject Stryper as a credible metal band. Cynical fans were quick to be critical of their lyrics because Michael was singing so openly about Christ. "You get that argument all the time: You can't mix heavy metal with God. Christ is not popular in [that] world. I always get a laugh out of that because God created music. Saying you can't mix God with music—heavy metal, specifically—is absurd.

"Going back to the '50s, I don't get the mentality of rock and roll is evil and only consists of sex and drugs. Rock and roll is just a type of music, [and] God created music. It's got a little heavier groove and a little edgier sound, but it's music."

The Christian audience policed Stryper lyrics to ensure direct references to their savior, while heavy metal fans often could not embrace the evangelism. But Michael Sweet saw little point in establishing songwriting guidelines in an attempt to placate both audiences.

"The most important thing to do with anything in life is follow your convictions and take a bold stance, whether you're fighting for cancer research or fighting for religion, fighting for your family or your job, whatever it is. That's what we do in this band. We give it our all. We don't sit and think, 'Okay, who are we going to offend or turn off?' We just do what we feel led to do and let the dust settle at the end of the day."

## LET THE MUSIC DO THE TALKING

Sweet does not believe anyone misinterpreted the lyrics to "More Than a Man" because they were so obvious. "How could you? It's black and white, plain and simple what they say and mean.

"It's scripture. It's translated a bit differently, but that lyric is scripture. And the Bible never changes, so those lyrics are always powerful to me. It's one of those songs that never gets old. That song—'Soldiers Under Command,' that's another one—I never get tired of playing because [it's] just so powerful."

"More Than a Man" has remained a crowd favorite at Stryper concerts, says Michael. "Everybody requests that song. Everybody. When I [ask] during the show, 'What do you want to hear?' most people yell out 'More Than a Man.' They're pretty powerful lyrics, hitting you in the face when you hear them at 112 dB."

He isn't sure exactly how much the metal genre has changed in terms of extreme references to religion and faith, but Sweet does think it has become more tolerant. "The world is more open-minded in every way, some good ways and some bad. The good ways are bands like Stryper going out and [just] being about music. It's not out of the ordinary now. You've got so many bands like P.O.D. and Switchfoot; it's really a pretty hip thing. If you're a good band, I don't think it matters what your message is. I think people are going to be drawn to the music and give it a listen. The music does the talking."

## 27

## MEGADETH

# Peace Sells

FROM THE ALBUM **PEACE SELLS...BUT WHO'S BUYING?** (1986)

The riff used for years as the lead-in to MTV News segments came from a song inspired by *Reader's Digest*. Dave Mustaine says he loved that magazine, and absorbing columns such as "It Pays to Enrich Your Word Power" helped develop an extensive vocabulary. "It would have 10 words. Each would have a definition, and you would see how many of them you knew."

He did that and also read the comics and stories, such as terror tales about someone hanging by a branch over a shark-infested lagoon. One of those stories was called "Peace Sells, Nobody's Buying."

"I thought, 'Yeah, for sure. What a bunch of shit *that* is.'" But the phrase caught his attention. "I thought, 'Peace sells, but nobody's buying...peace sells, but *who's* buying—wow, peace sells, but who's buying—I got it!'"

Changing the statement into a question was the beginning of the song, and Mustaine was excited by the concept. Faith, work ethic, and other life experiences, such as going to court, subsequently became the basis for the verses. "Getting to work on time and paying my bills, those are two really important things for me, because I'm old-fashioned."

*"Peace Sells" was part Marx Brothers, part life experience. But Dave Mustaine (pictured) says the inspiration for the title came from* Reader's Digest.

Mustaine admits to having broken the law several times and consequently going to court, where he was ordered to attend Alcoholics Anonymous meetings after being charged with DUI. "I used my keen alcoholic mind and convinced David Ellefson to go in my place," he scoffs. "He went to those meetings and got sober."

People might have misinterpreted other parts of the song, particularly references to God. Years later, fans would make an issue of Mustaine revealing a newfound faith. "People made such a big stink about me becoming a Christian, and yeah, I can understand why. Born-again Christians leave a lot to be desired, because of the stigma they have. There's not really a lot of people who can undo that in a way that can save the cause as a whole." But his devotion should have come as no surprise, considering the first line about talking to God every day."And I do talk to him every day, whether it's 'God, bless my food,' or 'God, get me out of this mess,'" he chuckles.

If the verses were autobiographical, the chorus about wanting a new social structure refers specifically to a generation, he says. Mustaine was beginning to carve a place for himself as a heavy metal lyricist, and those sentiments and others about becoming the President of the United States of America reflected his growing political awareness.

"It was about Joe Everyman. It just showed that no matter who you are, if you believe in yourself, you can do it. It also said something from the disgruntled side, where people aren't necessarily happy about being told what to do, knowing their opportunities are so much less than the next guy."

Still, Dave had no idea politically charged songs would be so successful. "There are a lot of people who feel the same way I do," he reasons. "They just don't know how to say it. Megadeth has been able to say things like peace sells, but who's buying, and things like 'Rust in Peace' and 'United Abominations.'"

# Groucho Marx

The lyrics unfolded easily, almost like *The Manchurian Candidate*, he says. Mustaine wasn't aware of that movie until he read about the 2004 remake in *TV Guide*. The similarity to "Peace Sells" made him wonder if he had seen the original Frank Sinatra film or read the 1959 Richard Condon novel and been subconsciously inspired.

But one part he readily credits as a Marx Brothers punch line: "'*What do you mean I'm not kind? Just not your kind.'* That's Groucho Marx, and people don't know that. People don't realize it's comedy.

"The problem is that society as a whole has become such filthy scumbags that unless you talk about somebody like that *all* the time, you are merely half of a human being." Mustaine—and by extension Megadeth—had been stereotyped as one-dimensional, preventing listeners from recognizing a more complex personality with a wider range of lyrical references.

"A lot of people think I'm just going through life, and I don't care about anybody but myself. But I'm *really* a very emotional, very sensitive person, especially when it comes down to the music."

Although Mustaine had several songwriting influences, none were predominant enough to directly affect him developing an individual style as a lyricist. "I don't think there ever was that deep of an influence on me," he says, although his playing bears an admittedly distinct European flavor.

He can't recall exactly when the title progressed to being a fully realized creative idea for a song, but it did happen in a rehearsal room in Vernon, California, where he and bassist Ellefson took turns living as vagrants. "We had been living off people, moving into their house and squatting on them, until they got fed up with it. It was my turn to be living in the studio.

"It was really a drag because of the way it felt. The moral feelings that I felt after living in that studio were really hard. I was losing my manners—I was really starting to become almost Neanderthal."

*Peace Sells...But Who's Buying?* was released shortly after they were there, and the lyrics to the song were actually written on a column in that rehearsal room. "Whoever came in after us, if they didn't paint that pillar—if it's still there, and there's still writing on that thing—I can only imagine what kind of an heirloom that thing would be, to have original handwritten 'Peace Sells' lyrics written on something you can cut out of this building."

# METAL MASTERPIECE

The success of their first album, *Killing Is My Business...And Business Is Good!*, made Mustaine realize that an audience was relying on him to write insightful metal lyrics. Someone counting on him was a cool feeling, he says, but also a heavy responsibility. The inspiration felt great, but it also required awareness and a fair amount of study. "It was difficult, but I tried to live up to it the best I could."

Feedback to the lyrics weren't nearly as surprising as the overall reaction to the song as a whole. "I was really excited about the success of everything. *That* was mind-blowing. That was a masterpiece, and I knew it as soon as the song was played live for the first time and people started singing along. I *knew* we'd struck gold. Still, to this day, when we play that song and people sing along, it's fantastic.

"There are some songs that have parts that are really enjoyable for me to sing. Parts of songs I used to *love* to sing because there were special effects, and our soundman would have problems doing the part." The crew would relish giving each other fines for missed cues and other failures. "There are all kinds of funny little things that take place when you get really advanced songs, and you need to depend on somebody to pull off their parts."

Mustaine didn't wonder whether the lyrics would be controversial, because he was so excited about the caliber of musicianship that established them as better than the first album. "I loved playing with David Ellefson. I often think about jamming with him—I still think about it."

*The original handwritten lyrics to "Peace Sells" were composed on a pillar in the Vernon, California, studio where Megadeth rehearsed and the homeless Dave Mustaine sometimes lived. (From left) Chris Poland, Gar Samuelson, Mustaine, and David Ellefson.*

# VIC RATTLEHEAD

Megadeth were in New York City to arrange the album cover artwork. The band was in the shadow of the United Nations building, eating ribs at Wylie's Steak & Rib House, when the idea developed to picture their skeletal mascot, Vic Rattlehead, as a real estate agent selling the annihilated remains of the United Nations headquarters. "The artwork turned out to be really important for us."

If Mustaine had any question that *Peace Sells...But Who's Buying?* was indeed the perfect title for an album and an anthem, validation came as the strangest of signs. "We'd gone to an art gallery in New York by this guy named Robert Longo. He had this huge statue of this alien dude made out of pennies. He had this belt around him, and lightning bolts being shot out of his ass. The pedestal said 'Peace Sells, Who's Buying,' and I thought, 'Wow, this is too uncanny.' It just made sense."

*The realization that fans were expecting him to write insightful lyrics that spoke for them was a double-edged sword for Mustaine. "It was difficult, but I tried to live up to it the best I could."*

Mustaine continues to watch lots of broadcast news, including segments about the president, and wonders why anyone would aspire to that office. "Once you get to the top, they destroy you." But the idea of that goal and the overall concept of "Peace Sells" remains strong. "I think the message [still] conveys the same thing, because I am still a person who believes in truth and justice and just treating people the way you want to be treated."

## 28

## ANTHRAX

# Efilnikufesin [N.f.L.]

FROM THE ALBUM **AMONG THE LIVING** (1987)

The fourth cut of Side A of the third Anthrax album was believed to have been written about John Belushi. The victim of a lethal speedball —a combination of cocaine and heroin—the beloved *Saturday Night Live* cast member and star of *Animal House* and *The Blues Brothers* was found dead in a bungalow at the Chateau Marmont in Los Angeles in 1982.

"It wasn't *specifically* about John Belushi," says Scott Ian. "It was maybe the same circumstance, but it wasn't about [him]. It was about anybody who has everything you could ever want out of life and throws it away with drugs. You could say it was about anyone on the long list of people, up until 1986, that basically wasted their life like that."

Belushi was periodically a news item throughout the decade, especially after *Wired: The Short Life and Fast Times of John Belushi* was published in 1984. Other performers whom Scott admired had also suffered fatal overdoses, but there was never a persistent urge to comment on their senseless deaths that he can recall—at least none so overwhelming to inspire a song.

"That's the problem with talking about lyrics for me, especially [from] back then. Other than things that are obvious, like Judge Dredd, I have no idea where the initial inspiration came from—not anymore, any-way," he laughs. "I just don't remember. Belushi had died years before that. It's not like I was sitting around waiting to write about [him].

"It must have been something that came across my radar at some point in 1986, when I was writing the lyrics. It would have been something that seemed interesting to me."

# MASTERING THE CRAFT

*Among the Living* was only the second album for which Scott wrote lyrics, so his approach was basically a hit-or-miss process. "It was all so new to me. I really didn't know what the fuck I was doing. I was just trying to do my best and write about things I understood or things I felt I had something to say about."

Although the guitarist was a fan of songwriters such as Pete Townshend, Bruce Dickinson, and Rob Halford, he doesn't think their influence had much impact on his formative attempts at writing lyrics. "I don't know that I really looked at any other artist and said, 'I really like what *he's* doing; I'm going to try and mimic that.'"

Instead, his method was very spontaneous. Once the subject of a song was decided, Scott was inclined to assimilate sudden lyrical concepts, rather than refer to a cache of snippets and phrases jotted down over a period of time. Those resources simply did not exist. "It's not like I was sitting around with books of lyrics. I was just starting, so everything was kind of off the cuff for me.

"That's why I wrote about Judge Dredd," he jokes. "If you pick any song off *Among the Living*, I was pretty much writing about what I knew and what my experience was."

# FOLLOW THE RIFF

Scott Ian founded Anthrax in 1981, but he was not the lyricist. That role developed as a result of need and also the desire to try his hand at the craft. "It was definitely a necessity once [singer] Neil Turbin was gone. I just kind of stepped up and took the reins. I felt, 'All right, I have ideas; let's see how this works.'"

He discovered that music would come first in the course of writing songs. "Yeah, always. Things seemed to gel with [drummer] Charlie [Benante]. He wrote most of the riffs, and those riffs were spurring [lyrical] ideas for me. Those riffs, they just spoke to me. They kind of told me what needed to be said.

*The style or capabilities of the singer (Joey Belladonna, pictured) were never contributing factors to Anthrax lyrics. "We would make it work, no matter what," Scott Ian says.*

"We're lucky in that we've had this really organic working relationship all these years, where it just worked—how or why I don't know. I'll hear music, and it will click with an idea in my head of what the song is supposed to be about, and I'll start hearing words."

If music was fundamental in producing ideas, formatting them into songs posed a greater degree of difficulty. "Writing lyrics, to me, is the most unnatural thing in the world because I don't speak in rhymes; I don't speak in verse." Referring to *Lobo: Highway to Hell*, the miniseries he scripted for DC Comics in 2009, Scott explains that writing dialogue outside the context of a song makes more sense. "I find it much more easy to tell a story without having to put it in lyric form. But, at the same time, I know how to do it."

# COLLOQUIAL HOOK

The band thought it was a cool song, he recalls. "They thought we had a really catchy hook with the N.F.L. chant." That acronym was a band colloquialism that stood for *nice fuckin' life*. "[It] was an expression for anyone we thought was a loser. You would use it as a derogatory term for someone you thought was an idiot—oh, N.F.L."

Scott thought it would work well as a chorus. "Chanting that part, it just seemed like a good metal hook. Luckily for us, Efilnikufesin—saying nice fuckin' life backwards— actually *worked*. It was easy to say, and people got it."

# ABSTINENCE

"Efilnikufesin" seemed to express an aversion to alcohol or drugs, much like the novelty title track from their *I'm the Man* EP released that same year. And magazine stories sometimes implied that Anthrax was a band of teetotalers.

But Scott insists they were never trying to be puritanical. "We were never anti. I just didn't drink a lot because I didn't like it. I got sick on my eighteenth birthday, and booze wasn't my friend," he laughs.

The song was meant in an observational sense, he explains, never intended to lecture or make a lifestyle statement about abstinence. "No, definitely not. The last thing I ever wanted to do was preach to anybody."

"We certainly weren't a straightedge band or anything like that. It was just kind of circumstance. I felt like me, Charlie, and [bassist] Frankie [Bello] were always too busy to waste time being hung over. It's really kind of where it was at."

Conversely, if the lyrics were not meant to rebuke, Scott says he was never concerned how anyone reacted to them either. "It's not something I ever worried about. We never cared what anyone thought about anything we did. If we were thinking that, we would have written *Pyromania*—that was the biggest record [then].

"If you worried about what anyone else was going to think, you would never be able to move forward as a band. No, we didn't give a shit what anybody thought, ever."

*(From left) Frank Bello, Scott Ian, Joey Belladonna, Charlie Benante, and Dan Spitz. The chorus for "Efilnikufesin (N.F.L.)" was actually a band colloquialism.*

# DRUG AWARENESS

Fans wanted to know if "Efilnikufesin" was a direct reference to John Belushi. So did writers covering the band for magazines. Scott just started saying yes. "You get tired of answering the same question for two years. Instead of a two-paragraph answer, you just boil it down to a one-word answer: yes."

Years later, what stands out most to him is not the misconception that the song was about the actor; he's amused that the jargon of their inner circle actually became the title and chorus. "I think it's hilarious that I took that expression and put it backwards, like I got away with doing that, in a sense."

The song seldom turns up in the Anthrax live set, but Scott still enjoys playing it. "It stays pretty fresh because we haven't played it for a few years. It's always fun to sing that chorus."

*(From left) Scott Ian, Charlie Benante, Dan Spitz, Frank Bello, and Joey Belladonna. Despite media coverage that implied Anthrax was a straightedge band, Ian says the lyrics to "Efilnikufesin (N.F.L.)" were never intended to be a lecture.*

Public awareness of celebrity drug-related deaths has multiplied since 1987, and the commentary of the song is still a caustic warning about the peril of drug abuse. "I guess so," he agrees, somewhat tentatively. "Look, people can get whatever they want out of it. That's always been my attitude. If people want to take the time to read my lyrics and examine them—or maybe learn something from them—that's great. But that was never the point.

"I was writing songs, and it's what I felt and wanted to say. Once it left my brain and went onto a piece of paper, people could get whatever the hell they want from it. If it's done anything positive for anybody, that's awesome."

# 29

## ANTHRAX

# Indians

FROM THE ALBUM **AMONG THE LIVING** (1987)

Charlie Benante came up with the riff that immediately struck Scott Ian as sounding like something adapted from Native American music. Once he made that connection, there was little need to hear more music for inspiration. "It was telling me right off the bat, *this* is what this song is going to be about.

"It just seemed like one of those perfect scenarios, where we didn't have to think too much about it. It was right there for us: I was going to write about how the American Indians got fucked."

The Manifest Destiny of the westward expansion of the United States during the 1800s happened at the expense of the indigenous tribes, resulting in forced assimilation and naturalization. Grievances against federal jurisdiction and the mismanagement of Indian affairs would continue through the twentieth century, when Scott thinks he read an article in either *Time* or *Newsweek* about Native Americans facing the worst circumstances of any minority in the country. "It was a problem that was completely swept under the rug. I couldn't understand, well, how does a country just turn a blind eye to these people who were here before us?"

*A magazine article and a guitar riff that sounded like a powwow prompted one of the signature songs from Joey Belladonna's tenure with the band.*

"I'm always a fan of the underdog. I'll take up the fight for the everyman. It struck a chord in me as a 21-year-old kid—these people have been getting fucked for hundreds of years, and they're still getting fucked. It was something I had feelings about, and the music certainly matched the subject matter."

Still, the song was never intended to be a rallying cry or to prompt awareness. There was no motive of social activism as the basis for the lyrics. "It was just an anger that I needed to get rid of. It was a cathartic way for me to put down on paper these feelings I had about this situation. That's pretty much almost any song I've ever written. It's just a way for me to express myself and get it out of my head."

Neither were parallels to his own Jewish heritage a motivating factor in writing about the displacement of another ethnic group. "I didn't make that connection because I didn't have any experience with that connection. My grandfather and that generation went through that. Of course I know all about the Holocaust, and I certainly appreciate what they went through. But I grew up as a middle-class kid in Queens who didn't have to worry about where his next meal was coming from."

# UNSPOKEN APPROVAL

The chorus was likely the first lyrical element written for the song, mainly because the corresponding music naturally prompted the refrain. "It just went along with the riff. I could be wrong, but I feel like that was the first part I had written. A lot of times I'll have a chorus first. I'll come up with an idea and work backwards from there. I just followed the melody that was already there, and it fit."

Although Scott can't recall any reaction from the band about the lyrics, that was normal for them. "I wouldn't hear anything. I would never hear anything unless there was something specifically that someone had a problem with. But, generally, I would write lyrics, and no one would say boo about it."

In fact, he can't think of a single instance of his lyrics eliciting any sort of animated response from the band back then. That changed when vocalist John Bush joined Anthrax in 1992. "We became writing partners, and we worked together on everything for 13 years. It was all back and forth between us. But before John, no, no one would ever really say anything. I would write lyrics, and we would go from there."

Bands are regarded as units, so lack of opinion about the sentiment representing the entire group might seem unusual. Scott reasons it's a sure sign of approval. "That's how I know I did a good job," he laughs. "Nobody in this band ever has a problem saying when they don't like something. Believe me, if people had problems with lyrics over the years, I certainly would have been the first one to know about it."

# COMPOSITION BOOKS AND FLOPPY DISKS

Scott, who was developing as a lyricist, had no totems or rituals to stimulate the writing process. But he was fond of the Mead composition books with the black marble-pattern covers. "I was always a fan of those. You can't really tear the pages out, [and] I would always write in those.

"Back then, I was still living in my mom's apartment. That's where most of it took place, in my little tiny bedroom in Queens. I had an electronic typewriter. Once I would be done with something, then I would type the lyrics and save them on a floppy disk. Then, that's it—they're official. They're done. I would make copies for when we were in the studio."

*Scott Ian reasons that the band (Joey Belladonna pictured) not commenting on his lyrics was a sure sign that they felt fairly represented by his ideas and statements.*

Unlike latter-era Anthrax songs, those typed copies meant the lyrics were set in stone. "Generally, yeah, unless something had to be changed for melody or phrasing purposes. Back then there wasn't much changing. Now, I fully expect that things are going to move, because we're so much better with ideas and melody lines. Everybody's involved, [so] I go in knowing I'm going to be moving or changing stuff to fit somebody else's idea."

Even though the melody was always the starting point for the lyrics, Scott admits he never considered how singer Joey Belladonna would have to adapt himself to deliver the words. Chuckling, he says, "We would make it work no matter what."

*Spreading the Disease* was mostly written before Belladonna joined the band, so his vocal style was never a factor in crafting the lyrics. That non-involvement also worked well for *Among the Living*, Scott says. "*State Of Euphoria*, not so much. We rushed that album because we had to get back out on tour. And then *Persistence of Time* is when I felt like we were trying to force the issue, to turn Joey into something he wasn't. That's when we realized it wasn't going to work anymore."

# SOCIAL AWARENESS

Anthrax were often dismissed as comedic because of farcical songs like "I'm the Man" and their affinity for colorful surf apparel. "Indians"—and songs such as "One World," about the 1986 summit meeting between Ronald Reagan and Mikhail Gorbachev—opened the bracket of social consciousness that was the territory of more "serious" metal bands.

Information absorbed by his subconscious would later manifest as song ideas. "Months later, I would get an idea based on music we were writing, and it would connect to something I had seen or read. That's pretty much how it would always work."

Scott remembers a favorable response to "Indians," particularly because the lyrics were more than a heavy metal cliché, like demons and *Dungeons & Dragons*, he says. "You know, horror or really violent imagery. There was a lot of positive reaction based on the fact that supposedly I was writing socially conscious lyrics.

*(From left) Scott Ian, Charlie Benante, Dan Spitz, Frank Bello, and Joey Belladonna. Although their collective personality was portrayed as silly,* Among the Living *addressed serious social issues, such as the Cold War and the plight of Native Americans.*

"I wasn't out to try to change the world. I was writing about things that were going on around me—or that I knew about or read about, whether it was books or comics, or magazines and newspapers—that were part of my life. I didn't have enough experience to write about personal shit, to write about feelings or emotions and relationships. I hadn't *had* any of that yet. I could only find things that interested me and write from an external point of view."

Despite his relative inexperience at writing about more personal subject matter, Scott never scanned the media as a premeditative search for ideas. "I wish it was that easy," he laughs. "It was never a struggle, but it's never been an easy thing. Still, to this day, I don't think writing lyrics is an easy thing to do. It's really hard for me to express myself and not have it sound cheesy.

"It's always been really important to be able to get myself across and not have it sound stupid. And a lot of the time I feel like [it] just sounds really lame because I'm putting it into lyric form. Nobody walks around *singing* their feelings. So, to me, that's always been the battle, to express myself in this context without sounding like *42nd Street* or *Phantom of the Opera*."

# MUSICAL LEGACY

"I don't cringe, no," Scott says, reflecting on "Indians." It's a commendable example of the quality of some of his earlier attempts as a songwriter. "I'm definitely proud of the lyrics in that song, how I was able to take something I had this feeling about and really get my point across. I think it definitely holds up, lyrically, musically—look, we still play it. It's still in the set, so that says a lot. I definitely still like it."

## 30

## DOKKEN

# Kiss of Death

FROM THE ALBUM **BACK FOR THE ATTACK** (1987)

AIDS—Acquired Immune Deficiency Syndrome—was classified as a United States epidemic by the Center for Disease Control and Prevention in 1981. During the latter half of the decade, fear of contracting the HIV virus that caused AIDS was far-reaching beyond the narrow demographic originally thought affected by the disease.

Touring musicians afforded celebrity status by magazines and MTV videos enjoyed a hedonistic lifestyle that included numerous anonymous sexual encounters. Data that HIV was transmitted through the transfer of bodily fluids worried the members of Dokken.

"We started freaking out because we were all single bad boys," remembers namesake singer Don. Azidothymidine had yet to be introduced, and the prognosis for long-term survival after diagnosis was discouraging. "People were dying left and right. How do you get it? Cough on you, sneeze on you—could you get it having sex? We didn't know."

The idea to write a song about contracting AIDS was inspired by an off-hand comment while the band discussed a new report about the disease. Public perception had been that it only affected intravenous drug users and the gay community, and someone remarked that a very attractive woman obviously would not have the disease.

"I'm like, 'Dude, I don't think you get it. The virus does not [exclude] the hot-looking chicks or rich people or educated people.' It dawned on me that it doesn't matter who you are, it will get you. That's when I started scribbling the words down."

Don says the opening line about a brief encounter came first, an analogy for a one-night stand on the road.

"It's saying, this girl is lonely. And now, because of sleeping with her, I'm a damned soul [who's] going to get AIDS. My ego has taken over my testosterone—like, cool, I'm getting this girl—and the price is death."

The Dokken trademark of lyrics about heartbreaking relationships had become tedious, he says. Those types of songs were harder to compose. "Anybody can write a song about lost love. But after you write it seven times, it's a redundant story. I might labor over a song like that for days, trying to come up with some clever line."

*Don Dokken began to panic once he realized that AIDS does not exclude rock stars living a hedonistic lifestyle.*

But venturing into different topics, such as AIDS, or the communist occupation of East Germany in "Lost Behind the Wall," was not arduous. In the case of "Kiss of Death," with the opening verse already written, the rest of the lyrics quickly followed. "When I know what I want to say, it's easy. Honestly, I wrote that song in about an hour."

# UNCLE BUTCH

Don's uncle, Butch, was afflicted with AIDS. Watching a family member struggle gave him a firsthand perspective on how the disease ravaged the body. "He lost an eye. Then he got sores, and he got skinny. He was weak and fragile, and every other week there was something else failing."

The singer remembers frequently seeing Butch throughout the sessions for the *Tooth and Nail* album. "There was a gay bar right across from where we were recording on Santa Monica Boulevard, literally 50 feet away. Walking out of the studio, I used to run into my uncle and all his friends. I'd invite them in to hear our songs, [and] I just thought they were really nice people. I thought they were cool, intelligent, and educated.

*Although "Kiss of Death" was not directly inspired by Don's uncle, watching him succumb to AIDS fueled the singer's paranoia that a one-night stand could afflict him with the virus.*

"Being around [him] gave me a better understanding of that whole thing. It really kept me from being homophobic."

Butch had been in a monogamous relationship with the same man for nearly 20 years. "I remember talking about it somewhat, and he said, 'I had a one-night stand, that was it. I cheated on my boyfriend one time.' "I thought, 'Well, that's all it takes.' And that was a little bit of the inspiration."

## AIDS AWARENESS

Initially, the band never made the connection between their sexual proclivity and being at risk. "Never crossed my mind. People said you got it from needles. There was that whole homophobic thing, that it's a homosexual disease. It was like, it's in Africa. It sounds terrible, but it had nothing to do with us. We don't live in Africa. We're not gay, and we're not shooting up heroin."

Everyone frantically called their doctors for information about how it was transmitted. "Do blow jobs count?" he laughs. "I remember that. And the doctor goes, 'Well, people have gotten AIDS from oral sex. If you have any kind of gum disease—you've got bleeding gums and she's got the virus—you could get AIDS.'"

It became increasingly apparent that AIDS was a communicable disease that could infect anyone. "We got very pro-condom, pro-paranoia, pro-everything," he laughs. "It kind of put a damper on the sex, drugs, and rock-and-roll thing."

## THE LOST INSTRUMENTAL

"Kiss of Death" was one of the last songs finished for *Back for the Attack*, probably second to last, Don thinks. The music was originally written as an instrumental track that would be replaced on the album by "Mr. Scary." On a break from the road, he discovered the music among his demos. "The riff, I just all of a sudden went, 'Wait a minute—and I wrote it.'

"The riff George wrote was very repetitive. He did that because he wanted a lot of room to shred. So, there were no confines of [being] limited on the melody. It was a very percussive riff, so I said, 'I'll write the lyrics percussive'—a bouncing-ball type of lyric, as I call it."

*(From left) George Lynch, Robert Englund as Freddie Krueger, and Don Dokken. George and Don's often contentious relationship produced a musical synergy that was the basis of the Dokken sound.*

The synergy between guitarist George Lynch and singer Don was a product of elaborate riffs and smooth, melodic vocals. "That song is very busy, that riff. I had to write this staccato melody that was totally out of character for my writing style, but it was the *only* thing that fit. George didn't leave me any room on the arrangement to do anything but that."

Don wrote the lyrics by scatting syllables over the melody. "I sometimes call it God. I hate to use that word a lot, but I think any writer that's a true writer, we have a gift and don't know exactly where it came from. You just *hear* it! It comes out of nowhere, and you're scrambling for the paper, scrambling for the pen, and you can't get the words down fast enough. Those are inspired moments that are wonderful."

# BROKEN-HEARTED LOVE SONG

Few people realized the song was about AIDS. "They totally got it as a love song, about how this woman sucked him into her life, then broke his heart and destroyed him. That seemed to be the general consensus, because you can interpret it that way. It makes sense, but the truth is, it's about AIDS.

"If they got *something* out of the song, and they relate the song to something in their personal life, then I've succeeded. That's what it's all about, right?"

He compares that misconception to the popular belief that "Lucy in the Sky with Diamonds" documented an acid trip. "According to the [Beatles] biographies, it wasn't about that. But for 30 years people believed it, and that's their right. If that's what they want to believe, it behooves us not to say anything."

But many fans have since come to understand his meaning over the years since 1987. Don says occasionally introducing the song onstage as being about a friend who died from AIDS adds some insight. "I'll make little comments, like wrap the rascal and double the glove," he laughs.

"I've had many, many fans say, 'After I heard that, I immediately listened to it again in a whole different light.' I've had lots of those comments."

He never really explained the lyrics to the band, either. "I didn't really go into any kind of dissertation on, you know, AIDS and my uncle, and groupies and the people you sleep with. I just said, 'I've got this idea for this instrumental, this big gang vocal—*with the kiss of death!*' We didn't have any songs on the album like that, and George and [drummer] Mick [Brown] both liked more of that gang vocal that was popular.

"They didn't *ask*—they didn't really care. They went, 'That's cool. Cool lyric, cool melody. Okay, we'll make it a song.'"

"Kiss of Death" has remained a staple of Dokken shows, although Don isn't exactly sure why it's popular. "[It] was not a hit. It never was a video. It was never played on the radio. It's an obscure track, but it became a cult track.

"I just think the guitar riff George wrote was really, really cool. It was a combination of the guitar, the groove, the arrangement—the stars aligned, and it all came together. It still stands up two decades later as a really in-your-face metal song."

# BETTER BAND LIVING

He had no clue how anyone might react to the hot-button topic, but Don claims the song was never meant to stir social consciousness. "I didn't say, 'Yeah, I'm trying to enlighten the world and warn people to have safe sex.' I wish I could say writing those lyrics was more of a benevolent state of mind, but it wasn't. It was written about how I got a reality check, that it could happen to me, not just my uncle.

"It was more about me sleeping with a different girl every night, and then I got paranoid that I was going to die—we all did. We would be on the bus, and every day there would be more and more on TV about it."

Despite new treatments and longer life expectancy, Don hopes the words still express the seriousness of AIDS and other sexually transmitted diseases. Now in his 50s, he cautions the backstage debauchery of younger bands. "I give them stories: Heads up, dude. That chick you've been talking to and making out with all night? I've seen her for the last 10 years. She's banged *every* band in rock and roll. Watch out for those baby-blue eyes. If your penis falls off, just remember I told you so."

## 31

## MEGADETH

# In My Darkest Hour

FROM THE ALBUM **SO FAR, SO GOOD…SO WHAT?** (1988)

Megadeth dominated the documentary *The Decline of Western Civilization Part II—The Metal Years* with "In My Darkest Hour." Powerful performance footage, cut with interview segments and studio scenes of Dave Mustaine in the vocal booth, dissociated their intensity from the overall giddy spirit of the other bands in the movie.

Regardless of the somewhat whimsical context of that 1988 documentary, the song was no laughing matter. Mustaine wrote the music when Cliff Burton died. The Metallica bassist died on September 27, 1986, when their tour bus driver lost control outside Dörarp, Sweden. Burton was thrown from the coach and pinned beneath it.

Mustaine, a member of Metallica until being ousted in 1983, wasn't told about his former bandmate's passing until he received a phone call from Megaforce Records executive Maria Ferarro. Not knowing the location of the funeral ceremony was also awkward, a move he says left people scratching their heads.

"When Maria called and told me that Cliff died, I was just totally rocked. So, I got in a car and went downtown—with Chris Poland—and we scored some heroin. We went back to the house we were renting, did our thing, and I wrote the song."

The music to "In My Darkest Hour" was written in one sitting when Cliff Burton died. But the song, he says, was also written in part because of problems he was having with his fiancée, Diana.

"When I started writing the lyrics for that song, it came out in two different ways. The first way was toward Diana, the second was toward Cliff. Now, Cliff was my buddy, and I loved him. There was no animosity at all. Diana was my fiancée, and I loved her. I didn't want to do anything bad to her either, but we had a very hot relationship."

The words were written about the difficulty of his relationship with her. "I was engaged to her, and I really loved her. I thought I was going to marry her, and it just didn't work."

The end of their tumultuous relationship was ugly, says Mustaine, calling himself a coward. "I didn't handle myself like a gentleman, and I certainly wasn't very brave about it. She ended up having to take therapy over it, because of what I did to her."

*The music was reactionary to news about the death of Metallica bassist Cliff Burton, but the lyrics to "In My Darkest Hour" were subsequently written about Dave Mustaine's relationship with his fiancée.*

*Mustaine says he did not handle the end of the relationship with his fiancée in a very gentlemanly or brave manner.*

He doesn't go into details—although the lyrics can be interpreted as overtly suicidal—other than saying if such circumstances happened to him, he likely would have sought counseling, as well.

Mustaine has always described the song as music happening first, then lyrics, but he says it's hard to remember exactly. "I think everything all kind of came at once." The song did not become a completed track, however, until he later refined it—a necessity, given the number of instances of musicians poaching each other's ideas. "The problem at that time was, there were so many people that would hear something, and they would *nab* it from you. If you had a song you wanted to try and record, really, you had to hide it until you were ready to go into the studio."

# COLLABORATION

"I'd been begging these guys to write something, because I wanted to be able to give them something for contributing to the record, so that we're all on it and it's not just written by me. There's actually a contribution in there from David Ellefson. He wrote something toward the end of 'In My Darkest Hour,' and I thought it was great, so we used it."

Timbuk3 had a Top 20 hit in 1986 with "The Future's So Bright, I Gotta Wear Shades." Mustaine says the optimism of that phrase conversely moved bassist Ellefson to write the lyrics of loss that became the last three lines of the song. "I'm pretty sure that's what it was.

"It was just like butter," Mustaine says about the simplicity with which the music and lyrics emerged. "It was like catching a fish and having it jump into the net. The song came out with an ease and comfort, almost like I had done this before. It wasn't difficult at all."

# LINEUP

*So Far, So Good...So What?* was the third Megadeth album, the first with a new lineup. Drum tech Chuck Behler replaced Gar Samuelson, a recurring scenario when Nick Menza joined the band two years later. Malice guitarist Jay Reynolds was recruited to replace Chris Poland, but was quickly displaced by his own guitar teacher, Jeff Young.

"That was a very interesting time with guitar playing, because a lot of the playing was that whole Tony MacAlpine overhand, kind of tap-it stuff."

Dave remembers turmoil soon developing because of Young, particularly his affection for Doro Pesch, when the guitarist found a note from the Warlock singer in Mustaine's luggage during their tour together. "He flipped because he was in love with her. He'd been giving her notes and flowers." He even stuck Doro stickers between the pickups on his guitar, Mustaine says. "It was just total madness.

"There was a *lot* of stuff going on with Jeff, especially after he quit." But during the indeterminate period before Megadeth hired another guitarist, Mustaine learned about the mischievous nature of his road crew. "His guitar tech goes, 'I'll tell you something that will make you feel better. I've been spitting in Jeff's water bottle every night.'"

*The* So Far, So Good...So What? *Megadeth lineup: (From left) David Ellefson, Chuck Behler, Jeff Young, and Dave Mustaine.*

# EMOTIONAL CONNECTION

The lyrics were admittedly dark, but Mustaine says a lot of people commented about being able to relate to the emotion of the song, thanking him for expressing their own despair. "I didn't really think that anybody was going to make that kind of connection, because there were some really intense feelings that were able to be dug up.

"The song got a great reaction, mostly stuff like it changed their life. A lot of people were saying, 'God, thank you so much for writing this song! I get it, and it's my song—I relate to it.'

"They were able to connect with the feelings in the song, and I thought that was great." That track was the beginning of Mustaine being able to write songs that went beyond an appeal of simply catchy melodies or chorus hooks.

Despite the desolate tone of the song, he doesn't think the lyrics stirred up any controversy. The metal media chose not to disparage or to overly exploit the song, surprising given the intense personal nature of a failed romantic relationship and the death of a friend.

"There's always going to be somebody not afraid to speak their mind. That's something that goes back to before I was even born," he laughs. "There's always going to be somebody who is going to disagree with what I'm saying. But for the most part, the press has been respectful, and the public is interested in what I have to say. The song got a great reaction. I don't think there's been anything too bad about it."

"In My Darkest Hour" struck a chord with passionate metal fans, but Dave says he isn't entirely sure why. "It could just be that time of year, that time of their life. It could be a word association game—who knows, man."

*Angus Young and Brian Johnson.* Back in Black, *Johnson's first album with AC/DC, was recorded in the Bahamas. The leadoff track, "Hells Bells," was basically a description of seeing his first tropical storm. "Sandstorm from the beach didn't fit,"* *he jokes.*

*The title for "Crazy Train" was inspired by Randy Rhoads's (right, with Ozzy Osbourne) effects pedal, which produced a chugging sound. "Even when he wasn't playing, you could hear that sound through the amp," remembers bassist Bob Daisley. "I said, 'Randy, it sounds like a train.'"*

*Former Quiet Riot guitarist Randy Rhoads's story about the headbanging fans in England was the jumping-off point for the catchphrase of the "Metal Health" chorus. Drummer Frankie Banali says that song was always the musical heart and soul of the band. (From left) Rudy Sarzo, Carlos Cavazo, Kevin DuBrow, and Banali.*

*Some listeners might have speculated that the title track on* Holy Diver *was allegorical, based on* Revelations 12:9. *But Ronnie James Dio says the point of the song was to illustrate the self-indulgence of humanity. "It shows extreme selfishness."*

*The lyrics to "Eat Me Alive" were intentionally nihilistic, like a film noir movie such as* Watchmen *or* Sin City. *Rob Halford calls the song a spoof, but the Parents Music Resource Center thought differently, ranking it #3 on the Filthy Fifteen, their list of objectionable songs.*

*"The Price," written in the bathroom at Led Zeppelin guitarist Jimmy Page's studio, was about a husband missing his wife and son. But the lyrical reference to Dee Snider's family was vague. "I always want people to be able to put their situation in the lyric, read their price that they're paying for their goal, their dream." (From left) Mark "The Animal" Mendoza, Eddie "Fingers" Ojeda, Snider, A.J. Pero, and Jay Jay French.*

*Shadows Fall singer Brian Fair says there was little illusion in James Hetfield's lyrics, giving Metallica a sense of realism that was appealing, such as in "Master of Puppets," which warned about the danger of substance abuse. "A lot of metal before that had almost a fantasy slant or the sleaze slant." (From left) Hetfield, Kirk Hammett, Cliff Burton, and Lars Ulrich.*

*Guitarist Kerry King says "Jesus Saves" was written to catch people's eye, not because of his childhood disbelief in religion. "People looking at an album back then would go, 'I can't believe Slayer wrote a song called "Jesus Saves."'" (From left) Dave Lombardo, Jeff Hanneman, King, and Tom Araya.*

*Anthrax were often dismissed as comedic because of farcical songs such as "I'm the Man" and their affinity for colorful surf apparel. But songs such as "Indians" opened the bracket of social consciousness that was the territory of more "serious" metal bands. (Clockwise from top left) Frank Bello, Joey Belladonna, Charlie Benante, Dan Spitz, and Scott Ian.*

*Information that HIV was transmitted through the transfer of bodily fluids worried the hedonistic members of Dokken. "We started freaking out because we were all single bad boys," remembers singer Don Dokken about the impetus behind "Kiss of Death." "How do you get it? Cough on you, sneeze on you—could you get it having sex? We didn't know." (Clockwise from top left) Jeff Pilson, Dokken, Wild Mick Brown, and George Lynch.*

*The music to "In My Darkest Hour" was written in one sitting when Cliff Burton died. But the song, Dave Mustaine says, was also written in part because of problems he was having with his fiancée, Diana. "I was engaged to her, and I really loved her. I thought I was going to marry her, and it just didn't work."*

*Bloody, poetic metaphors for emotional betrayal lent a gallant, almost Shakespearean tinge to "Close My Eyes Forever." But Lita Ford says the lyrics to her duet with Ozzy Osbourne were based on his unusual vision of being a fortuneteller. "It's Ozzy standing on a mountain, looking out with his eyes closed."*

*Ozzy Osbourne (right, with Zakk Wylde) was denounced by Christian groups as the chief antichrist of spiritual corruption. The lyrics to "Miracle Man" addressed the hypocrisy of religious leaders caught engaging in the same debauchery they alleged against Ozzy and heavy metal. "It could be [about] anybody being hypocritical and getting caught with their pants down," says bassist Bob Daisley.*

*"18 and Life" was a metaphor for the changes that affected Skid Row guitarist Dave "Snake" Sabo's brother after returning from military service in Vietnam. "Ricky became one of those guys who can't seem to do the right thing, and eventually something bad happens," says bassist Rachel Bolan. (Clockwise from top left) Bolan, Sabo, Rob Affuso, Scotti Hill, and Sebastian Bach.*

*Bobby "Blitz" Ellsworth says "The Years of Decay" was autobiographical about Overkill. "The road is common to all who tour, but this is how we perceived it to be, the best place to be, no matter how different it is from the nine-to-five norm. Regardless of the downs, the ups are still better."*
*(From left) Rat Skates, D.D. Verni, Ellsworth, and Bobby Gustafson.*

*"Cowboys from Hell" was steeped in attitude and gunfighter imagery. But Phil Anselmo says it was the work of guitarist Dimebag Darrell Abbott (pictured) that made the song come to life. "It was the riff. It was a massive anthem. It just had that feel, and the lyrics fit."*

# 32

## LITA FORD

# Close My Eyes forever

FROM THE ALBUM LITA (1988)

The haunting duet between Lita Ford and Ozzy Osbourne seemed to suggest the contemplation of suicide as a path to reconciliation after infidelity. "God, it really does," she agrees. "It does have that vibe to it. But when Ozzy and I wrote the lyrics, I don't think we meant it in that way."

Instead, the impetus for the song came from an unusual vision. "He said, in his thick, British voice, 'I see myself standing on top of a mountain, looking out with my eyes closed, almost like a fortuneteller'—which really doesn't make any sense."

The former Runaways guitarist was recording her third album when the Osbournes paid a visit bearing housewarming gifts. "Sharon and Ozzy came to the studio, and Ozzy and I started to play pool. We played pool...and we played pool...and we played pool."

Bored, Sharon eventually left the studio. The marathon billiards tournament then moved to an adjacent room off the studio that was equipped with a keyboard, guitar, and amplifiers. "We started to jam, [and] we came up with 'Close My Eyes Forever.'"

*Lita says the song developed sponta-
neously while they jammed, with Ozzy
singing over her instrumental noodling.*

Lita recalls the music and lyrics emerging together. "When you're writing with two
people, it kind of happens at the same time. Ozzy sang over the music as I was playing
it." The same dynamic happens between her and husband Jim Gillette. "I'll start playing
a guitar riff, and he'll come in and sing something over it."

The spontaneity of their unplanned collaboration was like a divine gift, she says. "It was
literally overnight. The sun came up, and I drove home with this new song. I remember
Sharon being pissed off at me and Ozzy because we stayed up so late and came home
the next day."

# TWO SINGERS, ONE SONG

The track was recorded as a duet, but Lita says it was not conceived as such. "No! Nothing was envisioned. The song wasn't envisioned; the lyrics weren't envisioned. It was just something that came out."

But the finished lyrics were not altered to accommodate two vocalists. "Any one song can be sung by two people. If you wanted to have it that way, it's not really difficult." *Wicked Wonderland*, the 2009 album that was her first in 14 years, also featured male and female vocals—her former Nitro vocalist husband singing the male parts—for no other reason than her wanting to do it that way.

No thought was given to anyone other than Ozzy singing on the track. The ex–Black Sabbath front man was one of the most popular male rock vocalists of that time, and Lita was the predominant female force of the genre. "And we were both managed by Sharon. So, it seemed like the thing to do was get together and do that song."

Rumors speculated about the existence of an unreleased version of the song that also featured her then-fiancé, Black Sabbath guitarist Tony Iommi. "No," Lita says, discrediting the hearsay.

# ROMANTIC TRAGEDY

The song outwardly seemed to describe the conflict and desperate turmoil of adolescent metal outcasts struggling with the confusion of romantic emotions for the first time in their lives.

Bloody, poetic metaphors for emotional betrayal lent a gallant, almost Shakespearean tinge to the words. Lita sees how one might suspect the song might have been inspired by the volatile passion of their teenage audience. "You would think so, but no, it wasn't at all. It's just Ozzy standing on a mountain, looking out with his eyes closed."

*The lyrics appealed to adolescent metal outcasts, many of whom were dealing with romantic emotions and relationships for the first time in their lives. But the song was actually inspired by Ozzy envisioning himself as a fortune-teller figure.*

# COLLABORATIVE PROCESS

But their jam session did not draw heavily from any preconceptions based upon his unusual daydream. There were no specific words or titles that initially primed their creativity. It was simply the spontaneity of random ideas. "It just came naturally. We just went in and started doodling around."

Although no particular songwriters specifically influenced "Close My Eyes Forever," Lita admittedly was a fan of Mike Chapman and Holly Knight, whose credits included hits for the likes of Pat Benatar, Tina Turner, and Aerosmith. Producer Chapman had a hand in writing a pair of tracks on *Lita*, and the album also featured collaborations with Mötley Crüe bassist Nikki Sixx and Lemmy Kilmister from Motörhead.

# SIGNATURE SUCCESS

*Lita* charted at #29 at the peak of its *Billboard* run, and "Close My Eyes Forever" broke into the Hot 100 top ten at #8. It would become her signature song, along with "Kiss Me Deadly." But Lita claims neither she nor Ozzy sensed it might become so revered.

"We didn't feel that. I think the point where I *really* felt like it was going to be something was when we were actually singing the lead vocals. Mike Chapman had us face to face in the studio, and I'm looking at Ozzy. I'm watching him sing his parts, and he's watching me sing my parts. It just felt like, 'Wow, this is *really* cool! This could be something.'

"I think then we started to realize that we had something on our hands and people were going to react—hopefully positively—to that song."

It became a source of strength for listeners who recognized their own resolve within the words. "A lot of people say things like, 'I remember when I broke up with my husband, and I used to listen to that song. It really got me through.' Or, 'My best friend died in a car accident. She used to love that song so much, and I used to listen to it for her after she passed away'—just really *wild* stuff that really touches your heart."

# CELLULOID FANTASY

The music video added to the foreboding interpretation of the lyrics. Shot in a very dark, desolate setting, the clip seemingly pictured Lita and Ozzy pleading with each other from isolated positions. That ambiance reinforced the feeling of separation conveyed by the song.

"The video is very deceiving because it looks like we're in two separate rooms. It looks like we're in two separate buildings. But we're not. We're together in one room. It's a train station. I'm on the ground, and he's up in this [alcove], but it looks like we're completely separated."

# NEW MILLENNIUM

"It was just one of those songs that got people through hard times, I guess you could say." Lita actively returned to performing in 2008 after a nearly 15-year hiatus, and "Close My Eyes Forever" remained a highlight of her set. During dates with Queensrÿche in 2009, it was performed as a duet with singer Geoff Tate.

"It's really cool. The audience does all the work. When we play it, I don't even have to sing the chorus, and then everybody sings *close your eyes* at the very end."

The song seems to still resonate as strongly, she says. "As a matter of fact, we're planning on doing a remake. But it won't be the same. It will be more of an up tempo, completely wild, digital version of the song."

# 33

## LIVING COLOUR

# Cult of Personality

FROM THE ALBUM VIVID (1988)

The attraction shared by beloved public figures and others cast in dark shadows intrigued Vernon Reid. "The great deeds of one character versus the evil deeds of another, raised to the level of legend or fame, the thing they have in common—that's what I wanted to talk about in the song."

Anyone to whom other people are willing to listen is the most dangerous person in a room, says Reid. "People like Charles Manson or Jesse James, whatever their bad deeds, have become anti-heroes. At the same time, Martin Luther King and Mahatma Gandhi and Malcolm X were icons in the other direction."

That essence of charisma, plus the idea that morally contrasting personalities are equally magnetic, inspired the lyrics of the most popular Living Colour song.

"There's an over-arching aspect of charisma that unites a fascist like [Benito] Mussolini to a popular figure like John F. Kennedy," Reid says. "It's the force of personality that raised them above paid bureaucrats and cranks to the level of leadership. The song is about that—the star stuff, if you will."

Just the juxtaposed song title itself was captivating. "Negative and positive are in that phrase," he explains. "There's something vaguely sinister about the *cult* of personality. Personality has the connotation of being positive, and cult had the connotation of negativity. Negative and positive are co-joined."

# POP CULTURE

The social and political landscape of 1988 was a culture bursting with characters that represented personality cults. The world was focused on the events that pointed to the dissolution of the Soviet Union and the end of Ronald Reagan's second term in office. The former actor, whose political affiliation shifted from Democrat to Republican years before his presidency, was perfectly suited for the global stage, according to Reid. "Reagan basically ruled by personality, because he played the role."

Although the lyrics reference historical leaders, Reid says the allusion was to celebrities. There was an ostentatious disposition that seemed to be running rampant in popular culture, he laughs. "Prince, to Jim and Tammy Bakker, to Boy George. Everything was kind of over the top, so there was a flavor of that.

"The cult of personality is about political figures, but that's really about our obsession with celebrity. The cult of personality is celebrity by another name."

The cut-and-dried assessment of celebrities as either good or bad, right or wrong, prompted the Living Colour guitarist to explore the complexity of human nature beyond outward appearances. "Say you have a baseball player who's a hero to his fans but an absolute horror show to his family. To his fans, the guy can do no wrong. But to his family, he's not a hero. That's a good example of what goes on in real life. The actor was wonderful, the politician was smiling, but you can never know the whole story."

*To Live and Die in L.A.*, one of Vernon's favorite '80s movies, also stimulated his thought about the limiting concept of good and evil. "The bad guy is *bad* through and through; the good guy is good all the time. The thing that's genius is the way each of these guys treats the women in their lives *completely* different." Secret Service agent Richard Chance (William L. Petersen) is cruel toward his informant paramour, while counterfeiter Eric Masters (Willem Dafoe) treats his girlfriend with tender care.

# MUSICAL EPIPHANY

Reid says writing "Cult of Personality" was one of the great days in Living Colour history. "Not so much because it became our most popular song, but the song was completely written in one session—literally, it came like an avalanche."

During rehearsal following a show at legendary New York City club CBGB, singer Corey Glover presented a new idea to the band. "I was trying to play what he was singing, and I stumbled on the riff, which is not what he was singing," Reid admits. "From that first phrase, the logic kind of revealed itself. It just took on a life of its own, and the song kind of wrote itself by magic."

A studious music fan, Vernon says he had always wondered just what it felt like, the inspired sensation of monumental songs coming together for his favorite bands. The day "Cult of Personality" was written, he knew. "I said, it was like *this*—not exactly the same, but this is what it was like—like an extended epiphany."

*The "Cult of Personality" riff developed from Vernon Reid's inability to mimic Corey Glover's singing.*

Less than a month earlier, Reid had written prose about personality cults, but without accompanying music. His prolific ideas that would become the lyrics to *Vivid* were scribbled in a little red notebook. "My notebook of dreams," he says.

A penchant for Peter Gabriel, whose 1980 *Peter Gabriel* album—particularly tracks like "Biko" and "Not One of Us"—influenced him. But the verse about one plus one adding up to three was subconsciously inspired by George Orwell's dystopian novel, *1984.* "There's a part of the book where Winston Smith is being held captive, and they're trying to break him. The torturer says, 'How many fingers am I holding up?' He gets beaten until the tormentor holds up three fingers, and he says four. The whole concept is reality is what I say it is, not what you see."

The impact of the book only became obvious in hindsight. "At that time, it just made sense to me to say that. I realized later on, that's what inspired it."

*Corey Glover and Muzz Skillings. The success of "Cult of Personality" was sometimes categorized by Living Colour being an entirely African-American rock band.*

# MESSAGE TO THE GRASS ROOTS

Reid liked the subject matter and felt good about the lyrics, but the reference to Mussolini, rather than Adolf Hitler, was a conscious decision. "I wanted the idea of fascism, but I was not going to give Hitler any honor." Besides, he explains, like the title of the song, the name Mussolini is also a contrast. "It's a much more pleasant sound. He's an evil man with a nice-sounding name."

The opening soundbite was supposed to be an excerpt from "I Have a Dream," Martin Luther King's 1963 Lincoln Memorial speech. "We approached the King Foundation, and it was really a lot of hassle. It just wasn't going to be workable."

Instead, Reid happened upon a Harlem vendor selling cassettes of Malcolm X speeches. An edit of his "Message to the Grass Roots" became the familiar opening to the track. "It's the voice of this iconic African-American social critic, talking about a language that everyone can easily understand, and *that* encapsulates what the cult of personality is."

# COMMERCIAL SUCCESS

"Cult of Personality" was the second single released from *Vivid*, and Vernon remembers they were shocked by its success. "We had total faith in the song. We believed in it completely. But so many times in life, you have faith and belief in something, and it just doesn't come true. Living Colour was the most unlikely band, so for the song to be a bona fide hit was completely overwhelming."

The reaction that meant the most to him was that of original Living Colour bassist Alex Mosely, who went on to play with Lisa Lisa and the Cult Jam. "When he left the band, I was pretty heartbroken. But his girlfriend had a baby, and it was a crazy situation—he had to make moves.

"We were at a conference, and he came to me, like, 'Man, you did it. You made history.'" Unlike forerunners such as Sound Barrier, who never enjoyed a hit single, the popularity of "Cult of Personality" thrust a rock band consisting of all African-American musicians into the awareness of a mainstream spotlight.

Their ethnicity, plus the lyrical pairing of Kennedy and Mussolini, turned heads, Reid remembers. Still, he never thought the song was controversial. He *does* recall someone hearing the chorus as "fucked-up personality."

"I thought, 'You actually think a song made it onto American popular radio with the phrase "fucked-up personality"?'" he laughs. "Really?"

Reid says that "Cult of Personality" was once ranked on a list of favorite right-wing rock-and-roll songs. "I thought it was wild that it made it to this list of songs for conservatives, because it's *exactly* the opposite.

"It was taken as a song against totalitarianism—and certainly it is against totalitarianism—but I'm coming to that from a very left-wing perspective," he laughs. "It's interesting that people from very different walks of life clued into it."

# OMINOUS APPEAL

The unmistakable nature of the lyrics is what Vernon thinks appealed the audience. "It invited people to think about something obvious, that maybe they hadn't thought about before. It's about larger-than-life beyond good and evil. The cult of personality is ubiquitous, and I think that's why it really struck a chord.

"We're fascinated by characters. Michael Myers, Hannibal Lecter, and Jason [Voorhees], we buy into that. We *love* our villains as much as we love our heroes—as much as we won't admit it. We have a fascination with evil figures, and we raise them to a level of iconic status. It's almost a viral human activity, and the cult of personality takes the sheet off of why that is. We identify, not with just the great and the good, but with the bad and the notorious. It's part of the human condition, and I think the song really brought a fresh conversation about the human condition."

# LASTING POPULARITY

Artists become very resentful of the music that got them noticed, according to Reid. But he doesn't feel that way about "Cult of Personality," grateful that it continues to affect an audience and became a popular *Guitar Hero* song. "It struck a chord because of the lyric *and* the music."

Reid believes every songwriter lives through the phenomenon of their music haunting them in unimaginable ways. Although he claims not to be mystical about things, he's certain that songs that resonate will unexpectedly come back at the artist.

*Podcast fan Vernon Reid was surprised
to hear "Cult of Personality" played
during some of his favorite episodes.*

An admitted tech podcast fan, Reid was surprised to hear "Cult of Personality" opening a Mac OS Ken podcast that wondered whether Steve Jobs would appear at the 2009 Worldwide Developers Conference. The irrationality of Apple stock directly affected by speculation about the CEO's health, based on his gaunt appearance, "that's *completely* the cult of personality," he insists.

The concept rings even stronger in 2009, with the media attention focused on Barack Obama. "Make no mistake; he is *completely* an example of what that lyric is talking about. They can say what they want about him—call him a celebrity, call him this, that, and the other thing—but right now the Republican Party are praying for someone to show up that has 50 percent of Obama's charisma."

He thinks it also applies to metal bands. The excessive number of artists and various subgenres of metal is like a factory mass-producing bands, Reid says. "What's going to cut through the noise is personality. There are going to be a lot of kids who can play crazy arpeggios. What's going to make the difference? It's going to be personality."

## 34

## QUEENSRŸCHE

# Operation: Mindcrime

FROM THE ALBUM **OPERATION: MINDCRIME** (1988)

Queensrÿche finished their *Rage for Order* tour in Quebec, and Geoff Tate had met people who invited him to stay and visit the province. "I thought, 'Yeah, let's try it out and see what it's like.'"

The singer ended up staying in Montreal for eight or nine months, learning his way around the city and absorbing the culture. The band had been considering the possibility of recording a concept album, so his eyes and ears were open to the environment, searching for ideas.

People such as French Canadian separatists, and a woman dressed as a nun seen previously in an Amsterdam discotheque, caught his attention, and he observed how they looked and what they said. "I was collecting characters in my head, waiting to find a theme, really, that would warrant a full-scale record."

Geoff knew immediately when he found that theme. "Yeah, I remember exactly when it happened and even what I was wearing," he laughs. "I was wearing a pair of jeans and a T-shirt and a black leather jacket. And I was freezing my ass off because it was like, 20 degrees below zero."

*Geoff Tate remained in Montreal for several months after Queensrÿche finished their* Rage for Order *tour. His experiences there greatly influenced the* Operation: Mindcrime *story. (From left) Chris DeGarmo, Michael Wilton, Tate, Scott Rockenfield, and Eddie Jackson.*

Walking through the snow to a corner store to buy a pack of cigarettes, he stood outside and smoked. An overwhelming urge led him inside the church across the street. "The Catholic churches, especially in Montreal, are very ornate, beautiful, with all sorts of pagan imagery mixed with the early Christian imagery."

The warmth and ambiance of lit candles sparked something in his imagination. "I'm sitting there, just kind of warming up and checking it out—and boom! It just hit me, this idea for this record."

Although he had already been gathering fragments of ideas, *Operation: Mindcrime* really started with his experience in the church.

# RUSH OF IDEAS

Tate quickly jotted down the sudden flow of thoughts in his notepad. "It just kind of came in a big rush, which is what happens to me. I get pretty taken with the whole thing, and it's sometimes a two-day rush of creative ideas."

The discussion about a concept album had started as early as the sessions for *The Warning*. The band had already flirted with interrelated topics on that album and *Rage for Order*. "We were stretching out musically to push the boundaries of our idea of metal. *Mindcrime* is really the culmination of those two records for us, moving in a certain direction [and] looking for a large-scale theme."

The title track was the first song written for the album, the guitar riff being the initial element. Geoff remembers hearing that melody in his imagination while in the church, and it became the basis for writing the words.

Lyrics came together quickly, he says. "Very fast, like a lot of songs. When I'm on a roll, it just kind of spills out. The majority of it is there in one sitting. Over the length of recording an album, I'll refine things, change some phrases that don't make sense— more or less fine-tuning it."

# MUSICAL STORYBOARD

It was the fourth track on the album, but Geoff doesn't remember knowing exactly where it would fit within the story. "No, I don't think I did. I'm guessing I was [just] thinking of it as a scene, establishing the first conversation with Nikki and Dr. X."

"Operation: Mindcrime" served as a summation of the story as a whole. The song provided a broad overview of the characters and the plot. But rather than storyboard the entire album, Geoff simply intended to establish the relationship between the characters. "Kind of like you do with a film," he says. "You have characterization and setups, things like that. Then you have conflict, as much as you can possibly pack into it."

To that degree the song became essential in setting the musical and lyrical tone for charting the rest of the story. "It gave us a map of the characters: the dominance that Dr. X had over Nikki; that Nikki was a junkie and Dr. X had this plan."

It definitely sketched out the nature of the characters—especially Nikki—something Geoff really liked. "It shows this kind of pathetic junkie who doesn't really have a direction, looking for himself in so many ways. I like that a lot about it."

Musically, the incorporation of classical guitar within the blues feel of the song was also something Geoff says he liked. "It's kind of mixing these modes together. That was pretty interesting for me at the time.

"If you listen to the music, there are several themes that keep reappearing throughout the record. The riff definitely set the tone: a bit sinister sounding, kind of raised eyebrow, not quite knowing—a little spooky. We also did that on *Mindcrime II*, the same half-step interval progression, to establish a soundscape."

Despite the relative lyrical content of each song and the connecting music, plus sound bites linking the tracks, a lot of people initially did not know the album told a story. "They had no idea that's what it was," Tate says. "I've heard many people tell me they first got the record, and maybe three or four listens in they began to realize this was a story. They would read the lyrics and start trying to figure out what was going on."

*Michael Wilton and Chris DeGarmo. Singer Geoff Tate says their guitar solos were the major addition to his initial vision of the song.*

# ONSTAGE FUN

The finished track was not drastically different from what Tate envisioned. Revisions were more musical than lyrical, definitely augmented by Michael Wilton and Chris DeGarmo adding guitar solos, he says. "That's probably the major addition to it."

"One major addition was Peter Collins, our producer, made a Hitchcock-like appearance in that song. He was the voiceover that goes, *and welcome.* I had to egg him on for a long time to do that," he laughs.

Geoff says the structure of the lyrics has made them always fun to sing. Different stage productions over the years have sometimes involved actors, but the lyrics being almost script-like also allows for the singer to embody the characters. "It's a bit of a play, and I get to play a couple different characters—dress up in different clothing and slap people around and fall down a lot," he chuckles. "It's a very physical show, but I like it a lot. It's really a lot of fun, it really is."

*The theatrical element and the physicality of performing* Operation: Mindcrime *has remained appealing to Geoff Tate through various stage productions over the years.*

# SUBJECTIVE LISTENING

Geoff had no idea how listeners might react to the song or the album. "I never do," he laughs. "By that time I had really learned that no matter what you write, people interpret it their own way."

Misinterpretation of his lyrics admittedly once bothered him because he wanted the audience to get his point. "It used to really upset me. It was kind of an ego-based point of view, I guess. You want them to understand what you're saying and talking about.

"But I learned that it's art, and people are going to interpret things in their own way, using their own filters, knowledge [and] experiences. There's no way you can dictate how they *should* hear it. And maybe they shouldn't hear it any other way than what's right for them." By the time *Operation: Mindcrime* was released, he had come to terms with that reality and learned to accept it.

# LONG TIME COMING

Queensrÿche took several years to act upon their plan to someday record a concept album. It took another year for *Operation: Mindcrime* to carry the band to the next level of commercial success. The album initially plateaued at the same sales level as the previous one. "It just hit the wall and stopped. That was our audience. That was how many people were interested or heard of Queensrÿche at that point.

"It had a really slow buildup, the way it was exposed to people." QPrime management wanted the band to come off the road and return to the studio. "We *really* didn't want to do that. So, we managed to stay out another month. During that month, Cliff Burnstein, our manager, called and said, 'There's a guy at MTV who wants you to make a video, and we think it's a good idea. It's going to be expensive, but we think you should risk it.'"

The band allocated their limited money and filmed "Eyes of a Stranger," based on the characters and storyline that originated with "Operation: Mindcrime." Their gamble paid off, and MTV frequently aired the video, Geoff remembers. "People saw it and became intrigued with the visual images. Within a month the album went gold. It went from 180,000 records to over 500,000 records in less than a month."

# 35

## QUEENSRŸCHE

# Revolution Calling

FROM THE ALBUM OPERATION: MINDCRIME (1988)

Sojourned in Montreal following the conclusion of a Queensrÿche tour, Geoff Tate started hanging out at Saint Sulpice, a cafe on rue Saint-Denis, not far from Université Laval. It was also frequented by members of a separatist movement determined to secede the province of Quebec from Canada.

"Today we would call it a terrorist group," he says, "and they were pretty scary people, into extortion, car bombings, things like that."

Their ideology provided the singer with another facet for the story that would become *Operation: Mindcrime*. Changing the world through radical idealism became a connection between the characters. "I remember coming home after a night of drinking and quickly scribbling out the whole verse and chorus sections and rough ideas for the entire album.

"The idea of takeover, doing whatever it takes to get your way— whether it means killing people, drugging people, assassinations—that extreme mentality was definitely inspired by that group in Montreal."

Geoff thinks only a couple of months passed between a revelation in a Catholic church that inspired the album and encountering the insurgents at Saint Sulpice. The idea that Nikki, Dr. X, and Mary could be conspirators was appealing. The next step would be finding music to sonically express an appropriate sense of danger.

"I remember searching out music to match that word. I wanted something very up tempo, very exciting. [Something] that had some muscle to it."

Guitarist Michael Wilton gave Tate different musical pieces and ideas, including what became the predominant riff, something Geoff says he really liked. It stayed in his head for a long time, until he and Michael spent several hours collaborating on the song. "It was really fast, actually. I went to his house, and we sat down and mapped it out and finished it that afternoon."

# POLITICAL AGENDA

Contrary to popular belief at the time, Tate interjected little of his political views into the lyrics to "Revolution Calling." The song was more an observation of the corrupt agenda of politicians and televangelists.

"Selling religion, and at the same time not following one's own words, that kind of thing was very evident to me. And that kind of heavy-handed economic dictatorship that the Reagan administration was implementing at the time. I didn't buy into the whole trickle-down economic idea. That was really obvious that the middle class was getting reamed, so other people—richer people—could make even more money. So, I thought, 'I'll just build that into the character. Why would he think any different, coming from the background he came from?'"

Nikki *did* somewhat reflect characteristics of a younger Geoff Tate, he admits. "Kind of idealistic, very humble beginnings. Not the Ivy League kid," he laughs, "but pretty much a lower-income family, that kind of thing."

More than making a statement, "Revolution Calling" was meant as another song to establish the relationship between characters. "What I was trying to do was establish characterization: This is Nikki—here is where he comes from, this is what he looks like, this is what he thinks. This is Dr. X—this is what he wants, this is how he goes about it. That was probably my major focus, really."

Activism was merely an aside to the story, color commentary about their personalities. Geoff is not even sure he hears any political message in the characters' idealism and wanting to change the world. "Don't we all want to do that when we're in our twenties?"

But some listeners were convinced they heard a subplot of anarchy. Interviews with the singer tried to corroborate the song—and, by extension, the album—as a literal manifesto.

*The* Operation: Mindcrime *characters were meant to carry the plot of the story, rather than convey any specific political statement. But Geoff Tate admits Nikki did bear characteristics similar to his own humble beginnings.*

Some journalists tried to imply that he intended to instigate revolution through a lyrical statement.

"I still get that to this day," Geoff says. "So many people cite *Mindcrime* as me talking about real extreme stuff, and that's definitely not me! It's the character. If you look at the lyrics I've written over the years, it's pretty obvious that I'm into social consciousness. I'm a pretty liberal-minded person. I'm into benefits for people, giving [them] a leg up."

Tate met with dissent during the tour for the album, too. Onstage, portraying Nikki, he would hold up a sign that read: *Would somebody please impeach George Bush?* "People were just raking me over the coals for that. It's [the] character! Obviously, I'm not that good of an actor, because they didn't believe the character," he laughs. "They believed me."

Still, growing up during an era of musicians who were advocates of social change likely affected him writing about revolution. Bands such as The Byrds, Jefferson Airplane, and Crosby, Stills, Nash, and Young might have been a subconscious influence on his song-writing. "Yeah, probably a lot of that seeped in."

# EXPLAINING THE MINDCRIME

The singer had spoken to guitarists Wilton and Chris DeGarmo during his stay in Montreal, briefly describing his ideas. He unveiled the full concept at Michael's wedding. "We're at the reception, and they started asking me, 'What's your idea on this?' So, we had a really long conversation over way too many drinks about the concept of the record."

*Singer Tate had briefly described some ideas to guitarists Michael Wilton (left) and Chris DeGarmo on the phone from Montreal. It wasn't until Wilton's wedding that he outlined the full concept to the band.*

Geoff jokes that it was like a browbeating inquest. "Everybody is asking all these questions. You start explaining yourself, and all of a sudden you feel like you're in one of those police station interrogation rooms," he laughs. But once he outlined the full idea, the rest of the band got excited about it.

"You know," he kids, "to this day I don't know if they even know what the album is about."

# THE COMMITTEE

Different lines in the verses flowed together and rolled cleverly off the tongue, such as the references to *Penthouse* and *Playboy* magazines. But Tate admits being unintentional with his wordplay. "Not consciously clever, no," he laughs.

Songs that develop as quickly as "Revolution Calling" might create a tendency to second-guess their caliber. Laughing, Geoff agrees. "Oh yeah, you do that—and that's good. You have to step away and get out of the creative haze and look at it as objectively as you can. That's where the committee comes in, and they tear it apart."

Queensrÿche uses a committee of band members and their producer to make decisions about quality control. "Collectively, you decide what's good and not good. We get into pretty heavy debates about this phrase or that. Does it help tell the story, or does it detract from it? It can get pretty heated."

"That's the deliberation we go through. Always." If the discussion sounds like it takes longer than actually writing the song, Geoff says sometimes it does. "Absolutely. It can get really tedious. But the committee has to come at the right time. You don't critique when people are on a writing roll. You wait until they sketch it out and explain their reasons for it, and then the committee comes in and says yes or no."

# ANARCHY IN THE 'RYCHE

Queensrÿche was the opening act for Metallica on their Damaged Justice tour. People were starting to pay attention to the lyrics, and Geoff says the audience had a tendency to respond furiously to the song. "There was actually a bit of anarchy at concerts, people getting pushed and shoved and beaten up, fires being set in the venues and things like that.

*Backstage with "The Committee."*
*Deliberation between all five band members*
*and their producer determined whether an*
*idea was worth developing. (From left)*
*Chris DeGarmo, Michael Wilton, Geoff*
*Tate, Scott Rockenfield, and Eddie Jackson.*

"I don't know if that was because of the *Mindcrime* album or the combination of Metallica and Queensrÿche and a bunch of young people all jacked up. Time and place, maybe. Both bands appealed to a certain segment of society that was, at that time, perhaps not doing too well economically. Maybe they were reacting to the character. Maybe they were feeling the [same] frustration and the words were ringing true to them."

# EXTENDED SHELF LIFE

Tate says he likes the song and still enjoys singing it quite a bit. "I like the whole album, actually. It was a wonderful experience to be part of. The band was working well together, and we had great rapport. The coming together of all the creative minds added to it and made it what it was."

*Operation: Mindcrime* and its revolutionary tale came to be regarded by many fans as the quintessential Queensrÿche album. There had not been a successful rock concept album in years, certainly never such a prominent attempt within the metal genre, and critics commended it as a classic.

Despite the album becoming almost singularly definitive in how numerous people have come to measure the band, Geoff says he would not reconsider any of the lyrical content. "I don't think so. I like the way it turned out. I stand by it, and I'm very proud of everyone's effort. Both [*Mindcrime*] albums tell an interesting story, one that has a lot of different levels that people can latch onto at different times in their life, depending on their experience.

"I'm glad that people have accepted the record and love it so much. I'm *glad* they talk about it. I'm glad they [still] debate about it on forums. It was kind of a new thing for people. Whenever you can be part of something that hasn't been done before, it's a wonderful experience to affect an audience like that."

## 36

## NUCLEAR ASSAULT

# Brainwashed

FROM THE ALBUM **SURVIVE** (1988)

Seven years before Filter had a hit with "Hey Man, Nice Shot," the 1995 song about the televised death of Pennsylvania state treasurer Robert "Budd" Dwyer, his press conference suicide cued John Connelly to scrutinize media indoctrination.

"There was a lot of strange stuff going on. Very high-up politicians were being investigated. All of a sudden, somebody would commit suicide, and it was like, 'Oh, it was *this* guy! He did it all.'"

Reporting on impropriety that ended with inconclusive events, such as the death of a solitary suspect, confounded the Nuclear Assault singer. His observation of the faulty media was an omen of the shortsighted coverage of the Whitewater scandal and the suicide of Deputy White House Counsel Vincent Foster in 1993.

"Are you honestly going to say that the guy who committed suicide is responsible for all the shady stuff that happened? Wait a minute—while this guy was alive, you were running down every available lead, all leading back to the Clintons. This guy commits suicide, and all of a sudden it's a dead end; he did it all."

The George Santayana quote about those who cannot learn from history being doomed to repeat it, in light of the Dwyer suicide in 1987, illustrates what later irked Connelly about coverage of Whitewater. "The press is supposed to be the annoying voice in the back of the room, asking questions the government doesn't want asked. You want to be the Fourth Estate, be the Fourth Estate—bug the government, don't be their buddy."

The media agenda, and its position turning on a dime, was the motivation to write "Brainwashed." But the lyrics also addressed other forms of media indoctrination, such as commercial radio and television sitcoms that dull the intellect. Even music itself, he says, can be a form of indoctrination. The industry charting trends and determining what genre to sell—even specific types of songs—also deadens the mind. And the mainstream in 1988 graded metal fans as little more than a community stamped from an empty-headed mold, easily conditioned by the media.

"Metalheads have *always* been treated like the idiots of society. Punks as well," he says. "You could refuse a guy with long hair a job, and nobody would bat an eye. A cop could roust a guy, and nobody would bat an eye—well, he must be holding drugs. He's got long hair, he's got a leather jacket—he's got that look—he must have done something.

"It was socially acceptable. Was there ever going to be a Civil Rights movement for us? I doubt it. It's always been easy to marginalize heavy metal, easy to marginalize punk. We've always been fringe. We've always been [on] the outskirts of society, looking in and poking and prodding, saying this is wrong."

"Brainwashed" was a commentary about the media machine and also a plea for the metal audience to think for themselves, rather than be programmed.

"It hit at the media. It hit radio, television, and newspapers specifically, in order: This is what these people are feeding you, and they're shaping your opinions without you knowing it."

Organized religion utilizing the media outlets was part of that doctrine. Cardinal John O'Connor, Archbishop of the Roman Catholic Archdiocese of New York, crusaded against the moral threat of heavy metal—notably Ozzy Osbourne—prompting Connelly's aunt to write a furious letter to the pontiff: *My nephew's a good boy. He's not one of these Satan-worshiping people that you scream about, and you shouldn't lump everybody together like that!*

*(From left) Glenn Evans, John Connelly, Anthony Bramante, and Dan Lilker. Nuclear Assault instigated though, Connelly says. "We offered ideas. The person on the other end of the speaker has to start asking questions." (Frank White photo.)*

# ARCHITECTURE OF THE SONG

John doesn't recall any fragments of ideas existing before Dwyer's suicide, but lyrics were always the last thing to happen before the band entered the studio. "It's always hot, fresh—the latest topical subject. It's current events, really." He estimates that 70 to 80 percent of Nuclear Assault lyrics were actually written in the studio. "It was occasionally nice to roll the song out before we went to record it, but on the whole it wasn't necessary."

Lyrics are an accurate portrayal of whatever was going through his mind at a given moment. "I don't want to say everything was entirely sensible or accurate," he laughs. "But it's certainly a reflection of where I was at the moment they were written."

Dan Lilker and John wrote the music, but the latter was always the primary lyricist. "We made a decision fairly early, after one or two demo tapes, to focus on socially conscious lyrics." It was a conversation over beer, parked in Connelly's parents' driveway in bassist Lilker's car, that established their credo: "Let's make the lyrics mean something. We don't have to do other heavy metal topics. What is 10,000 guys charging side by side—with all apologies to Manowar, that's what they do—it doesn't mean anything."

Musically, for the most part, the idea was to write short songs. "Lyrically, the philosophy was always cut to the core, hit the point, make the point and get out. Regardless of whether the song is 30 seconds or the rare five-minute tune, the lyrics are very incisive, very much like cutting with a scalpel to get to the point."

That hit-and-run style was very much the influence of Wendy O. Williams and The Plasmatics. Their guerrilla lyricism impacted John to write words that were simple and direct. "She had the art of delivering a very simple message, repeating it three or four times, punching it through. Don't elaborate, don't get complicated. The Plasmatics did a lot of fun, goofy stuff, but she also did some *really* serious social critiques."

The lyrical ideology of Nuclear Assault was never just John's opinion. "Mine was not the only point of view. If you had a point of view you wanted to get across, and you said write a song about this, okay, great. I can do that. If it was something I *absolutely* disagreed with and couldn't bring myself to do, feel free to do it yourself."

The decision was made that songs would be credited to the entire band, to lessen internal competition and generate income for everyone. "The way payments were made, back in the day, if they're not credited as being a songwriter, they got almost nothing. It was our attempt at side-stepping the issue," Connelly says. "It sort of worked, but it led to other issues."

# MUSICAL FRAMEWORK

The sociological concepts of Nuclear Assault songs were like listening to a homework assignment, John jokes. The rapid-fire tempo and musical structure made absorbing the messages somewhat difficult. It also made maintaining the lyrical criteria a challenge.

"The syllables *have* to be synched to the music, to the melody. It's all got to be precise. There can't be rushed [or] multiple syllables in a single syllabic statement." He doesn't know if that's because the song wouldn't flow or he simply couldn't sing it. Regardless, he says, "The meter has to be there.

"The way I write music, in a sense, it's dictatorial. When a piece of music pops in my head, in a lot of cases it's an entire composed piece. The percussion, the bass, the guitars, the melody, they're all fitted together in a specific way. The whole thing, at the end, is like a piece of clockwork."

That overbearing way of songwriting is irritating, he says, calling it a sickness. "It's annoying. But, lyrically, it makes the job easy because it has to do *this*.

# AFFECTING AN AUDIENCE

Connelly doesn't recall "Brainwashed" prompting any specific dialog with the fans, certainly not to the extent of "Trail of Tears." Response to that track, also on *Survive*, was sobering, he says. "On a number of occasions, I had people pull me aside and say, 'Dude, I did not commit suicide because of those lyrics.'

"It makes all the years of poverty, the years of homelessness—literally being homeless, living in a tent—all the hardship go away. It was worth *something*. It *did* something. With another tune, a guy said, 'This song made me quit drugs.' Okay, mission accomplished. Those are the high points. All the rest of the crap, it's all pretty trivial at this point."

Controversy over Nuclear Assault lyrics was reserved for the tongue-in-cheek "joke" songs, such as "Mother's Day" and "PSA"—literally the text of New York City public service advertisements posted on subway trains. People in the city got the joke, he says about that eight-second track. Outside New York, he's not sure fans understood the humor.

"Never underestimate the ability of people to not get a joke." That's the moral of "Hang the Pope" and "Lesbians," he says. "It's like, 'Dude, it's a gag. It's a joke; lighten up.' It broke up the seriousness of everything else we did." Strangely, it was drummer Glenn Evans who bore the brunt of contention. "We used to look at each other like, 'He didn't write the song; he didn't sing it. Why is Glenn getting death threats?'"

# THINK FOR YOURSELF

"Brainwashed" denoted the instigation to think that was the root of most Nuclear Assault songs. "Nuclear Assault *always* instigated thought," John insists, "whether it was the stupidest jackass things we did—*a la* 'Hang the Pope' or 'PSA' or 'Lesbians'—or the most brain-crushing lyrics ever produced. We offered ideas. The recipient has to think. The person on the other end of the speaker has to start asking questions.

"I represent a viewpoint. I never said—or would ever claim—that my perspective or my viewpoint is the correct viewpoint. Come to me, talk with me—argue with me! Exchange ideas. In theory, that's the way our country is supposed to work. It's an exchange of ideas, an exchange of concepts."

The viewpoint of "Brainwashed" is more relevant with time and the prolific availability of imprecise information. "History repeats itself. It does the same thing over and over. I never claimed to be a visionary. I'm an historian. Times change, people do not. We do the same things, regardless of how economies change, regardless of how technologies change."

Nuclear Assault was more than entertainment. "To that degree, were we a propaganda arm? Yeah, I guess so. We were a propaganda arm for, 'Hey, wake up. Think. This is your society, take an active part in it.'"

## 37

**SLAYER**

# Mandatory Suicide

FROM THE ALBUM **SOUTH OF HEAVEN** (1988)

Although his brother served in the military, with no active campaign at the time, he never experienced the guerrilla warfare of "Mandatory Suicide." Instead, movies were the inspiration for Tom Araya to write the song.

The Hollywood trend of latter '80s war films, such as *Platoon* and *Hamburger Hill*, provided good material from which the Slayer front man derived the bloody lyrics. "There were three or four of them about the Vietnam War. I took ideas from the movies and put them to words.

"One of the movies had a soldier picking up a stuffed animal, and it blew up," he remembers. That booby trap scene from the 1987 Stanley Kubrick film, *Full Metal Jacket*—in which Crazy Earl (Kieron Jecchinis) was killed—launched his imagination.

"That was the first thing that came to me. I started writing different things—just ideas—and it just came together." Tom had no other lyrical thoughts for the song prior to that. It was simply a case of trying to describe movies. "I went home and started writing, trying to remember and write what I saw."

The vivid imagery made it easy to assimilate words. "I just tried to re-create the scenes and write them in a poetic way."

The darkness of his narrative was affected by the mournful style of another writer, he says. "Yeah, Jim Morrison. The way he wrote his poetry influenced me, helped me create that song." Araya wrote with a tone similar to that of The Doors singer's style—unsettling, yet alluring, almost an exhilaration of death.

# NATURALLY COMPATIBLE

Guitarist Jeff Hanneman had already composed the music that would become "Mandatory Suicide." Tom's first lines and his random notes about the movies seemed to fit the overall ambiance of the instrumentation. "I didn't really have to try very hard. When I put the words to that music, it kind of fell into place."

Separately written but naturally corresponding words and music is generally how some Slayer songs happened, he says. "We did the same thing with 'Dead Skin Mask.' I had lyric ideas; Jeff came up with the music—it just fit together."

*Jeff Hanneman and Kerry King. Their lyrics denigrating religion and analyzing Nazi surgeon Josef Mengele drew fire from conservative moralists, shielding equally graphic songs such as "Mandatory Suicide."*

But Araya wasn't sure his hit-or-miss scribbling about war movies would form cohesive lyrics. The spoken ending of the track was essentially the singer reciting his notes. Nonetheless, there were few revisions during the recording process.

Approval from the rest of the band was typically understated. There was no profound analysis or spirited response, the norm for Slayer. "It was like, 'Wow, that's cool,'" he laughs, "like any other song we write."

# LYRICAL AWAKENING

Despite the violent phrases and thought-provoking message, there was little debate about the song. "A lot of songs I think people would remark about or find interesting, they don't. There are a lot of songs we've written that I think could really spark a conversation. But those aren't the songs that people talk about," Araya chuckles. "'Angel of Death,' or a song that shits all over religion, those are the songs that get reactions."

Slayer fans might not have been cognizant of the underlying morality of the song, but Tom believes they eventually came to understand the significance of the lyrics—just like he did as a kid. "Growing up, I listened to all kinds of music. It wasn't until I hit my teen years that I realized the messages of some of the songs."

For example, he says, "Revolution" was one of his favorite Beatles cuts. "I really liked the heaviness; I liked the groove of the song. I liked the words, but never really understood [them]—and then it hit me: I'm like, wow! John Lennon was the start of the civil revolution in America.

"That song said a lot! He believed in the Constitution enough to write about it in a song, and the U.S. government gave him shit for it. He felt peace was the answer. America, at that time—the government—didn't want to hear it."

# MURDER SONG

The lyrics to "Mandatory Suicide" have become more relevant in the years since the release of *South of Heaven*. "The things I wrote about are still happening, with people fighting for democracy and snipers shooting people in the streets because they don't want them to do that. Now, they're not booby traps; they're homicide bombers. People find [other] people and blow themselves up in the middle of them.

*Guitarist Kerry King. "Mandatory Suicide" has become part of an onstage trilogy that belies the overt gratuitousness in favor of a greater social consciousness.*

Araya's lyric about the cheapness of blood was an observation about the insignificance of human life in the context of ideological warfare. "[That] line stuck out, and always sticks out whenever I sing 'Mandatory Suicide.' That rings true now. You can kill 80 people with one shot, to prove a point or make a statement. That's how cheap it is.

"To me, it's all murder, and that's what the song was about."

# POLITICAL STATEMENT

"Mandatory Suicide" has remained an integral part of the Slayer live set. The song has become part of an onstage trilogy with "Chemical Warfare" and "Born of Fire." The lyrics initially heard as gratuitous now reveal a deeper social consciousness, and Araya says there's a method to the madness of grouping those three songs together. "Yeah, there kind of is, believe it or not. I bring up the questions: Are you willing to die for *your* freedom? Are you willing to die so that others may be free? We do [those] three songs in a row, and they're pretty intense."

"We've got it easy. We have Americans that go out and fight for freedom. That's hard for the soldiers because they're fighting for freedom for people who aren't standing up for themselves. Eventually, the tide turns, and the people win. It takes a long time for that to happen, though."

People dying in the name of freedom was the fundamental message of the song. "That's the strongest message the song sent. Sometimes people have to fight for their freedom. You can't just let people tell you how to run your life, tell you how to live."

The song is still agreeable for Tom to sing because it continues to remain pertinent to world events. But he does hear the lyrics differently through the context of Iraq and Afghanistan—and especially Africa, he says. "The civil unrest going on in Africa, that's the one we should be paying attention to. Those are the countries that need help. We need to stop what's going on before it gets worse. But there's no money to be made, so no one's going to want to put energy into Africa."

# THE CYCLE OF HISTORY

The sentiment of the song was purely observational when Araya wrote lyrics that retold the war movies. But he thinks it's gained meaning as an anti-war statement to stand alongside later Slayer songs. "'Mandatory Suicide,' in the descriptive sense, is no different from 'Flesh Storm.'

"Any song about war is relevant because there's [always] war going on. Everything in Vietnam is happening in Iraq. Everything that happened in North Korea is happening in Afghanistan."

History repeats itself, and he points out that the revolving door of enemies and alliances is cyclical. "The Russians got into a war, the Americans helped the enemy," Araya says about the Soviet conflict with Afghanistan throughout the '80s. "Now, the Americans are going through it. The Russians left, and the Americans try to crush the enemy they were [once] helping."

The same thing has happened in the Middle East, he says. The Bush administration opposing Iraq in 1990—and again in 2003—reverses the backing of the Reagan administration throughout the 1980s. "It just cycles. That's how it works. That's the way of the world."

# 38

## JANE'S ADDICTION

# Jane Says

FROM THE ALBUM **NOTHING'S SHOCKING** (1988)

Perry Farrell was a single musician trying to survive in Los Angeles without much money. He found a two-story house big enough to accommodate roughly 12 people with whom to split the rent. People would come and go, he recalls. "The kids that rented the house, they were kind of flaky. They were musicians, and they didn't hold jobs."

One month, when they were short on the number of tenants needed to make rent, Jane came. Perry says he was not acquainted with her. "In fact, I'm not even sure how she was recommended to come and see our place."

Farrell remembers observing his roommate as a very odd girl. She was smart, he says, a Smith College graduate who wore glasses and came from an affluent family in Arizona. Jane was a little bit more cultured than her housemates, someone inclined to enjoy wine and cheese on weekends. "But she was in love with the notion of being a femme fatale, hanging out with musicians and kind of slumming it."

She could never hold down a job. "In fact, to this day, when I see Jane, she's asking me if I know where she can get a job," he laughs. "There's just something about the girl—it's almost like she invites trouble [and] drama into her life."

# MELANCHOLY ADDICTION

"It's funny; people look at junkies as poor slobs. Maybe they're poor as a result of becoming junkies. But they don't really start that way because you don't have enough money to be constantly shooting drugs. It's when you get signed to the contract and get the money that you really get to do all the drugs you want."

Music is an art form driven by mood enhancers, he believes. And a house that was home to musicians, plus the fact that the neighborhood was also home to numerous drug dealers, meant someone was always holding. "There weren't many of us smoking crack—crack cocaine came a little bit later, actually—but a lot of us were beginning to shoot heroin and cocaine."

*Drug abuse ironically fostered an uninhibited stream of consciousness that Perry Farrell tapped into to write a song based in part on his own heroin addiction.*

Songwriting is about telling a good story, and Perry says good storytellers have the ability to embellish a story to make it really compelling. "Jane Says" was a dark tale hard to resist. But the melancholy addiction of the lyrics was the point of the song, not necessarily a singular portrait of his roommate. And, admittedly, it was also about him.

He explains that although singular subjects might inspire a song, his writing has often been a composite of more than one person. "So, yes, at times it was definitely a self-reflective observation about life.

"This was more of a song for people who have gotten into drugs and have a hard time getting out." The denial of an addict swearing to quit after one last dose was specific not only to him, but also to his target audience. "I'm going to kick tomorrow—*everybody* knows that feeling, so I decided to use that as the chorus."

His own lifestyle may have made Perry passionate to write about heroin addiction, but Jane as a character made for a much better story. "There's nothing like a good drama, and she was certainly that."

Jane was seeing a Mexican drug dealer who Perry thinks was only 15 to her 21. The age difference alone was interesting enough to write about. But he eventually became aggravated by her inability to pay him, rather than bartering with sex. Farrell says she did not understand how many women remunerate their drug dealers the same way. "They've got five girls showing up every morning, ready to blow [them]. If you don't pay them their money, you're going to get your ass kicked."

# UNINHIBITED CREATIVITY

Perry says he writes every day. "I have just gotten into the habit of waking up and writing. The solitude of sleep gives me a chance to think about things from yesterday. I wake up and [have] a good hour's worth of writing in me."

That isolation created by slumber is similar to writers who seclude themselves in remote locales to stimulate creative flow. Inebriation also produced the same result. "Drunk, or when I get fucked up, it's very good to write. So, being as I was in that state a lot, I wrote about those kinds of things because that's what was happening around me—and it was happening to me."

Unlike other lyricists, Farrell says he composes without referencing already written music. Hearing songs in his sleep, Perry will often wake up and remember the words as a repetitive groove that lends a rhythm to the lyrics. "A lot of times I go back and don't remember what the groove was, if I didn't record it.

"A lot of times instrumentalists just sit around playing guitar to write something. Some bands start writing a bunch of grooves and hand it over to the singer. The singer is caught where he is going to have to now write a [lyrical] groove. They'll be *forced* rhymes because there's a forced groove and a forced conclusion. Now you're trapped, and the song starts to get real stiff. But when you write lyrics [first], you're telling stories."

# JANE DOESN'T RHYME

Something worth repeating can sum up a song and encourage further development. Such was the case with "Jane Says," which began with the opening line about Jane being tired of her abusive drug dealer, Sergio. "That was maybe the most original line I had, or the most profound." It could have unfolded into a love song about Jane and Sergio or possibly been used as a chorus. But that would have lent more of a typical pop slant that was different from what he had in mind.

Farrell explains that the human ear is acclimated to listen for rhymes. "[The lyrics] don't rhyme at all. But you don't notice because I've got a good *story*. That's how you can get songs that seemingly sound genius: *How could he do this?*"

"Jane Says" was essentially written as a poem and later set to music. That allowed the words to not follow a lyrical rhyme scheme and eventually become polyrhythmic to the music. "I like to not rhyme. I like to write within the [lyrical] groove. I don't like to write right on top of the rhythm of a song. [That's] what I call stale—I even say stinky. If a song is coming out stale, I'll tell the guys it's starting to sound stinky.

"Many groups, that's how they write. That's why, when you listen to a song, you go, 'This group is not super. They're good, but I just don't know why this song is not great.' Because it takes dimension; it takes stereo; it takes polyrhythmics to make a song rich."

The varying process is something he compares to growing trees. "There's not an ideal, perfect system for the way a tree grows. None of them is the same. Every single tree is different." And adhering to that approach has allowed Perry to find beauty and success in songwriting.

*The anticipation of an extended intro creates a musical high for the audience when Perry launches into the opening line of the first verse.*

# ALTERNATIVE LIFESTYLE

The exact moment when "Jane Says" became a song, bassist Eric Avery was playing an acoustic guitar. "To tell you the truth, he was playing something that sounded like another song." Perry thought he heard a David Bowie tune, but the music kindled his imagination for those lyrics. "I just jumped on the groove, and it started to come together.

"Eric was basically puttering around with 'Rebel Rebel,' and I started to sing something different."

And Farrell cautions against being uncompromising about revisions. "Don't expect your song to be done. Human beings tend to want to come back to familiarity, so nine times out of ten they're going to write something they've heard before, which is okay. You've got to go back and knock the edges off of it. Find where it's really average and throw in a major seventh or a fifth, and you'll find newness in the song. Those are all writing tricks, and you can find genius in the final hour when you're putting your song together."

Although he can't say he emulated anyone specifically in writing the lyrics to "Jane Says," Perry does admit having looked up to songwriters such as David Bowie and Lou Reed, Ian Curtis and Mick Jagger—the greats, he clarifies. "They spoke about a life that was an underground, alternative life, before there was the term 'alternative.' These people were living in this beautiful subway system of life that *I* was living in. It makes for beautiful stories. The people you run into—the people you love—are all interesting characters, so you can write great stories."

# MEASURE OF SUCCESS

Perry says audiences love to sing along with the song, especially the line about Jane's inability to hit Sergio. "Everybody gets down to that part of it. I also love the very first line, just singing [it], because they know it's coming. It's kind of like a rush that's about to come. We have a long intro, and then when they hit those lyrics, they're high."

He can't remember what the rest of the band thought about the lyrics, or really how their audience reacted to them back in the day. "I was so high, I would just do the shows. I never really got a chance to know the audience or hear reactions."

Warner Bros. staff would tell him when the track was getting airplay and that people liked it. But he explains that sometimes an artist at the center of a whirlwind can be oblivious while it's happening.

"I was certain we were going to be a success in the underground because that's where people couldn't stop me. I knew we would be respected [by] people like the Nick Caves and the New Orders of the world. Those are the people I wanted respect from, and over the years I've come to know that they appreciate my music. *That*, to me, was success. But as far as pop culture, my ambition was not pop culture."

That's the price a songwriter pays for singing about heroin and *ménage à trois*. Perry says his wife reminds him of that whenever he laments about Jane's Addiction not becoming a more widely known band. "That's pop culture. But it's funny because 'Jane Says,' even though we were talking about hard drugs, still ended up to be probably our most popular song."

It's a result of the period of life he calls the age of discovery, when young men and women start learning about themselves through experimentation. "I think that's why [the song] has become so popular and touches everybody. They all feel that I'm speaking to them, because I really am."

Farrell reasons that people either create the trauma of hard drug use or find themselves surrounded by people living it, particularly in 2009. The whole kick-tomorrow idea, so many years later, is now understood as a drug issue that affects a global society.

"People get buried with drugs. We see shows on television now, like *Intervention*—I mean, it's pop culture now. After all this time, yeah, the idea that you can have a drug problem and be tragically trapped and buried—basically losing your grip on life over drugs—that happens every day to people who are members of our family, our neighbors, and the people we work with."

# 39

## HELLOWEEN

# I Want Out

FROM THE ALBUM **KEEPER OF THE SEVEN KEYS PART II** (1988)

Helloween reached a global audience with their third album. The German band that evolved over several years through a succession of formative groups was in MTV rotation and playing gigs with Anthrax on the Headbangers Ball tour in the United States. Thousands of people saw the band at Monsters of Rock festivals in the Netherlands, Italy, Spain, and England at Donnington Park, when Guns N' Roses famously filmed their "Paradise City" video.

The band was gaining a reputation as pioneers of what would become the power metal sub-genre when founding guitarist Kai Hansen abruptly quit the group. But there had been warning signs. "I Want Out," the breakout track from *Keeper of the Seven Keys Part II*, was rumored to have been his statement of dissatisfaction with the band and their record label. "That's true," he confirms. "That was the basis of the lyrics."

But writing a song to voice his feelings about the situation and the will to change it was not on purpose, he says. "I didn't immediately realize what this was about. It just happened to *be* that song."

# OPEN LETTER OF DISSENT

Hansen says his original intent was to express a general sense of life situations that feel conforming or socially oppressive, such as parental control or the rigid authority of the classroom. "Take any situation you dislike. You come to a point where the only thing you can think about is, 'I want out. Let me out.'"

Initially, Kai was not conscious of how much the song actually reflected his own discord. The band dynamic must have affected the sentiment of the words, but it was not a conscious objective in writing the song. Hansen admittedly felt cynical once he realized the clear source of the frustrated lyrics. "I was still in the band while we recorded that album. I was already thinking about [leaving], so it was kind of weird."

Kai doesn't think it dawned on his bandmates that the song was about his own discontent. "They didn't even think about it or realize it. And if they did, they didn't say so."

None of the lines in the song is directed toward any specific person. "No, absolutely not," Kai says, chuckling. "I wouldn't do that. I didn't think about the song as a kind of internal affair. That would be very bad."

Abandoning the band he formed, especially when it was starting to earn international praise, was difficult. "That was pretty tough, actually. I was thinking to myself, 'This is bullshit. You're not serious. That's your band—that's your *baby*. That's the thing you worked on so much, the guys you want to be with and everything.'

"But a few things came together, so it grew more and more into something that was looking realistic, instead of being a weird idea." His simple life philosophy was love it, change it, or leave it. "If you cannot love it anymore the way it is, you try to change it. If that doesn't work, you better leave; otherwise, you end up stuck in an endless black hole."

"I Want Out" would illustrate to up-and-coming bands that their partnership might not always be agreeable. "A band cannot be in harmony all the time," Kai laughs. "It's like a long-term relationship, only it's not a man and a woman. It's four guys. There will be tension, there will be fights. There will be things that are not good and not nice. But the recipe is not to avoid these things. The solution is to get along with these things and in the end have no bad feelings, even though you have different opinions—'Well, this fucker, he sucks, but I still love him.'"

# SPONTANEOUS CREATIVE METHOD

The songwriting process was not a conscious method based on forethought. It was a combination of having a starting melody and the spontaneity of singing random words off the top of his head. The full significance of his subconscious lyrics would reveal itself in hindsight. "It just comes out naturally, along with the music, then suddenly I realize the meaning."

Music was the predominant starting point for "I Want Out," but the finished lyrics were not pieced together to fit the instrumental structure. "I have this kind of gift that when I hear music or start writing music, I immediately imagine the lyrics. It's an instinctive feel that's based on phonetics." If the phonetic flow sounds right, the right words quickly follow, he says.

"I still do that today. I have some key words or maybe some ideas, and I don't know what the meaning should be. I just start singing on the demo tape as it comes out. Most of the time, 80 [or] 90 percent makes sense."

The dissatisfaction at the heart of the lyrics was revealed through the course of refining the song. The original chorus centered around the idea of a phoenix rising. Hansen disliked the concept, and his freeform technique of singing along bore the *I want out* phrase. "Then, it all started to make sense."

His lyrical mentors were just about anybody who ever wrote a memorable hard rock or metal song. "It goes from A to Z. There's definitely Rainbow as an influence, in terms of writing a song. Judas Priest, Maiden, Sabbath—even the Sex Pistols. I have a very commercial taste, I guess, so all the songs that are kind of metal hits, in a way. Every good song is something I can look up to and say, 'Right, that's the way to do it.'"

# CONJURING THE CHORUS

Kai lived in a small apartment where most of his songwriting took place. "I had a small eight-track tape recorder and a drum computer and a little Zoom device to get guitar sounds [without] disturbing the neighbors too much."

The initial melody had chords that recurred in the main riff. "In the end, I didn't really like it, and I changed it to another riff." The original idea would resurface years later with Hansen's next band, Gamma Ray. "I picked up that melody again in 'Rich and Famous.'

The riff there has a melody on top, and that was actually the melody line I had initially for the chorus of 'I Want Out.'"

Once the new melody prompted the titular phrase, it was not long before Hansen developed the song. "Pretty short, actually. I don't know if I had it [subconsciously] before, but consciously it was there for maybe one week. It became so much of a *need* to write that down or record it."

Changing the original phoenix rising chorus to the new liberating sentiment accelerated writing the song, starting with the first verse that spoke about being pushed into societal constraints from birth. "The rest of the lyrics were coming out pretty quick, just by singing. I didn't even have to work on it so much."

*Video director Storm Thorgerson misinterpreted "I Want Out" as a dark, ominous track, until he met the band and understood their underlying silliness and sense of fun. But no one recognized the song as a literal statement of guitarist Kai Hansen's feelings.*

# KEEPER OF THE KEYS

Kai thinks his "I Want Out" lyrics originated more as a personal statement rather trying to maintain the *Keeper of the Seven Keys* concept. "I didn't even think about the concept."

Maintaining an overall concept was not difficult because only two songs were actually part of the theme. "'Keeper of the Seven Keys' and 'Helloween' had more of this story to follow. The rest of the songs don't really have the storyboard. The rest of the songs were independent from that. We just kept writing lyrics that popped into our minds or that we thought were worth writing."

Even Storm Thorgerson misinterpreted the context of the song. A graphic designer renowned for iconic album covers such as *Houses of the Holy* and *Dark Side of the Moon*, his interpretation of the song was an ominous and depressing treatment for the video.

The band wanted something uplifting—even cheerful and funny, says Hansen—which confused Thorgerson. "Even dealing with serious themes, we always had a wink of an eye. It was never taken so serious, and we were never sinister guys.

"He thought we were like, the bad metal guys that want a video like, the world sucks and all that. *I want out, fuck you!* He got to know us and realized that's not us."

Overnight the director developed a different idea, and filming commenced the next morning. The silly video recalled the absurdity of Beatles movies such as *Help!* and *A Hard Day's Night*. "It actually did represent the way we were, yeah. He had a total plan, and we didn't even know what it would be. He just told us some bits and pieces, and that was fun."

# UNIVERSAL SENTIMENT

The simple message of the song still stands out, Hansen says. "Those lyrics don't get out of date. It's something everybody can understand very easily, and everybody can *feel* those lyrics."

The appeal is the universal, rather than songs limited to specific situations. "If somebody tells a sad story [about] drug addiction, this can only be felt by people who have been drug addicts, for instance. But these lyrics are something that *everybody* knows about. Everybody can *feel* those words very clearly. I didn't get any feedback that told me somebody didn't really understand those lyrics.

"These lyrics pretty much fit everybody, in general. They reflect thoughts that everybody develops during life. I think we have all felt the situation of 'I Want Out.' You can try to fuck with me, but you won't get too far—I'm out.

"There were many reactions to the lyrics, mostly coming from fans saying, 'Man, you spoke my mind! I am—or I was—in that situation, and it was so good to listen to that music and sing along with it and get strength out of these lyrics.'"

# 40

## METALLICA

# ...And Justice for All

FROM THE ALBUM ...AND JUSTICE FOR ALL (1988)

Metallica changed Matt Heafy's life.

The Trivium frontman admittedly knew nothing about heavy metal before discovering them. He was only aware of pop punk and mid-'90s modern rock radio playlists, until someone suggested he listen to *Metallica*—The Black Album.

"It blew my mind because I had *never* heard metal before. Ever. I copied it to tape, because you couldn't burn CD-Rs [then] and listened to it every day until I could finally get to a store and [buy] it."

Heafy actually failed the audition to join his first band because he couldn't play "Dammit" by blink-182. But Metallica inspired him to rehearse. "I started practicing all the time, and I got really good at guitar."

"No Leaf Clover," from the 1999 *S&M* live symphonic album, was his entry in an eighth-grade talent show. Original Trivium vocalist Brad Lewter, whose sister performed in the same pageant, invited Matt to audition. "The band had been together for about two weeks, and my tryout song was 'For Whom the Bell Tolls.' I nailed the song and made it into the band.

"Thanks to Metallica, I not only learned what metal was, I was able to get a tryout into Trivium. Sure, I could have found out about metal another way, maybe through another band, but I didn't. I found it through them."

# COMPLETE PACKAGE

It wasn't their music or lyrics alone that affected him. It was the whole package. "Obviously, it was the music first. And then, to be able to see how those lyrics were there, too—I had to know everything involved with this [thing] that I loved so much.

"When it came to Metallica, it felt real. It sounded real. There are so many positive bands that are heavy, and people [sing] positive things. But it's nice when you can show there *is* darkness in the world. Songs need to reflect that, so you can get over it in your own life by *hearing* that other people have those same feelings."

The singer started with the 1991 *Metallica* album, followed by the *Garage Inc.* compilation and the *Load* and *ReLoad* albums. He was unfamiliar with their older thrash pedigree before hearing *...And Justice for All* in drummer Travis Smith's early-model Dodge Dynasty.

 "This thing was falling apart," he recalls. "He had taken out the back seat so he could put his drums back there. I was sitting on this back seat chunk, and he played me *...And Justice for All* out of a Walkman that played [through] one of those [adapters] into the tape deck.

"[It] was the first of the older records I heard, and I couldn't believe it. It blew my mind. Not only did they sound super heavy, they were faster."

# BROKEN JUSTICE

The lyrics to the title track of *...And Justice for All* were a scathing commentary about the inequity and corruption of the justice system. James Hetfield wrote about manipulation that tarnished judicial fairness. "People can relate to that because it's something a portion of the population has always seen and felt.

"Most metal bands never really touch on sociopolitical things going on in the country or the world. [They] typically don't go into politics in the right way. Sometimes it's a little bit too much in one direction or the other. The way they did the lyrics on that song was tasteful and very gripping, and very real about the darkness.

"It's interesting; the record's got a white cover and white album [sleeve]. Everything seemed like it should be brighter, whereas it's really about this dark way the world could be."

Heafy says he loves the epic way in which Hetfield expressed such repugnance by using different types of language. "Some of the things are as direct as they need to be, and other points are kind of veiled in mystery, and it always hits the nail on the head."

Matt was born less than two years after the release of the album. It was already 11 years old by the time Trivium formed in 1999. But ...*And Justice for All* remains important to young fans and new generations of metal bands. The key, he says, is that Hetfield wrote lyrics that retain their relevance.

"You need to make them general enough, where they can become timeless, applicable to any time. That's the thing [he] definitely pulls off. A topic like the justice system—or government, religion, or war—something that's universal, it's all about how that song-writer wrote the song."

Although Matt is sure he's taken ownership of the words and recognized his own experiences within them, it's in a more general sense. "It's things I had already learned by the time I started learning about the lyrics to that song. [But] I think it's great that he put his beliefs out there, so people who want to be into him can see what he's about. He puts it all out there, versus hiding the way he really feels."

# LONGER SONGS

The track is nearly 10 minutes long, and Matt himself is no stranger to extended songs. When it comes to writing lyrics in those instances, he thinks Hetfield's example demonstrates the importance of good dynamics, so the words don't come across as drawn out or boring.

"Every single verse is just as interesting as the previous [one], and every word is just as meaningful as the next. Some bands repeat things or don't write too many words. It becomes nonsense or perhaps kind of blundering. But that song is a focused direction from start to finish."

But it was a subconscious lesson, he says. "We never picked apart the structure or looked at how they did it and tried to interpret it in our own way. When we created, whatever came out, came out as products of listening to our favorite bands. We listened as fans and never really thought past that."

To that end, the influence of James Hetfield impacted Matt beyond that of a lyricist. His influence was more as an individual. "Seeing through interviews the way he is as a person. I've met him a couple times, and the way he speaks to people, there's such a power and an aura about him. With James, it's commanding, but also engaging and fun, when he feels like it.

"Not that I would sit there and take notes, but growing up as a bright-eyed kid watching him, I think I learned from seeing how they do it. They had everything together. They had the persona on and off stage; they had the music, the lyrics, the song structure, the production. It was the entire package. And it still is the entire package when it comes to that band. That's what's so influential to everything."

*(From left) James Hetfield, Kirk Hammett, Lars Ulrich, and Jason Newsted. Trivium frontman Matt Heafy says Metallica had everything together in terms of music, lyrics, and persona. The entire package is what has sustained their continued relevance, he says.*

# INTERPRETING THE MEANING

Given the reverence he feels for Metallica, it's interesting that Heafy says he never wonders what James would do in order to jump start his imagination in a songwriting bind. "No, I don't. I just go for it. It's great to have your heroes at the start, to help you get moving and get going in the right direction—be that foundation of where you're going to go with [your] band. But I think those bands also help people who learn from them to create in their own way.

*Some listeners speculated that the scathing commentary of "...And Justice for All" was reactionary to no criminal charges being filed in the 1986 death of bassist Cliff Burton. Jason Newsted (pictured) succeeded him in Metallica for a little more than 14 years.*

"I never really delved too much into meanings of everything, exactly what those songs mean," he says. "I like to have my own ideas on what everything is."

Some listeners have speculated that the angry distaste for corrupt justice was reactionary to the questionable circumstances of the death of bassist Cliff Burton in a 1986 accident. The driver maintained that black ice led to the tour bus skidding off the road and over-turning, throwing Burton through a window and subsequently crushing him. Investigators found no evidence of slippery road conditions, and charges were never filed against the driver, whom some suspected to have been intoxicated or asleep at the wheel.

"Since I don't know his interpretation, I would ask him, 'What does this song mean?' I would like to know where it came from, where he was when he wrote it. Was he sitting at a park bench? At a table in his house? It would be nice to know the setting and scenario to where that song came from."

# INFLUENCE OF A LIFETIME

"It's really amazing to see the countless bands that would not exist if it were not for [Metallica]. It's so crazy to think that a [single] band got me into a new style of music. A band got me to where I am now.

"I was getting into this [album] in '98 and '99, 10 years after when I was 12. I said, 'I want to do that for a living. I want to be in a band that can travel around the world and play in front of cool people who know my songs.' I've been able to do that, [and] I always remember that it was my heroes who helped start me into this."

# 41

## DANZIG

# Mother

Danzig was not a band that projected the typical rock and roll spirit of good time excess and mischievous rebellion. Namesake singer Glenn Danzig was inclined to incorporate arcane lyrical themes that created an extremely dark ambiance and evoked erotic and supernatural imagery. "The stuff I sing about is not your normal stuff," he admits. "A lot of people, well, maybe now they sing about it. But back then they really didn't."

The menacing lyrics to "Mother" could have been interpreted in numerous ways. The song was a literal scenario of an immoral boy dating an innocent girl naïve to darker pleasures. It also made sense to mean a band familiarizing its audience with a sinful style of music. The words could even constitute a negative religious commentary, as suggested by the John Bunyan quotation from *The Pilgrim's Progress* that launched the original music video.

Glenn says his songs were purposely written to create multiple translations on different levels, some he never even intended. "The whole girl thing, I didn't *ever* think of that, but that's cool." The principle essence of "Mother," though, was an attack against censorship. "It was the whole PMRC thing, which really infuriated me. Really, that's what it's about."

The Parents Music Resource Center had already cast its shadow over contemporary music—especially hard rock and heavy metal—by the time he wrote the song. "I was just furious about the whole thing. I saw the trials, and I was *infuriated*. You don't even know how mad I was. When I'm writing [about] stuff like that, I have so much hatred, so the song just pours out."

The September 1985 hearing before the Senate Committee on Commerce, Science, and Transportation was described as a forum to call public attention to music that supposedly endorsed activities of questionable morality. It was stated that the proceedings were not a prelude to legislation, but the clear agenda was censorship as dictated by a sectarian group of political wives.

# SPONTANEOUS CREATIVITY

"Mother," like all Danzig songs, he says, was meant as both an observation and a personal statement. "All of the above. They're informative, observational—they're personal. They're everything. Whatever I need to make that song happen, I will put [it] in there."

The New Jersey native describes his creative process as different for every song, but always spontaneous. Glenn says he never followed a specific songwriting regimen. "When a song comes to you, it just comes to you. I don't have a notebook. I just grab a piece of paper and write down chord patterns and the lyrics.

"Sometimes songs take a long time, like a year and a half. You're constantly tearing apart and putting them back together, changing arrangements and lyrics. But with that song, it wasn't like that. The whole song came to me right at once, maybe a half-hour. Some songs happen like that, and that was one of those."

Glenn formed The Misfits in 1977, then disbanded the legendary punk group six years later and formed the heavier Samhain. The release of *Danzig* in 1988 showed the singer further refining that metal sound, and the stylistic progression affected his approach to writing songs. "It changed in that it was more focused. I had been doing it for so long, it became easier and easier, but also harder at the same time. Every record, you want to try and top the [last] record."

But there was no collaboration with the rest of the band to enhance the songs, so Glenn doesn't really know what they thought of the lyrics "I don't think they even *know* the lyrics," he laughs.

*The occult ambiance of Danzig and "Mother" led to multiple interpretations of the song. But singer Glenn Danzig says the lyrics were actually inspired by the PMRC and his distaste for censorship. (From left) John Christ, Eerie Von, Danzig, and Chuck Biscuits.*

# SPECIAL SONG

Danzig says he could tell immediately that the song was distinctive. "I knew right when I wrote it, before I even showed it to Rick, that it was going to be a really popular song—at least in my catalog. Whether or not it was going to be a hit, you never know. But I knew I had written something very special. I even called [producer Rick Rubin] and told him I wrote this incredible song."

That's not to say the singer had any expectation about how he thought people might react to the track. "I just thought it would be a great song for people who enjoyed my music."

He can't recall which line or phrase first came to mind. But once the basic premise of the song was established and the lyrics written, revisions throughout the recording process with producer Rick Rubin were more structural than lyrical. "When we started working with Rick, it became more arrangements, really—like, 'Okay, let's put the guitar like this instead of that, put a stop here,' things like that."

# CENSORING ANTI-CENSORSHIP

It was reactionary to the censorship advocated by the Parents Music Resource Center, but the song was also a defiant statement as an alternative to the vapid state of the music business as a creative enterprise. "You had MTV shoving this really soft, crappy music. I would see a lot of bands actually writing that kind of stuff, just so they could be on MTV."

The original video for the song represented little of the lyrical intent of the song. Glenn says that was mainly because he did not direct the clip himself. "I'd have an idea here or there, [but] it was a lot of [Rubin] and some of the other people he worked with."

Ironically, MTV banned the video for the song that condemned censorship. It featured black-and-white close-up shots of Glenn and footage of guitarist John Christ and drummer Chuck Biscuits. But a sacrificial bird and the ritual of its blood traced in an inverted cross across the midriff of a woman positioned on a demonic altar likely disposed the Broadcast Standards and Practices of the cable network from airing it.

"It kind of became infamous," he remembers. "There was a lot of music censorship going on, and there was a lot of censorship focused on Danzig—and actually a lot of [Def American] acts like Slayer and the Ghetto Boys. It seemed like Rick [Rubin] had all the bands that were being banned. Of course, every kid was like, 'Wow, I want to know about this band!' They didn't know about Danzig or Slayer, [but] they *wanted* to know about it."

# TWICE DENIED BY MTV

It was somewhat strange to be an essentially underground artist with a mainstream audience liking a song never intended for them. Glenn just shrugs it off to having become so infamous, they attracted attention. Danzig was touring Europe to support their third album when they learned response in the United States was growing. "We had a call from our booking agent, and they told us we sold out the whole lawn at Irvine Meadows, like 10,000 people."

A second version of "Mother" was taken from material compiled for a documentary Glenn was directing at the time. The song finally reached a larger audience when tracks recorded at the Irvine Meadows show were released as the *Thrall: Demonsweatlive* EP in 1993. Its popularity the second time around was surprising, he says. "It was pretty unexpected.

"We did the *Thrall* record, really, because Biscuits had no money," Glenn laughs. "We needed to get some money into his bank account, so I had to convince the label to do an EP." The success that bands such as Metallica and Nine Inch Nails had with *Garage Days Re-Revisited* and *Broken*, respectively, led to Def American Recordings consenting to its release.

"So, we put some money in Biscuits' account so he wouldn't starve and then went on the road. We came back from the end of the tour, and they were like, '"Mother" is a hit. Your song has been going crazy at radio.'"

The continued irony of MTV refusing to add a new performance video for the song to their rotation was funny, he says. The interactive Video Jukebox Network, an on-demand music video service, forced their hand. "I think you paid 25 cents. People would call up and type in a number, and the song got played. Radio was playing it, [too], so they had to play it."

# FREE SPEECH ADVOCACY

Ultimately, Glenn recalls no controversy during the second run of "Mother" at radio and MTV. He suspects the Democratic Party was trying to make voters forget that the Parents Music Resource Center had been spearheaded by the wife of Vice President Al Gore.

"Even though they tried to kill it when it first came out, they couldn't, so there you go." But Danzig really doesn't know why his multi-layered attack against censorship affected listeners. "You'd have to ask them," he laughs.

The anti-censorship message of the song continues to be relevant beyond its 1988 and 1993 release, more so in latter years. Danzig says governmental policy and actions are never fully disclosed because the media fails to clearly report all available information pertinent to a given news story. People then form opinions based on limited facts. "It's pretty scary. I see [them] trying to control what people think and say, people who might not agree with the government."

Glenn says he has no preference between the studio and live versions of the song. He equally likes both videos, as well. But the live version seems to be closer to his heart. "It's live and it's crazy. When the audience starts singing along, it's just explosive."

It still affects him every time Danzig performs the song live. "It's incredible. I wrote the song hoping everybody would love it, and it seems like most people dig it, so it's cool.

I wouldn't change a thing." But despite being arguably the best known song in his catalog, Glenn just laughs when asked what stands out most to him about the lyrics. "Nothing. It's just another song to me. I know it's special, but I like all my songs."

## 42

## OZZY OSBOURNE
# Miracle Man

FROM THE ALBUM **NO REST FOR THE WICKED** (1988)

The battle to save misguided souls from the spiritual corruption of heavy metal was a raging storm during the latter half of the 1980s. Allegations that his music advocated suicide denounced Ozzy Osbourne as the chief antichrist. Organizations such as the Moral Majority, a rightwing Christian lobbyist group, and the Parents Music Resource Center, which prompted a Senate hearing to explore the inherent danger of song lyrics, were a sanction for some extremists to slander not only him, but the entire musical genre.

Fervent televangelists recognized an opportunity to promote their own agenda by asserting the threat of moral jeopardy from their TV pulpits. Pointing pious fingers helped further the ministries of Jerry Falwell, Jim Bakker, and Jimmy Swaggart.

Bakker, host with then-wife Tammy Faye of *The PTL Club* program that was the cornerstone of their evangelical empire, was revealed in 1987 during a Federal Grand Jury probe into fraud and conspiracy charges to have had an affair with church secretary Jessica Hahn.

The following year, Swaggart confessed during a tearful broadcast that he had sinned. Photographed consorting with a prostitute outside a Travel Inn motel, the Assemblies of God hierarchy defrocked him, leading to his ministry being reclassified as nondenominational.

Bob Daisley remembers that teary performance being notable news during the writing and recording of *No Rest for the Wicked*. It directly shaped "Miracle Man," and the original lyrics even called Jimmy Swaggart by name. "We thought, 'Well, we might be a bit near the bone there. It might cause problems.' So, we called him little Jimmy Sinner.

"I like that line," he laughs about referring to him as a clown. "There he was, a born-again Christian, preaching to people and trying to brainwash [with] this threat of hell—do as I say or you'll go to hell—and all this shit. And then he gets busted in a cheap motel with a hooker. It was laughable."

# TRUTH IN ADVERTISING

Although the song was a direct reference to the sanctimonious minister—who was ironically the cousin of rambunctious singers Jerry Lee Lewis and Mickey Gilley—Daisley wanted the overall allusion to be to any deceptive leader. "It could be anybody being hypocritical and getting caught with their pants down.

"In some ways, this song is a little judgmental. But I suppose I was being judgmental on a person who *was* judgmental, if you know what I mean—preachy, then being hypocritical about it."

The outright dishonesty angered Bob into writing the lyrics. "I really don't care if somebody wants to go to a motel and shag a prostitute. Good luck to you, Jimmy. Go and have some more fun—it's called life," he laughs. "But don't go telling other people they're going to hell with all this other fairytale bullshit they push down people's throats."

Writing the words was enjoyable because it was an outlet to express his contempt for the programming leaders use to create and maintain power. "I felt strongly about the mind control that goes into religion, controlling people through threats of hell. People are brainwashed. Sadly, a lot of them believe it. Personally, I got some satisfaction out of poking fun at such a silly situation and the hypocrisy involved. But they *still* follow it! God, sometimes I do not get it.

"I don't think religion goes with philosophy or spirituality. I know many religious people who aren't spiritual and philosophical. But I know very philosophical and spiritual people who aren't religious."

*Apostolic teenagers at a Midwest concert venue, warning that Ozzy Osbourne (pictured) songs were satanic doctrine, were surprised to learn that Bob Daisley was the lyricist.*

# MANIPULATED BY THE DEVIL

The Australian bass player admittedly doesn't know whether the phenomenon of tele-vangelists targeting rock and roll was prevalent outside the United States. But since the birth of the genre in the 1950s, many factions have crusaded against it to establish power. "All the church people and the Bible Belt brigade were preaching that [it] was evil and the devil's music. They said that about blues, too. It was like an expression of ignorance."

That sad illusion is illustrated by a story from the *Bark at the Moon* tour. Waiting for the equipment to be ready for sound check, Bob remembers soaking up the afternoon sunshine outside the venue. A group of teenagers unknowingly asked if he would be going to the concert. "I said, 'Well, I kind of have to.'

"But that's Ozzy Osbourne!" they protested. "He's evil. He's being used by the devil." Trying to make their point, they asked if he had ever heard the lyrics. "And I said, 'Well, actually, I write them.'"

Surprised, they started telling Daisley that *he* was being manipulated by Satan. "I said, 'No, you're very misled. There's nothing negative in the lyrics. I try to keep them philosophical or have some kind of message, so you've been misinformed.'"

# RETURN TO THE LAND OF OZZ

Ozzy and the latest lineup of his band had been working at John Henry's, a London rehearsal studio, when he called Daisley, who had been working with guitarist Gary Moore. "He was drunk, and he wasn't happy with the way the songs were going. He said to me, 'Bob, come and salvage this fucking album for me, will you?'

*Bob Daisley was a songwriter and played bass on* No Rest for the Wicked, *but Ozzy's Black Sabbath bandmate Geezer Butler joined him on the road. (From left) Zakk Wylde, Ozzy Osbourne, Randy Castillo, and Geezer Butler.*

"So, I had a meeting with him and Sharon, and I went back and started rehearsals with them."

Working together again was not the strained relationship some might expect, following the first time Bob and drummer Lee Kerslake sued for unpaid royalties and the reinstatement of performance credits. "I sued Don Arden—Sharon's father—and Jet Records. [Ozzy and Sharon] were actually helping us in our lawsuit, so it was a natural thing that I would work with them again."

Bob wrote and played on *No Rest for the Wicked*, and he says Ozzy asked him to return on a permanent basis while they were in Los Angeles. "I suppose I gave it consideration, but I didn't answer yes or no. I was told probably halfway through recording that album they decided to take Geezer Butler on the road. So, I just co-wrote the music with Zakk, and then wrote the lyrics. I wasn't even there for the mix. I just left, and that was it."

"Ozzy and I have always got on very well together as friends. It's been a bit of a love/hate relationship—not real hate, but that's the expression. We had a knack for getting on very well together and being mates. We liked the same sorts of things musically, which, being together, easily gave the music its direction. We also had a knack of pissing each other off," he laughs.

# FAMILIAR ROUTINE

"Miracle Man" was musically in progress when Daisley joined the sessions in late 1987. Although it had been eight years since their relationship started with *Blizzard of Ozz*, Bob says his conscious approach to writing with Ozzy basically stayed the same, despite the succession of musicians since the original foursome.

"It was a different band. It was the Ozzy Osbourne show. It must have had some kind of effect on me. But on a conscious level, I just got on with it and made the best product I could."

Like their previous collaborative efforts, he says Ozzy contributed vocal melodies and the phrasing that inspired how he would write the lyrics to fit the songs. The process was one that combined the integral contributions from him, Ozzy, and new guitarist Zakk Wylde.

*Guitarist Zakk Wylde (right) would be part of the songwriting core with Ozzy and Bob Daisley, much like Randy Rhoads had been on the first two albums.*

The title might have come from Ozzy himself, or maybe keyboardist John Sinclair, but Bob can't remember for sure. The idea to write about Jimmy Swaggart might have been kicking around his imagination for a little while, but likely not very long he says. "A couple of weeks or something, then I probably spent a day on it. I was staying at a place in Universal City. A lot of lyrics for this album were written there at Oakwood Apartments."

# RELIGIOUS HYPOCRISY

Bob remembers the band loving the song. It was a controversial situation that was current in the news and at the top of people's minds. "I expected it to be a bit controversial somewhere, but I didn't know from which angle. I thought the song might get some praise from people saying, 'Yeah, it's about time something like this was said.'"

Reading the lyrics to some of his Ozzy songs now, Bob jokes that some of them actually aren't bad. "Certain lyrics that I've written, I think, 'Yeah, I like that, that's good.' That was one of them. I liked my expression of what I said in the song. It did have a little bit of personal satisfaction."

Daisley thought there might be a backlash from Jimmy Swaggart supporters or possibly the overall Christian community. "I thought they might take it personally that it was a slant on their religion. But I really didn't care. I thought, 'If you want to have a dig at anybody, have a dig at Jimmy.'"

But he *did* wonder whether people would understand the reference years later. "When Jimmy Swaggart got busted and was actually on TV crying, that was fresh in people's minds. But I remember thinking, 'God, down the track a few years, are people going to even know who Jimmy Sinner is?'"

Nearly four years later, Jimmy Swaggart was again caught in the company of a prostitute when stopped by the California Highway Patrol for driving on the wrong side of the road.

That idea he tried to convey in 1988 may not have the same impact as a reference to Jimmy Swaggart. But the lyrics can be applied to other religious controversies that have occurred in the years since. "I suppose it doesn't necessarily have to be just him. It could be interpreted in a generalized way about any religious figure who commits hypocritical acts and gets caught, like all these Catholic priests that get busted for pedophilia. Somebody will come out years later and say, 'He did this to me when I was a child.' It's still going on."

## 43

## SKID ROW

# 18 and Life

FROM THE ALBUM **SKID ROW** (1989)

Ricky, the protagonist of "18 and Life," was a character loosely based on Snake Sabo's brother. "He essentially raised me, because my dad left when I was really young."

The guitarist's second oldest sibling had been his childhood hero, but his brother was not the same after returning from military service in Vietnam. Snake wanted to write a song depicting a happy, energetic, and exciting young man, completely changed by war and struggling to adapt.

Bassist Rachel Bolan, his newfound songwriting partner, latched onto the idea. But the challenge was an inability to exact the mindset of a broken veteran and channel it into a song. None of their ideas seemed good enough to honor his brother. "That was me more than anything," Snake admits. "The story I wanted to tell, because it was so near and dear to my heart, nothing would have been perfect.

"It was a changing point in his life, his brother going off to war," Rachel says. "He was a little kid and didn't know if he was going to see his brother again."

Bolan suggested taking a less specific approach than the precise story of a particular person, to something indistinct that could work as a metaphor for Sabo's brother. "It just started turning into something that became more universal. Ricky became one of those guys who can't seem to do the right thing, and eventually something bad happens."

The nascent songwriters never guessed how many people might know someone like the troubled character they were fleshing out. "We had no idea," Rachel says. "We were just writing what we thought was a good story." But the finished song still contained analogies that alluded to the original concept, such as the idea of a solitary soldier walking the streets."Even though it's a fictional story, I still felt it was a metaphor for what my brother had gone through, to some degree. It wasn't the exact story, but it *was* about being young and innocent, and all of a sudden this tragic thing happens. The storyline is similar in its cause and effect."

# LYRICAL STORYTELLERS

Sabo had the formative elements of the song, such as chord patterns and what became the first line of the opening verse. "I had that line, and that's all I had." But the minute he played the opening notes on an unplugged electric guitar, Rachel knew it was an idea they would pursue. "I was like, 'Dude, that's *haunting.*' It gave me chills.

"We knew this could be something really, really special—for ourselves. It's not like writing a song for the sake of writing a song, which we never really did," Snake says. "We just wrote songs to see if there was a bond. And there was; it was so obvious.

They wrote other songs, and Rachel says there were lots of laughs. But "18 and Life" was different. "I just remember us being really serious, absolutely *focused* on this song. It made us feel like, 'Wow, we really told a story about someone.' I remember that, clear as day, working on that at my parents' house and at Snake's house, when he still lived at home."

There were lyrical storytellers whom they both admired. "Bruce Springsteen, who always told a good story within his songs, comes to mind," Rachel says. "He always had characters, like folk songs set to rock. Steven Tyler was another one who always seemed to create a movie within his lyrics, and that's what we were doing."

Fictional stories were their mainstay during the early years, mainly, says Bolan, because age had not yet allowed the life experiences that would later become a source of lyrical ideas. "We didn't know what the hell we were doing back then, so we wrote stories and put them to music, basically."

He remembers "18 and Life" being written over the course of two or three days, at night after Snake finished work. "We would write until we couldn't keep our eyes open. I remember how hard we worked on that song, to make sure we *loved* everything about it."

# KING OF THE OPENING LINES

Their lyrical goal has always been to create imagery that people can visualize. Rachel says it usually starts with Snake and his talent for coming up with great opening lines. "There's no one better at it than Snake. He'll come up with a line that will create such a picture in my head, I'll know right where he's going with it. That was the case with a lot of Skid Row songs. It's kind of like a handoff type of thing: Here's an idea, these are the opening lines, run with it, boy!"

At first, the opening line told of Ricky having a heart of gold. "We changed it to *heart of stone*," Bolan says. Another idea that changed was him being best friends with a bottle. Originally, "bottle" was "devil." Devil was too cartoonish, Rachel says. "Devil just sounded—and no disrespect intended—too Black Sabbath or Ronnie James Dio for a band like us. The word devil just didn't sound right. We were talking about a kid gone down the wrong track, so I said, 'What about bottle?'" Changing that word led to a clever lyric about tequila being the corrosive fuel that sustained Ricky. The song was nearly complete when they presented it to the rest of the band. Rachel guesses they must have liked it. "They played it," he laughs.

*Snake Sabo says no one in the band was likely to predict "18 and Life" would be such a big hit. (From left) Sabo, Rob Affuso, Rachel Bolan, Scotti Hill, and Sebastian Bach.*

"No one was ever like, 'Oh, this song's going to be a hit'—not in our circle of five people, that's for damn sure!" Snake says. "We just looked at it like, it feels really good to play, and it makes sense to us. It didn't hit us like a tidal wave or anything like that. That came afterward, with the success of the song."

Still, Sabo must have suspected its potential during the demo process with producer Michael Wagener. "We were in the control room listening to it, and it's the first time I ever got chills to one of our own songs. It's happened a million times to me with other people's music, but that was the first time for one of our own."

Rachel guessed it when they played the track for Jon Bon Jovi and Richie Sambora. "You have peers who have had great success, and when they say, 'Man, this is special,' and give you the thumbs up, it's a cool thing."

# MAKING THEIR MARK

"We were so young, and that was our second single. People just *knowing* something we did blew me away." The first time Rachel heard it on the radio was in New York City while doing press. He was in a cab at a red light, and the song was blasting from another cab while two kids in the backseat sang along.

Hearing them singing along to *Casey's Top 40*—singing along with his band, a song he co-wrote—left Rachel taken aback. "I was like, 'Wow, we've kind of made our mark in rock-and-roll history.' It was a really good feeling."

Atlantic Records had not planned to release "18 and Life" as the second single. The label originally wanted to follow up "Youth Gone Wild" with the sure hit, "I Remember You."

"What was prevalent in those days was that you go with the most obvious track," Snake explains. But the band felt prematurely releasing "I Remember You" would inhibit subsequent singles and effectively end the lifespan of the album. Rachel, Snake, and singer Sebastian Bach, in Las Cruces, New Mexico, pleaded their case via conference call with A&R executive Jason Flom.

"We kept making our point, that this is a story people get. People understand it. We see the reaction in the audience. They finally said, 'Okay, we'll trust your judgment.'"

*(From left) Snake Sabo, Sebastian Bach, Scotti Hill, Rob Affuso, and Rachel Bolan. Skid Row at the Moscow Music Peace Festival in 1989. "18 and Life" affected people beyond the radius of the garages, bedrooms, and New Jersey record store where it was written.*

# MUSIC VIDEO

Director Wayne Isham developed a video treatment that featured two outcast teenagers and a tragic shooting, making the dark lyrics edgier. Some scenes were considered too graphic for MTV. "Their Standards and Practices was like, 'No, this is a bit too far,'" Snake remembers. The scene in which Ricky aimed the gun at his friend's head was cut, and also the shooting segment that was followed by a shot of blood running down the sidewalk.

Despite the distressing tone of the video and the hopelessness of the lyrics, reaction to the song was surprisingly favorable. "People just took it for what it was and somehow —I don't know how—turned it into a positive," Rachel says.

# STRENGTH TO SURVIVE

"People still, to this day—people in their 40s now—say how much that song helped them get through hard times. That absolutely *blows* me away." Bolan recounts a MySpace message from a woman who met him during their first tour, saying the song saved her life. "I totally remember [her], because she had scars on her wrists—she had slit her wrists. That song brought her out of the bad place and inspired her to do better with her life.

"That is probably the ultimate compliment you can get as a songwriter," Sabo says. "You were able to touch someone at the core of their being through a three-and-a-half-minute song that you put together in a music store, a garage, and a bedroom. You can't be humbled more than having something like that happen."

*The haunting beginning of "18 and Life" performed onstage includes the ritual of Snake Sabo and Rachel Bolan (pictured) needling each other. "I'll go, 'Man, you are the worst bass player in the world,'" Sabo says.*

People still sing the opening verse out loud when they recognize the band checking in at airports and hotels. And Rachel says he hears more than anything that people had a troubled brother or friend named Ricky. "Everybody knows a person like that. I can probably name two of them in my life. Whether they're 50 or 15, they know a person like this—like Ricky—where you just can't help a person who won't help themselves."

Rachel says he still loves that point in the live set, when the sustain of the final note of the previous song resonates, and nothing is said to introduce "18 and Life" as he counts it off to Snake. "As soon as they hear the first three notes, the place goes nuts, and I just *love* seeing the reaction of the crowd. With most people you can tell they're either reliving their youth or thinking about that person they knew, like Ricky."

Playing the song arouses good memories for Snake, and the sight of an audience enthusiastically singing along is an overwhelming high. "I have to put my head down, like, thanks. I've taken nothing for granted, whether it was back in the day or now. Seeing people singing the lyrics all the way through, I'm just going, 'Wow, we actually *wrote* this!'"

The songwriting bond and friendship formed years ago is affirmed every time the song is played live, says Sabo, during the solitary beginning of just guitar and bass—just him and Rachel. "We'll whisper something stupid in each other's ear. I'll go, 'Man, you are the *worst* bass player in the world.' And he'll go, 'Yeah, but everybody *knows* that you suck, and you're playing horrible right now.' By doing stuff like that, I think that's a moment where he and I are just kind of celebrating the history of writing that song, having been able to play it and enjoy it for so long."

## 44

# W.A.S.P.

# The Headless Children

FROM THE ALBUM **THE HEADLESS CHILDREN** (1989)

W.A.S.P. was backstage in Toledo, Ohio. Blackie Lawless remembers the arena shaking from the force of the audience stomping their feet in anticipation. Staring in the mirror, applying his stage makeup, he could see the rest of the band getting ready behind him.

"I looked up and said, 'Are we going to continue like this, or are we going to do something of true musical merit?' You could see the look on their faces, like, 'Man, he's blown a gasket—it's all over now.'"

Two weeks left of the tour, and the singer was counting the days until the first chapter of the band would finish. It was a defining moment of clarity, he says, the culmination of a thought process that gained momentum when *Sounds* magazine ranked their latest single better than those of U2 and ZZ Top but judged W.A.S.P. as capable of doing something far more significant.

Fashioning himself into a character that was equal parts Zorro and Dracula, Blackie and W.A.S.P. were primarily viewed as salacious entertainment. Lawless initially thought his main goal was to be famous, but becoming that changed his perspective. It became clear what he really wanted—or did *not* want—and harder to ignore the feeling of responsibility that came with the realization that people were affected by his songs.

"Artists are supposed to provoke thought. If you ain't doing that, then you're just some guy churning out music." He realized there needed to be a change. "If I'm going to stay in this, I have a responsibility to myself—and to them—to try to say something positive."

# HITTING THE FAN

The first W.A.S.P. album was an accurate musical representation of the mindset of the band at that time. *The Last Command* was genuine, too, although to a lesser degree, he says. Sustaining the pace of a breakneck cycle of recording and touring had become creatively numbing by the time their third album was released in 1986, and Lawless was admittedly adrift.

*Blackie Lawless questioning his artistic integrity worried the other members of W.A.S.P. that their run was over. (From left) Steve Riley, Johnny Rod, Lawless, and Chris Holmes.*

Blackie had reached a point where songwriting was more about maintaining a level of success by catering to audience expectations than about writing more serious lyrics that better reflected himself. *Inside the Electric Circus* did not represent his true mindset. "I made a dishonest record. You get lost inside the process and lose yourself, and you don't know who you are."

His frustration detonated during a *Hit Parader* interview that went beyond the character of Blackie Lawless. That conversation revealed passionate opinions about a number of social issues. "It was a pretty angry interview. A lot of it had to do with politics, but I was just stripping down the veneer, those layers of untruthfulness."

The unprecedented volume of mail in response to the magazine article was overwhelming. "I never received letters from an interview [before]. People were saying, 'Why didn't you say this before? We knew you felt this way, but you would never say it.' I thought, 'If I'm going to make records, I'm going to have to make something that's what I believe. And if I can't do that, maybe I should start thinking about doing something else for a living.'"

*Blackie Lawless initially created himself as a character based on elements of Dracula and Zorro. By the time W.A.S.P. released their third album, reality was beginning to dominate his ideas about the band and himself.*

Capitol Records was opposed to the idea of reinventing the W.A.S.P. brand at the potential commercial expense of alienating its fan base. "They were quite happy with 'Blind in Texas' and 'Wild Child.' When I told them where I wanted to go, they didn't like it. When they heard the demos, they liked it even less."

Gambling with the popularity built over the better part of several years, Lawless trusted his conviction, which became the foundation of everything he has since tried to do.

# INSPIRED DREAMS

Blackie says he dreamed the music and lyrics for the title track of *The Headless Children*. "It was about six o'clock on a Saturday evening, and I sat down on the couch. I thought, 'Well, I'll take a nap for a second.'"

Starting to doze, the song began playing in his mind, like falling asleep while listening to the stereo, and he rushed to jot down the lyric and record the music before the idea faded. "All songwriters can tell you the same story, that we've all had enough bad experiences of being lazy, saying I'll do that in the morning—you get up and it's gone forever.

"There's an energy that starts flowing when a song is happening, and sometimes it's hard to [keep] up with it because it's happening so fast. It's almost like taking dictation. That's such an exciting process because you *know* you're experiencing that magic you hear songwriters talk about."

The song exploded into consciousness during the onset of sleep, but Blackie figures his mind was already leaning toward composing that sentiment. "You look at it and go, 'Okay, yeah, I *have* been feeling like this for awhile.'

"It's your subconsciousness having compiled all those little tidbits you've picked up from watching the news or engaging in conversation with a friend. You're *constantly* filing stuff away. You're assembling it, and you don't know it until the guard at the door of your subconsciousness starts to drift off a little bit and lets out what's in there."

The national and global social and political climate of the time affected his thought process. "Totally," he agrees. "I would say a good 50 percent." If half of songwriting is the writers themselves, he explains, the rest is their surroundings. And the world around Blackie Lawless was chaotic.

# PLEASE GOD, HELP US

Crack cocaine was about to blow up into an epidemic. AIDS was becoming more prevalent in heterosexual cases. The Berlin Wall had yet to be leveled, and tension between the United States and the Soviet Union was escalating. "There was a lot happening, where it was making the world politically tense."

The USSR seemed on the edge of instability. "We found out a year later that, yes, that was the case. When you've got a country that's becoming desperate, they're capable of anything. It's like a wounded animal. It's that kind of scenario—if I'm going down, I'm taking everyone with me. That's *really* where ['The Headless Children'] came from, a geo-political environment [and] the tension in the air because of that.

"If you look at the lyrics from that perspective, it's a cry—literally an outcry—to God saying, 'Save us from this.' Every time God has to intervene, it usually gets pretty hairy. If you're asking for *that*, because what we're doing on our own is even *worse*, that's desperate."

The song questioned if the world was on the verge of apocalypse. But the intent of the song was not a plea for divine intervention in the form of nuclear holocaust, to clean the slate of humanity. "No, it's precisely the opposite. It's like, 'We need divine intervention to keep us from going off this cliff.'"

Listeners who were chorus-driven might have interpreted the song from only the titular lyric. "People will do that, so a lot of times you'll get someone taking the idea of headless children and thinking it's a bunch of kids running around helter-skelter. In reality, they would not be wrong," he laughs. "It's all of that, but not the specifics of where I was coming from.

"I'm talking about direct references to God, [and] some folks don't get that. If you look at the lyrics from an apocalyptic point of view, you'll see it from a totally different perspective."

# FOUNDATION FOR A CAREER

*The Headless Children* revealed an artist developing his potential to an unexpected degree. The prior catalog of sing-along anthems and lyrics that were often innuendo—in some cases not very subtle—made it easy to underestimate Lawless and W.A.S.P. as a creative force.

"That song, and that record, really solidified being able to move forward. That was the beginning of what would be the bridge that would cross us over to getting out of where we came from, giving us a real career."

It was caustic beyond the caricature of overtly sexual lyrics and extreme stage theatrics. "In terms of comparison from where we started, that record was far more dangerous— for the right reasons. The thought process was pretty hostile and frustrated with the social environment. The music ends up being a reflection of that."

He still hears the venom in that album, audible anger at having previously made what he calls a bad record. "I hear the hostility, not just at a global scenario, [but] my *own* situation of not having been as honest as I should have been. I was singing about stuff that was crap. I was interested in not just redemption in the world's eyes, but for *me*!

*Blackie Lawless in 1984. Less than three years later, he would start thinking about presenting himself and W.A.S.P. in a way that was less gratuitous and more hostile— ultimately more dangerous in a topical sense.*

"It's almost like you got up to bat and struck out the first time, and now you're really mad. You're breathing fire when you come up the next time. That's kind of where I was."

# MOVING FORWARD

It was the line in the sand between their history and how W.A.S.P. would progress with more serious messages. The song and album cast Blackie in a different light as a more thoughtful lyricist than the inane stereotype that burdened heavy metal bands and their audience. *The Headless Children* also created a division between fans of the earlier material and people more interested in the new social and political commentary.

There was a lot of schmaltz happening at that time in hard rock, he says. "There was a lot of junk coming out. It was borderline pop disguised as this type of music." It contaminated the metal genre, ultimately leading to its perceived death with the advent of grunge.

The timing of the song and the honesty of its aggression made it genuine. That is what still stands out most to him. "That truthfulness [is] a really sacred thing, and I had lost it prior to that. That whole idea of truth—what do you feel—put it on paper and put some music to it. Put a backbeat to it. That's the secret to writing songs. Write down what *you* feel. That's really what I think all great songwriters have in common."

The global events of the beginning years of the new millennium have made the plea for God to save humanity from itself just as applicable in 2009. "When we get to a point as people where we can no longer govern ourselves, we need something that puts it back in perspective, and for me that's faith. When we start losing sight of the idea of do unto others the way you want them to do you, all hell starts breaking loose."

## 45

## KING'S X

# Over My Head

FROM THE ALBUM GRETCHEN GOES TO NEBRASKA (1989)

Doug Pinnick was admittedly a pretty scared kid who had trouble sleeping. Late at night, though, he would hear voices from the bedroom of the grandmother who was raising him, like she was talking, maybe even singing. "She might have been having a nightmare or something, for all I know. But I always felt comfort in it, because I could hear her."

That sound of what might have been evangelizing soothed Doug and made him feel not alone in the house. "I don't know if she was praying, but she was very religious, so I sort of took that idea and put it in 'Over My Head.'"

If she was singing anything, it was probably the old Negro spiritual "Over My Head I Hear Music," he reckons. "I don't know for sure, but it was a fictitious story in my head, from my grandmother."

"Over My Head" was written in 1982, seven years before being released on *Gretchen Goes to Nebraska*. Pinnick remembers writing the riff, specifically the chord at the end. "When I hit that chord, it didn't sound right. I didn't like the song, and I thought it sucked, so I buried it for probably five years."

The band and then-manager Sam Taylor accidentally heard the demo when they were working on *Out of the Silent Planet*. Doug mistakenly cued "Over My Head," rather than the following song on the cassette. "I played just a second of it, and I go, 'Oh no, not that song.'" But they pressured him to reluctantly play the whole song.

"I played it for them, and they *loved* it! And Ty made me promise that I would always play anything I wrote, regardless of whether I thought it sucked or not."

## MUSICAL CORNERSTONE

The song was envisioned as a cross between AC/DC and Jimi Hendrix. "It's a combination of those two, plus my gospel upbringing," he says. "I love the four-on-the-floor AC/DC, where it just rocks. There's no holds barred. You just bang your head because it sounds good, and 'Over My Head' has that kind of vibe. And the riff was a real Hendrix kind of riff."

*Let Love Rule*, especially the dynamic structure of the title track of the Lenny Kravitz debut album, also affected him. "The chorus didn't lift; it kind of went down instead. Normal pop songs, usually, when you get to the chorus, it's a big bang. With 'Let Love Rule' it was the opposite. I thought that was really cool, so I brought the chorus down like he did."

The other significant influence was the church he attended as a teenager. "They had some incredible musicians, and I got to watch highly emotional singers firsthand, every Sunday morning—watch the crowd jump up and down, people running out in the streets, screaming and praising God. It was pretty crazy and very exciting at the same time. And it's always stuck with me. I believe that whatever we put in our music is whatever impressed us when we were growing up. That's a part of it—that, and Led Zeppelin and Black Sabbath and Chuck Berry. It was a combination of all that stuff."

## GET STONED, TAKE A WALK

Words or hints of lyrical phrases didn't exist in Doug's mind prior to composing the music. They never do, he says. "Everything I write, first I write the music. After I get the music done, then I get stoned and go walking," he laughs. "Somehow, lyrics come to me, and I go immediately and do it. But I never think of lyrics until way after the song's done."

*Doug Pinnick and Ty Tabor.*
*"Ty made me promise that I would*
*always play anything I wrote,*
*regardless of whether I thought*
*it sucked or not."*

The chorus, he says, was the words that came first. "I went, 'Whoa, what do I do with this?'" he laughs. Pinnick says he started thinking about the minister from his adolescence. "Basically, it's me imitating the pastor I sat under when I was a teenager. He used to do a lot of phrasing, like *aye-aye-aye* and things like that, so I put it all in there."

That wasn't the only childhood church experience he mimicked. "The end of the song, where we're all singing, it sounds like a church choir or congregation. Everyone's talking and laughing, and it was really my interpretation of the church that I grew up in and the music that impressed me to this day."

The similarity to the Negro spiritual made Doug think he was on to something. But the close lyrical proximity worried him that it might be considered stealing. "I took a chance and decided to do it. I found out the old spiritual was [public domain], which means anybody can use it."

The lyrics were not tailored to fit the musical structure, and Pinnick thought he made a mistake and wrote an inadequate song. "The song doesn't make a lot of sense. Everything's done backwards: The chorus is lower; the lyrics are sort of repetitious. I just thought it was a boring song. But, to my surprise, everyone seems to love it."

Bandmates Ty Tabor and Jerry Gaskill loved the lyrics, but they never specifically commented on them, he says. "They never challenge my lyrics, ever. They just say, 'That's a good song, let's do it.' Sometimes," he jokes, "I don't even know if they listen [to the lyrics]."

# CHRISTIAN DOGMA

Writing spiritual songs was a challenge because he didn't want the words to sound presumptuous, and Doug knew some listeners would consign the lyrics to Christianity. "It's always been hard for me. In the early days I was a full-fledged Christian. But I didn't want people to think we were a Christian band trying to save the world. We were just a rock band, and we just wanted to make music and be judged for our music, not anything else.

"At the time, it was not a cool thing to be called a Christian band. That's probably why I buried the song and didn't want the rest of the band to hear it. We never said we were, and never told the media or anybody that we were." Regardless, Pinnick says Christian became another label people used to describe the band, like metal and progressive. "They put every name in the genre when they named King's X."

But wanting to be viewed as a secular band backfired within the pious Christian community. Pinnick's songs cultivated a certain degree of controversy because of his stark sentiment, especially back then. He was writing lyrics that reflected misgivings about religion and God and his place in all of it. "I wrote a lot about the way I felt—you know, my confusion about religion, my dissatisfaction of being in Christianity, and the mystery of God."

*The Christian community that initially embraced the spirituality of Pinnick's lyrics became disillusioned by his dissatisfaction with organized religion.*

It was the influence of U2, who Doug distinctly remembers first hearing in 1980, that revealed a nondenominational way to sing about faith. "Bono sang spiritually, but it wasn't religious or preachy. It was more about how he felt and the shortcomings of his faith and how he felt about himself." Pinnick identified with that approach because Christian music, at the time, "was all about pointing the finger and giving people an ultimatum. I didn't want that. I don't believe in that bullshit. Bono opened my heart up to just speak what I felt."

# BACKLASH

"Many, many Christians rallied around King's X. When I wrote about my dissatisfaction with Christianity, I think I kind of confused them." He heard about arguments during church youth group meetings, questioning the band's devotion and faith. "Back then, it was a dividing point. Either you were Christian, or you weren't. And you were not accepted unless you preached Jesus from the altar. We didn't do that. We played our set, and we drank, we smoked weed, and we cussed, and they didn't understand. We confused the Christian world, to the point where they rejected us and our music was banned from Christian bookstores."

In hindsight, Pinnick thinks he should have sung more controversial lyrics. "If you're not making waves, people don't pay attention to you. Sometimes we watered everything down to make everyone happy." The result, he says, was that the people not paying closer attention didn't get it. "That was one of the reasons King's X didn't sell a lot of records, because I didn't put my risk deep enough for the world to see me bleed," he laughs.

*The song Doug Pinnick initially hid from the band became the centerpiece of their live performances for the next 20 years.*

# IF IT WERE UP TO ME...

The *Gretchen Goes to Nebraska* version of "Over My Head" was nearly identical to his demo, but Doug goes into preacher mode onstage when the band plays an extended version. He laughs, admitting that from show to show, he doesn't know what to say. "When I walk up to the mic, I have a blank slate in my head. When I'm done, I'm kind of amazed that I did it again." It's gotten to the point where he has a different sermon for each tour, not really knowing what to say next time.

The biggest surprise, given his aversion to the song, was that so many people liked it. "I'm quite pleased, even though, if it was up to me, no one would have ever heard the song. It became a big part of our set. We've done that song, from the time we recorded it, at every show. We have not missed doing 'Over My Head,' to the point where it's like, 'How can I reinterpret it, so it's not boring to me or the people who have heard us do it for twenty years?'"

# MOONWALK

Sam Taylor wrote the treatment and directed the video for "Over My Head." The performance video had a brief scene with a grandmother sitting in a rocking chair. "Joey Gaskill, Jerry's son, was into Michael Jackson and could dance real good," Pinnick remembers. "We put him in front of her, while she's rocking in the chair, and he danced. There were a couple scenes where he's spinning around while she's laughing. It gave you that feeling of the grandma and the grandson, the whole warm feeling. In the black community especially, a lot of grandparents raise their grandchildren, and I was one of those products."

He thinks that idea is a story that made people like the video and the song. "The story is what people really want to hear. You can make up great lyrics, or you can make up great poetry, but if you aren't telling a story, people kind of don't pay attention to it. I think one of the biggest reasons people like the song is because I was telling a story about a grandma and my life with her."

# MUSICAL REVIVAL

"Over My Head" sounds innocent to Pinnick. The lyrics were not any sort of rousing statement, so he's still comfortable hearing them. It's a song he can comfortably sing, without feeling penalized for now having different feelings about life. "A lot of the other early songs, I just don't want to do them because I don't believe the same anymore. I just can't get behind the lyrics. But 'Over My Head' is one of those songs I think I'll be able to do forever because it's a story."

Playing the song live feels more like a novelty, rather than a vigorous spiritual revival. But, he says, a King's X show is sort of like going to church without religion, so they use the song as a rallying point to get the audience involved and make them feel fulfilled. "It seems to be the show-stopper every night. I see the crowd react—young and old, whoever they are—and they all get into it and sing along. It's just one of those songs that makes people feel good, so I hope it still means something to people."

Doug's own faith has changed, to the point that he doesn't know if anything exists. "I don't subscribe to any religion or even say I believe in any type of god. I just live my life the best I can."

But he does think everyone has a spiritual side. "It seems like just about everybody believes in *a* god of some sort, whether they go to church or believe in Jesus or Buddha or whatever. At the end of the day, I think people feel safe when they have some sort of faith and believe in something. This song kind of strikes a chord with people, not necessarily to believe in any particular religion, but it just makes them feel spiritual, and I think we all long for that in some way."

# 46

# Practice What You Preach

FROM THE ALBUM **PRACTICE WHAT YOU PREACH** (1989)

Chuck Billy had just finished watching Pantera when he came up with the title of the next Testament album and its lead track. In Texas filming the "Trial by Fire" video, the members of the band went to see Pantera, as they regularly did whenever they were in the Lone Star State. "They always used to play this club," Chuck says. "They were the local band in town, so we always used to go watch."

The entire band was together and having a good time. "We were all drunk," the singer says. Leaving the club, Chuck vividly remembers the idea hitting him while getting into the van. "I was like, 'Oh, I got the name of the record: *Practice What You Preach*.' And, being called Testament, it kind of fell right into place and made sense.

"Everybody said, right at the same time, 'That's it! That is so perfect. That's the *right* title for the record.'"

No idea since has collectively hit them with such force, and Chuck would never again feel so certain about a lyric or title. Ideas never just popped into their heads, he says. "Everything else since then has been throwing around names and titles. But that one, it was the situation. It was just so weird because we were *all* together, sitting in a van, and there it was."

The title was the perfect sentiment for what would be a major turning point in their career. It made sense for Testament, who were ready to shift from albums such as *The Legacy* and *The New Order* to music that would be slightly more accessible to a larger demographic. "We were kind of in a crossover point, coming from just thrashing to trying to be a little more polished.

"We were trying to appeal to a broader audience, but still playing heavy metal. So, we *were* practicing what we preached." Testament returned to San Francisco, excited and armed with a title and its ethos. "That was the very next song we started working on and writing."

*(Clockwise from top left) Chuck Billy, Greg Christian, Alex Skolnick, Louie Clemente, and Eric Peterson. Testament was venturing into major label territory with a more refined thrash sound on* Practice What You Preach. *(Courtesy Adrenaline PR.)*

# CHANGING DIRECTION

Testament had been signed to the indie Megaforce label and distributed by Atlantic Records. *Practice What You Preach* would be their first album released solely on the major label that had been home to the Rolling Stones and Led Zeppelin. "We're thinking, 'Wow, we're on Atlantic Records. They're going to do great things with our music.'

"We had a guy coming down, listening to the demos and telling us what kind of songs he wanted—what kind of songs they could pitch to radio," Chuck says. The band had never worked with A&R people or label executives who surveyed their creative process and proposed a specific direction. "It was a different thing for us, at the time, because we were always on our own, just writing metal songs. All of a sudden, we had someone whispering in our ear, telling us what kind of music to write."

Bands such as Testament had become the new trend attracting mainstream interest. Thrash became viewed as a hot commodity, and in the wake of Metallica, major labels were signing comparable bands away from their indie label beginnings.

The title guided the direction of the lyrics but was also meant as a guidepost to remaining true to themselves. "We were young kids thinking, 'Hey, we're selling records! We're going to be rock stars.' But, in reality, we were still just a bunch of kids making metal music."

# SOCIAL CONSCIOUSNESS

If Pantera indirectly inspired the title, singers such as Bruce Dickinson and Ronnie James Dio were role models to write lyrics with much more meaningful content. "We were trying to get away from cliché heavy metal lyrics," Chuck says. "You know, gloom and doom, graveyards and stuff like that. We wanted to have relevant topics."

"Greenhouse Effect" was probably the most obvious social statement Testament had made to that point. Rebellious teenage metalheads probably weren't aware of the global warming trend, but the topic was important to the Chuck. "I was really concerned with the planet, and that was a big issue. It was like, 'This is a reality, and it's affecting everybody in the world.' That was a message, a reality we all have to pay attention to."

Another statement was "Sins of Omission," guitarist Alex Skolnick's idea inspired by the Tiananmen Square protests in China. "That was kind of his baby, his music—a lot of lyrics were his. He really felt strongly about that and wanted us to write about it."

The topical subject matter presented on *Practice What You Preach* revealed the band members growing beyond the usual thrash lyrics of malevolent imagery and violence. To that end, the title track was a statement that they were indeed practicing what they preached, incorporating ardent social themes while musically remaining faithful to metal despite a comparatively refined approach.

# CREATIVE PROCESS

"I'm not really one to write [lyrics] before the music. I don't think I've ever written a song—just the lyrics—without the music," Chuck laughs. "I'm always inspired by the music. Listening to the music always leads me to the lyric."

Starting with the title, "Practice What You Preach" came together quickly. "We knew that was going to be the title of the record, so it was something we really focused on and had to make pretty strong. Eric [Peterson] had a riff, and it just happened that the riff fit the chorus. Once we had the chorus, it came together really fast."

*Chuck Billy thought of the title for "Practice What You Preach" when the band saw Pantera in Texas. Eric Peterson (pictured) had a guitar riff that fit the chorus, and the song came together very quickly. (Courtesy Adrenaline PR.)*

Chuck calls the chorus one of the biggest hooks on the album, and the finished song was the result of a collaborative process. "Alex and Eric contributed a lot of lyrics; it wasn't just me presenting my ideas. We all kind of put our two cents in. All three of us used to sit down and put our heads together and write a lot of those songs."

The Testament songwriting process starts with guitarist Peterson unveiling a riff. Chuck will outline the structural elements in a rough arrangement of the song. "I kind of tell him, 'Okay, let's do a bridge here, a lead section here.'" Once Eric restructures the song, Chuck says he starts writing lyrics.

# EXPECTATIONS

Chuck expected fans to react to the changed musical direction more than the lyrical content. "We were thrashy young kids," he says. "The next thing you know, we're getting a little more defined."

But the song itself was received fairly well, in part because of the big chorus that generated more radio play for Testament. The result was a turning point. Longtime fans expected the band to remain a classic thrash band, not readily wanting them to evolve into a more mainstream sound. But, he points out, the band was relatively young and musically still discovering themselves when *The Legacy* was released in 1987. "A lot of the guys were still naïve and just didn't know any better."

Still, given the gamble of label executives directing the band in a somewhat different direction, Chuck insists they wouldn't have altered the music or lyrics. "We believed in everything we put out. And if it did cause controversy, good. It's stirring things up and getting people to talk about it."

The appeal of the message of "Practice What You Preach" was its subjectiveness. "Practice what you preach is such a big statement. You can interpret that any way you live your life. It's like, you've really got to believe in yourself. Be confident in what you do and believe in yourself."

"We actually had people writing to us, telling us how those lyrics helped them and got them out of bad times, as far as people even wanting to commit suicide." The first time their lyrics affected anyone to such a powerful extent made the band realize their stylistic change had been a good move. "At that point, it was like, 'I think we're doing the right thing and writing the right type of lyrics for this band. If it's getting that far, to touch people like that, they're working and we need to keep doing what we do.'"

*Alex Skolnick and Chuck Billy.*
*Writing Testament lyrics was a*
*collaborative process between*
*them and guitarist Eric Peterson.*
*"All three of us used to sit down*
*and put our heads together and*
*write a lot of those songs," says*
*Chuck. (Courtesy Adrenaline PR.)*

Maturity doesn't make Chuck Billy hear "Practice What You Preach"—or any
Testament song, he says—differently. "The lyrics are still relevant, and they still have
the same meaning. It's definitely one of the best songs we wrote, ever. The lyric, the
melody, and the music all flow together so good. It's a song we've played our whole
career, and it's never been out of the set."

The lyrics are just as strong now because of the strength of their meaning. "It was such
a positive message. It meant something. That's kind of where we stayed our whole
career, lyrics that have meaning."

At the time, he admits the band wondered whether the musical and lyrical changes
showcased by *Practice What You Preach* were a good idea. "Twenty years later, I'm
thinking, 'Man, that was the best thing we probably ever did,'" he laughs.

OVERKILL

# The Years of Decay

FROM THE ALBUM **THE YEARS OF DECAY** (1989)

Overkill had released three studio albums and a pair of EPs by the end of 1988. *The Years of Decay* would be their first major label release on Atlantic Records. The band was beginning to get magazine coverage and MTV exposure on *Headbangers Ball*. In the eyes of metal fans, it was an exciting, lucrative lifestyle, and being on tour was the culmination of living the dream.

The reality was far from glamorous. In fact, singer Bobby "Blitz" Ellsworth, who only bought his first brand-new car around the time of that album, sometimes found himself sleeping in that car. "One of the greatest misconceptions is that if you're promoted—if you're heard and doing bigger shows—that equals financial compensation. It wasn't necessarily the truth."

Metallica was on the verge of being recognized by a more mainstream audience, but most thrash bands attracted only a niche market, mainly through college radio programming and miles of hard touring. The title track of the fourth Overkill album was about that grind of a musician's life on the road. "Those were huge touring years for us. There were probably, at minimum, 150 shows in every 12-month period."

The song could have applied in a general sense to any touring band in the genre, but Ellsworth thinks the lyrics were meant in a more autobiographical way. "Obviously, the road is common to all who tour, but this is how *we* perceived it to be, the best place to be, no matter how different it is from the nine-to-five norm. Regardless of the downs, the ups are still better.

"The highs are higher, but the lows can be lower. Somewhere in between you feel like you come out ahead.

"Those mass touring days really made us what we are," Ellsworth says. "It was the culmination of everything we thought it should be, to be on the stage where you eventually became comfortable. We eventually became at home. We said, 'This 30×20 slab of wood, with the lights above it and smoke machines and amplifiers on it, is now ours."

But the song was not meant to implore sympathy for the hardship. Blitz says it was more like a painting, and the lyrics were brushstrokes that portrayed a picture of their life and the sentiment that it was worthwhile. "It's based on a factual account with an abstract pick of words."

# COLLABORATIVE EFFORT

At the time, Ellsworth says their songwriting was more of a group effort. Nearly half the topics of their songs were based on a group consensus. It was guitarist Bobby Gustafson who initially suggested the idea of writing a song about being on tour.

"I remember [him] bringing it up, saying this would be a great way to put something out that was different for us."

Gustafson was a real motivator when it came to recommending ideas for songs topics. "The guys could bring stuff that I would take and say, 'Well, there's an interesting topic.' I would take it from that point and finish it. I really just filled in the blanks."

Overkill rehearsed in the Flatbush section of Brooklyn at Fast Lane Studios. "There was a red carpet in that room," he remembers. "I think we had pictures from *Hit Parader* on the wall, [and] we would draw mustaches and put breasts on bands we didn't particularly like. There were Budweiser and Heineken bottles laying around, full ashtrays.

"The original idea came up in that smoke-filled room. It developed over the course of weeks or even a few months." They scheduled long periods of pre-production prior to recording an album, during which time songs would be written. The band would convene every day, regardless of having an idea to build upon.

"Sometimes there would be four guys sitting in a room, and nobody's talking the whole time. What would break the silence was a beer opening. We thought it was necessary to spend that amount of time with each other. That's how these and other lyrics on that record developed."

Blitz remembers it being one of the last songs completed for the album. Writing the lyrics started with the first line about the touring road taking its toll. "Just that simple. From there, it just kind of blossomed into a black rose thorn bush," he laughs.

"When it comes out of one guy's mouth, into another guy's ears, it opens the world of possibilities, especially with regard to songwriting. And that's where this specific [song] came from. Somebody stood up and said it. It was [then] necessary to take it to the next step, and the next step was completion of a full song."

*(From left) Bobby Gustafson, Bobby "Blitz" Ellsworth, D.D. Verni, and Rat Skates. "The Years of Decay" was a collaborative effort between the four band members, but Gustafson came up with the initial idea to write about being on the road.*

# LONGER SONGS

Overkill started in 1980 with the punk mentality of fast songs that were short bursts of intensity. *The Years of Decay*, the title track in particular, revealed the band experimenting with slower and longer songs.

"We wrote 'Skullkrusher' around the same time, which was also a long song. What was fun—*is* fun, still to this day—is to be able to challenge yourself. We're a metal band; we know that. But it doesn't mean within that realm there are not different things to explore. If you walk a straight line, [this] is taking a step to the left, but keeping the line in sight with regard to what you know. That's what I did, lyrically. I took a step to the left, but kept the line in sight. That kind of exploration, especially for a young band at that time, gave us the opportunity to find out new things about ourselves.

"It was one of the things necessary to show that a band like ourselves could do more."

Bobby defines himself as someone more inclined to live for the day. The result was spontaneity and not documenting lyrical ideas in notebooks for future use. Besides, he admits, he never expected Overkill to become a career. "I never thought it would have gone past two records, and that was our fourth. By the time *The Years of Decay* was happening, I thought it was a free pass. I was enjoying the moment."

# WRITER BY NATURE

Some Overkill songs were cases of lyrics first, such as more melodic, sing-along songs like "In Union We Stand" and "Bastard Nation," he says. But music was typically the formative element of their songs. "The more in-depth [songs] were really about getting down the riffs, the arrangement—like building a house. That was the foundation and the walls. The lyrics and the melody would be putting the roof on top of that house."

Blitz says there's no rule of thumb for how quickly he writes lyrics. Some songs were finished in a single pass, but that's the odd instance, he says. "Sometimes, it takes me three months."

Ellsworth is a writer by nature. He was a communications major in college who took elective literature courses. "I always loved Shakespeare [and] real old stuff. It just so happened that when [Overkill] came about, it was a perfect match to my interests. The lyrical content of some of the stuff we presented with music was perfect.

*(From left) Rat Skates, Bobby Gustafson, Bobby "Blitz" Ellsworth, and D.D. Verni. Ellsworth says he never expected Overkill to last beyond two albums. In his mind, anything after* Taking Over *in 1987 was a free pass. Two years later, they would begin experimenting with longer, slower songs, such as "The Years of Decay."*

"I recently cleaned out my office and found a whole bunch of short stories [that] pre-date Overkill, all the way back to my teens. So, lyrically, it was always there for me. I never thought of myself as a lyricist, but I always felt the putting together of words was really important. I felt that way when we [wrote] songs.

"So, when it came to 'Years of Decay,' even if I didn't know it outwardly, inwardly I was prepared to do the song."

# LONG AND WINDING ROAD

Ellsworth thinks fans loved the song. "This was the record where we first showed more. On this song, we showed variation with regard to what we were doing. It didn't *have* to be fast to be heavy. I think the reaction from people was, 'Wow, we never expected this from four lunkheads from Jersey and Staten Island.'"

*Bobby "Blitz" Ellsworth (pictured) never thought of himself as a lyricist. But elective literature courses in college, plus an inclination for writing short stories, inadvertently prepared him for the task.*

It gave people a different, more realistic view of life on the road. But Blitz isn't sure people took the meaning in such a literal sense. He thinks listeners equated the "road" with their own path in life.

"I think it just became identifiable to what their road was, because everybody has [their] road. If you perceive anything with any depth, you always apply it to your own situation and how you feel about that situation. I think that was the overwhelming quality most people got out of it."

The road—both literally and figuratively—has changed for Bobby Ellsworth. He's married, and there's a lot less alcohol, he jokes. And Overkill tours less. "Instead of those 150 to 200 shows a year, we're in the position to consolidate, play [just] the A-markets—bigger, more promoted shows. It's not a Tuesday night in Bumfuck, Idaho, for instance. It's Tuesday night in Chicago.

"Is the road still home? I think it is. The road is still home because we learned to make it work for us. That helps all the way around because life changed. Guys have families, the whole bit. There's Overkiddies running around. That's all about life, and we're still able to do both sides of it."

Blitz says the sacrifice of so many miles logged on the road have been worth it. "Oh, are you kidding? I wouldn't trade a fucking minute of this. We made it work as a business, but we made it work as a business we love. I'm probably one of the [happiest] people in this industry. How can a guy have so much angst and keep a smile on his face? Well, that's because it's been a great road, not a sad road."

## 48

## PANTERA

# Cemetery Gates

FROM THE ALBUM **COWBOYS FROM HELL** (1990)

New Orleans was an underground hotbed for a new direction of metal in the latter half of the '80s. Musicians who would be prominent leaders of various subgenres in the following years—including members of Crowbar, Eyehategod, Goatwhore, and Down—made up a tight-knit community.

Mike Hatch was significant in that scene. "He was the guitar player in a band called Shell Shock, a hardcore band that broke a lot of barriers for up-and-coming underground bands," says Phil Anselmo. "They were *the* band that broke the mold."

Phil describes him as a good friend and a sweet person. His suicide was something no one expected, he says. "I was so much younger, and that really affected a lot of us, at the time."

The suicide of another good friend—Henry—also affected the singer. His life seemed full of promise, and Anselmo says he never would have guessed someone with so much character would kill himself.

"He started messing around with cocaine at a very young age. He was way too young for all that stuff. He hung himself in his own bedroom— I can see his bedroom right now in my head—and his mother found him. I was close with his mother, and she cried endlessly."

Anselmo says he did not want to be literal in writing about the deaths of his friends. The lyrics instead were abstract with understated references to specific people. "Obviously, you always leave lyrics open to interpretation, where it can fit anyone else's life. I wanted to be more hypothetical, but most definitely about something real.

"I left it where it wasn't so pointedly direct, but something [about] this thing called life, where we're going to be emotionally tested over and over, not to mention physically, and the mental aspect of all the emotions."

They were tough times, Phil says. Writing the song was meant to establish a bond with the audience through the commonality of the hardship of life. "We were on the same wavelength as them, just living our lives and feeling these heavy emotions. The listeners can take that and apply it to any situation. We're going to be facing adversity, losing people we loved along the way until we hit the dirt."

*"Cemetery Gates" went through several drafts before Phil Anselmo was comfortable with the lyrics about the suicides of his friends and his difficulty in dealing with the loss.*

# CATHARSIS IN SONGWRITING

The deaths of his friends were growing into a storm of misery by the time he remembers putting pen to paper sometime in 1989. "Believe it or not, I went through a lot of different drafts on that particular song. There are certain songs that pour out, but 'Cemetery Gates,' yeah, it definitely took me a couple of drafts before I felt comfortable. I do remember going over it several times until it was what it is."

Despite the revisions, Phil knew he was on to something. "Oh, of course. The whole time there was a subject. There was circumstance. I guess for that particular era, if you want to call it a power ballad—much to my chagrin—that's really what it was."

Going over the lyrics in his mind, Anselmo says the line that suggested he should have cried came first. "That would mean I am not a man who would automatically break down under those circumstances. I have, of course. But that particular lyric right there, what I'm trying to say is, holding on to that particular baggage, I should have cried. I should have let it go right then and there, and I would have not had that hanging over my head."

Phil describes himself as the type of person who keeps feelings buried inside, so writing the words was a catharsis, like a lyrical crying. "When it comes down to the hardcore facts of the situation at hand, no matter what it may be, I tend to spill my guts through music."

# THE CREATIVE PROCESS

Music normally comes first in his process, followed by a lyrical spearhead that fits the mood of the instrumentation. But "Cemetery Gates" was a case of being predetermined to write about his emotional affliction before hearing compatible music. "In hindsight I do believe I did have that want to do this particular song, to address this particular situation." The song developed as a tailoring of the music and lyrics to fit each other. "It was a little bit of both, I figure. I think the lyrics sit right where they should."

Compassion from the rest of the band was a key factor in Phil presenting such personal lyrics for a song and wanting them to write music fitting enough to carry them. He says there was no struggle in being so personal, especially once they knew the details. "They heard me out, and they got it. Once that was out in the open and I explained the chapter in my life, it came pretty easy [to them]. It was understood."

# PESSIMISTIC SINGER

*Cowboys from Hell* was the fifth Pantera album, but their first released on a major label. Phil had no expectation about how anyone might respond to the song. "No, I really didn't. I wasn't very concerned with how people would react, but I didn't expect much, I'll say that. I'm always a pessimist first, especially back then."

Neither the album nor the single charted in the *Billboard* 200, but both represented a pivotal juncture in the heavy metal timeline. The genre had become contaminated with so much languid music, grunge became a more legitimate alternative. *Cowboys from Hell* represented a hopefulness that the next generation could reinvent metal and restore its viability.

"I'm the type of guy, even when everything might be rosy and great, who will kind of look to the, 'Well, what if *this* happens?' type of thing. I'm not paranoid, but instead of expecting the best, just expect whatever comes. If it happens to be all positive, then fine. I've lived with both, so either way it doesn't bother me."

*There was an element of naïve youth in the lyrics to "Cemetery Gates," says Anselmo. "I didn't know how much more life was going to test. I didn't realize how many times life is going to crush your heart."*

But people telling him how the song affected them, buoying them through hard periods of life, made it obvious that Phil touched a nerve. "Mission accomplished, you know? There's a sense of accomplishment there, yes. There's no better compliment than having a true fan—which is really what counts to me—come up and say what they *do* say about that [song]. It does mean a lot."

There have been people who asked whether the song related specifically to Mike Hatch, especially anyone from that New Orleans music scene. But Phil has also heard different, broader interpretations. "Of course. You have a person from across the globe who applies the song to their life. Or they attempt to dig inside my mind and apply a plot, a story— something that would fit my life without knowing [me]—yeah, I'll have to correct them," he laughs. "It's like, 'No, not quite.' But that's only been few and far between."

# HINDSIGHT

Maturity and time have made it hard for Anselmo to say what stands out most when he reflects on the lyrics so long after writing them. "I addressed the situations at hand at the time in my life. There's a bit of naïve youth there—what I mean by naïve is, at the time I didn't know how much more life was going to test. I didn't know. I didn't realize how much, and how many times, life is going to crush your heart. I think of the song as not necessarily immature, but comparative to the way I would put lyrics today, I think I took it pretty easy on the listeners," he chuckles. "I was pretty soft.

"I had a lot of school friends that ended it early, man. To be so young and see no light at the end of the tunnel, I don't know. A lot of times, I think people hell bent on suicide have the mentality that this will show them. They act as if they'll be able to see the entire scene unfold and watch their own funeral—see who shows up, see who cries the most. But they're terribly mistaken. It's not a game. It's not any kind of retribution, and there's not much of an epitaph there [for] such a young person."

## 49

## PANTERA

# Cowboys from Hell

FROM THE ALBUM COWBOYS FROM HELL (1990)

Pantera was a Texas-based band full of rambunctious piss and vinegar. The title track of their major-label debut was steeped in that attitude and gunfighter imagery. Its larger-than-life posture became a rallying cry for their fans and a beloved sobriquet for the band.

"Honestly, it just was what it was," says Phil Anselmo. "It's about attitude, so I guess it's about the band and whatnot, sure. But it definitely wasn't autobiographical," he laughs.

Anselmo says it *was* his transition from earlier Pantera songs to writing less clichéd lyrics. "That was probably one of my last songs that was not gut-level street truth. I don't think there's much depth there. It's more of an anthemic song."

The high-noon gunfighter imagery had nothing to do with expressing anything personal like other Anselmo life experience songs. "But it definitely has attitude," he says. "It definitely has the hook. That particular song was more the hook novelty of the whole thing."

"Cowboys from Hell" was a remnant from their days of paying dues on the club circuit. "It happened to be one of the few leftover songs that reflected more of our old style." The album itself was what Phil calls a growth spurt for the band. "I've always said Pantera never truly evolved into what we were really about until *Vulgar Display of Power*."

# SECRETS OF SONGWRITING

The title was one of the first things when Phil was formulating the lyrics for the song. But knowing whether a title will develop into a profound statement is an inexplicable process, he says. "I'm going to have to take the John Lennon point of view and say, 'If you're a songwriter, that's what you do.' That's how it rolls. Sometimes you wake up, and it might be a personal feeling. Sometimes it might just be a song like 'Cowboys from Hell.'

"All you're doing is writing songs. Really, that's what happens. I can't get any deeper than that, man," he laughs.

His process tends to start with a general idea, followed by a deliberate series of construction. "Syllables are always a fantastic thing to follow, triplets and different cadences [where] you can use your voice. I've never felt it was an absolute must to have rhyming words or anything like that."

# RESPECTING THE RIFF

"Honestly, it was the riff," Phil says. "It was a massive anthem. It just had that feel, and the lyrics fit. I guess I was young enough to still write those types of songs, and it worked out."

The whole song, he explains, almost seems like an extended guitar riff. "The whole thing gallops and turns into this churning riff. Even the middle is really a lick that people would normally use in a lead situation. I look at it now and marvel at Darrell— and Rex is playing just as tight as Dimebag—and it's really a lot of hard playing. That blows me away, man! It really blows my ass away."

"Pantera had such a groove, I absolutely felt like I had to definitely make a bold state-ment with the lyrics. You really need to add to that groove."

The instrumentation might have been different from typical metal songs, but meshing lyrics to the unorthodox structure was not difficult, he says. "No, not at all. It was very unique because there were really no musicians quite like them. Once I was in the creative force of Pantera, I was pretty clear on where I stood. It was a four-way input, so it was no problem there.

*Dimebag Darrell (pictured) prompted the lyrics with a riff that Phil Anselmo heard as a foundation for an anthem.*

"It wasn't really upping my game. It was more or less having the freedom to play my game.

"They came from a traditional metal school. I grew up with the metal they grew up with, but I didn't stop there. I [also] grew up with bands like Agnostic Front and the Righteous Pigs." Traditional metal, in Anselmo's mind, had run its course. "I was like, 'I'm out to crush tradition.' I brought an appreciation for the underground."

# GOOD GUYS WEAR BLACK

The decision was later made to also name the album *Cowboys from Hell*. Anselmo was a New Orleans native, but the rest of the band—brothers Dimebag Darrell and Vinnie Paul, and Rex Brown—were Texans. Pantera had already been playing the song in clubs before signing with Atco Records. "In Texas, hell yeah, it worked!"

Even though the "good guys wear black" sentiment went over well in the Lone Star state, they had no clue how the rest of the world would bite on that track. "I don't think we cared, you know? It was such a done deal in our minds. We had been playing it for over a year before we got signed, so it was like, 'Take it or leave it, motherfucker,'" he laughs.

*The phrase "cowboys from hell" came to define the Texas-based Pantera, and the song itself became a staple of their live shows. Says frontman Phil Anselmo (pictured), "There was no way we were leaving that building unless people heard 'Cowboys from Hell.'"*

The band still did not realize it was a defining song, or that fans were starting to refer to them as the literal cowboys from hell. "I don't think anything really started to culminate in our minds as a proven commodity or a force to be reckoned with."

During their first tour with Suicidal Tendencies and Exodus, Anselmo says nobody knew them, but he remembers someone from one of the other bands' crew insisting they would soon be a headlining band. "Once again, the pessimism in me, I'm like, 'Nah, you're out of your fucking mind.'

"It's like a delayed reaction, if you know what I'm saying. Once *Vulgar Display of Power* came out, and word got out and we started doing our own shows, that's when those [older] songs became staples. *That's* when the realization [hit] that these songs meant something to people."

It would remain a mainstay in their live set throughout the duration of the band. "Oh yeah, there was no way we were leaving that building unless people heard 'Cowboys from Hell,' or they would throw a fucking fit."

# LYRICAL DEVELOPMENT

In retrospect, Phil thinks the lyrics are kind of childish, a little funny. "Look, I felt I was beyond that even then. It's nothing I would have written a year later, nothing I would write today. It just fit. It fit like it should have."

Even though he's progressed as a lyricist, he doesn't look back with creative regrct. "Put it in perspective, [and] I'm fine with it. There it sits, and it is forever, and I have no qualms about it. It is what it is, and I'm cool with it.

"If I wanted to scrutinize myself and look back 20 years plus, and say, 'Oh Jesus, how childish,' well, I look back at other things I've done and cringe worse."

The bottom line is people still listen to the song and enjoy it so much, and *that* is cool to Phil Anselmo. "Of course, yeah. That goes without saying."

## 50

## MEGADETH

# holy Wars...The Punishment Due

FROM THE ALBUM RUST IN PEACE (1990)

Northern Ireland had been immersed in religious-based political unrest for some 20 years. Nationalists—mostly minority Roman Catholics—sought liberation from Great Britain and the unification of a single Ireland. Protestant Unionists supported the British government. The opposing paramilitary Provisional Irish Republican Army and Ulster Volunteer Force exchanged violent attacks that periodically seemed like preludes to full-scale civil war.

Megadeth was on tour with a date in Antrim, 20 miles northwest of the capital city of Belfast. Dave Mustaine ventured out to mingle with fans and discovered bootleg T-shirts for sale outside the venue. The malice directed toward the singer took him aback. "This little kid, like 13 years old, spit on me."

Incensed, he returned to the building and demanded the sale of unofficial merchandise be stopped. "I said, 'Go get that box of T-shirts right now'—because that's how we lived back then, merchandise and what little money we made off record sales and playing live—and I got a message that there's a guy out there selling it for The Cause."

The messenger spelled it out for the curious Mustaine. "The Cause is the IRA—and this guy explained it to me so innocently. He said the Protestants think they're better than the Catholics; the Catholics think they're better than the Protestants. The Cause is trying to bring equality between the two.

"I went, 'Fuck, that sounds great!' He goes, 'By the way, if you make a smiley face in your Guinness, you'll have a drinking partner.'"

# ANARCHY FOR ANTRIM

A smiley face traced in the head of a draft and still visible at the bottom of the glass is a sign of a good pour. Mustaine was coyly engaged in conversation and received the good cheer of his newfound mate, eagerly imbibing Guinness.

*The result of Dave Mustaine's onstage rant in Antrim was an outbreak of violence. Megadeth was forced to leave the hostile venue in bulletproof busses.*

"And by the time he finished telling me [about The Cause], I was like, 'Okay!' I get onstage and say, 'This one's for Antrim! Give Ireland back to the Irish! Anarchy and Antrim!'"

The audience split into Catholic and Protestant factions and fighting broke out. Bomb-sniffing dogs were brought to the venue, and the band was escorted to their hotel in security coaches.

Bassist David Ellefson refused to speak to Mustaine the following morning. Asked if he even remembered what happened the previous evening, Dave, laughing, replied, "Yeah, I drank." Ellefson reminded him that they were extracted from the venue in bulletproof busses. "I went, 'Is that rock and roll, or what? Man, that's so *metal*!'"

But he mulled over the possible consequences and realized his actions demonstrated poor leadership. "I jeopardized everybody's safety. As much as we were serious bad boys, we didn't want to be stupid boys." Mustaine also pondered the hostility between Irish countrymen over religious and political differences.

# NOTTINGHAM ROCK CITY

The band arrived several days later in Nottingham to play a gig at the famed Rock City. "That club will forever be famous," says Mustaine, "because I wrote 'Holy Wars' there." It would also be the day that set the stage for Chuck Behler to ultimately lose his job to drum tech Nick Menza. "Nick got up and started playing with us. He was so good, and I was so inspired, I penned the song."

Dave jokes that the starting point for the song was probably something like, *oh shit*, he laughs, "because I was in so much trouble." He thinks inquiring about religious beliefs was probably one of the first lines. "The whole episode had come because I asked that guy what was going on. He told me, and he snookered me."

# THE PUNISHER

Religious antagonism and the potency of Nick Menza may have prompted Dave to write about the situation in Northern Ireland, but "Holy Wars...The Punishment Due" consisted of two separate lyrical sections. The latter half of the song was based on his favorite Marvel Comics character.

*(From left) Marty Friedman, David Ellefson, Nick Menza, and Dave Mustaine. The* Rust in Peace *lineup would be regarded by many fans as the definitive version of Megadeth.*

"The Punisher was what I would be like if I was a superhero—just a no-shit kind of guy. I loved the comic. The thing I identified with the most was that he was just a normal guy. Something happened, and he got pissed. He started to fight, and even though his vigilante ways weren't necessarily legal, he stood for what was morally right."

The Punisher first appeared in the pages of *The Amazing Spider-Man* in 1974. Frank Castle was a military veteran whose family was silenced after witnessing a mafia murder. His retaliation against their killers—and subsequently all criminals—appealed to Mustaine's sensibility.

"The song was written before I got married and had a baby. But after I got married and had a baby, it just kind of reverberated in my head." Mustaine says that part of the song still makes him imagine what he might have done, had someone threatened his young family. "Every time I sing that, I think of Pam and Justice."

He also enjoys watching the audience physically react to the vengeful lines about not making any more mistakes. "When I sing [that], I see everybody roll their eyes up in their head, like a one-armed bandit. I love that! I love that audience interaction."

# DANGEROUS LYRICS

He had no idea how people might react to the tempestuous lyrics, and he didn't care. During the *Rust in Peace* days, his attitude was brazen, rebellious. Megadeth—and Dave Mustaine—were intimidating. "I didn't care. I was dangerous. That's right about the time where my martial arts training was at its fiercest. I was training every single day, for almost two hours a day."

Although there was no outward controversy specific to that one song, he does remember people condemning Megadeth as a whole. "People threatened to burn my records." But, as he remarked at the time, "you gotta buy those records to burn them, so go ahead, baby. You get one play off of it, make it a good one."

*Mustaine's martial arts regimen fostered a dissenting attitude on* Rust in Peace.

# FAITH AND CONFLICT

"I don't think anybody can get through life without having somebody to confide in. Everybody needs something to believe in, whether it's God or Buddha or whatever. I've believed in God since I was a kid. It's been me and my imaginary God that I've never seen but I believe in."

The abstract message of the song was belief and faith, says Mustaine, despite the literal inspiration being his experience in Northern Ireland. "'Holy Wars' is just my own interpretation from my own mistakes. Some people can identify with other parts of it because religiosity might be their thing."

The lyrics are vague about who is warring over God, and many listeners took their interpretation from the video. The Benjamin Stokes and Eric Zimmerman–directed clip featured performance footage cut with scenes of Middle Eastern conflict.

"The video inspired a lot of questions, whether I was an Arab hater or not. I hate the devil, but I don't hate any people. There are people I don't like very much," he snickers, "but I don't hate anybody."

It *could* have been interpreted as applicable to the tension of that region. "The threat we were dealing with back then was Saddam Hussein. We had just come out of dealing with the Ayatollah Khomeini, Moammar Kadafi, the Shah of Iran—all of those things."

# MODERN SIGNIFICANCE

"I don't remember anything prior to that that was really that strong about politics outside of my own country." If "Peace Sells" marked the beginning of Dave Mustaine writing political lyrics on a national level, he thinks "Holy Wars" was the start of being a politically global songwriter.

The lyrics have taken on significant meaning in the years since Mustaine incited chaos at that gig in Antrim. His portrait of civil disorder could be applicable to the 2009 election of Iranian president Mahmoud Ahmadinejad. "I know young people who are Iranian, and they have already stated they don't want this guy. They want a new government.

"The young people are going to win because we're not fighting hand-to-hand combat anymore; we're fighting with computers. We can completely obliterate the entire Middle East with the push of an Enter button. It's going to be a civil war, and it's going to come down to a bloody revolution."

# Index